Ashwani Gujral's brilliant academic background spans engineering and finance. He is BE (Electronics and Communications) from M.I.T. Manipal, 1993, and MBA (Finance) from Georgetown University, Washington DC, USA, 1995.

Mr Gujral writes regularly for the leading US specialist magazines and journals on trading and technical analysis, including *The Active Trader*, USA; *Stock Futures and Options*, USA; *Futures*, USA; *Trader's Source*, USA, and *Technical Analysis of Stocks and Commodities*, USA. He is also a Technical Analysis Consultant to Reuters India Ltd.

Mr Gujral also features regularly as an expert over CNBC, NDTV and Zee News Channels to offer comments on the Indian economy and the stock and derivatives markets. Since 1995, he has been trading stocks and derivatives for a living.

How to Make Money Trading Derivatives is his first book.

"Ashwani Gujral has taken great strides at bringing technical analysis to the Indian financial markets. This book encompasses all facets . . . . It's a must read for anyone interested in technically trading the Indian markets." *Jayanthi Gopalakrishnan, Editor, Technical Analysis of Stocks and Commodities Magazine, USA*

"India is the world's largest and most exciting frontier of speculative markets. Ashwani Gujral has cemented himself as a pioneer in the field and will help numerous Indian market participants graduate from passive investors to traders." *James Holter, Editor, Futures Magazine, USA*

"As a trader and writer, Ashwani Gujral has the natural ability to break down a contract, market or product and tell traders how it works and what it means to them. His straight-forward style should help any trader trying to filter out what is needed in trading India's derivatives markets."

Jim Kharoof, Editor, Trader's Source Magazine, USA

"Gujral's book is heavily under-priced for the great ideas it offers so liberally." *Hindu Business Line*

AF516665

Spontaneous Reader Comments

" The more I read, the more I fascinated got"
Saikat Dasgupta

"I found your book interesting, enlightening and practical"
Aravind Gandhi, Mumbai

"The unique thing about this book is that the author shares with us his experiences on a particular trade. It has specific pinpointed examples rather than more conceptual knowledge. In recent times, this is one of the best books on trading and managing money." www.*traderji.com*

How to Make Money Trading Derivatives

An Insider's Guide

3rd Edition

Ashwani Gujral

VISION BOOKS

www.visionbooksindia.com

Dedication

This book is dedicated to my biggest trade so far
my wife, Anubha
and my highest profit
my daughter Rtunjya
and I am still long on them.

They stood by me not only while I wrote this book
but also while I learnt trading and
through the inevitable initial failures
but continued to believe I could succeed.

www.vision**books**india.com

Disclaimer

The author and the publisher disclaim all legal or other responsibilities for any losses which investors may suffer by investing or trading using the methods described in this book. Readers are advised to seek professional guidance before making any specific investments. This book is meant purely for the purpose of investor and trader education.

First Published 2005, Reprinted 2005 (5 times)
Reprinted 2006 (5 times)
Revised and Expanded Edition 2007
Reprinted 2007 (4 times), 2008 (4 times), 2009 (Twice), 2010 (Twice), 2011
3rd Edition 2012
Reprinted 2014, 2015 (Twice), 2016 (Twice), 2017, 2018, 2019, 2020, 2021, 2022, 2023

ISBN 10: 81-7094-853-3
ISBN 13: 978-81-7094-853-7

Published by
Vision Books Pvt. Ltd.
(Incorporating Orient Paperbacks and CARING imprints)
24 Feroze Gandhi Road, Lajpat Nagar 3
New Delhi 110024, India.
Phone: (+91-11) 2984 0821 / 22
e-mail: visionbooks@gmail.com

Printed at
Ashim Print Line
38/2, 35 & 36 Sahibabad Industrial Area, Ghaziabad
Uttar Pradesh 201010, India.

Contents

Preface to the 3rd Edition

A lot of water has flown under the bridge since this book was first published in February 2005. The book has been widely read and appreciated by Indian investors and traders and I would like to thank the large number of readers who have said so many kind words about it. Indeed, it were the mails I received from readers far and wide coupled with my publisher's insistence that motivated me to add two extra chapters in the book's second edition on some enduring lessons to be learnt from the way the markets moved between February 2005 and June 2006.

The first of the new chapters (Chapter 13) deals with stock selection, in which we look at how to choose suitable stocks for trading. Personally, I believe that this chapter is the second most important one in the entire book, next only to the one on money management (Chapter 12). This is so because it's futile to apply the right techniques to wrong stocks.

In the other new chapter (Chapter 14), I describe how I dealt both with the top forming around May 2006, and then the 40% correction from that top through June 2006. As the market went through a huge rally and then an equally sharp 40% correction, I thought it was an appropriate occasion to add some of my new learning and experience for the readers of the book.

For the book's third edition, I have added a new chapter (Chapter 15) which describes the last hour trading strategy which I have honed and perfected during my television shows on ET-NOW. It provides a new dimension to the way day traders approach the last hour in the market.

I plan to continually add more chapters as my trading life unfolds, sharing my experiences and research with the readers.

While you won't become an expert technical analyst or trader merely by reading this book, I hope it will nevertheless sensitize you to the issues faced in trading.

January 2012 ASHWANI GUJRAL

Preface

Let's first be clear what this book is not.

This is not a book on technical analysis although it does discuss technical methods, specifically in chapters 2, 3 and 4 and uses it in almost all the others. Technical analysis is a vast field and it's not possible to discuss it in its entirety in one book. Neither is it necessary to do so in a book on strategies for trading derivatives. Profitable trading does not depend on the knowledge of a large number of theories, rather it depends on successfully implementation of a few. I have tried to discuss technical analysis in a simple manner and one that can be implemented by traders having elementary knowledge of the subject. An important part of successful trading is also money management and psychology which most books do not get around to discussing at all but which are covered in some detail in separate chapters in this book.

Secondly, this is not a book written for a theoretical view of either technical analysis or derivatives but as far as possible tries to discuss the practical insights I have gained in more than eight years of trading — a period which saw recessions, booms, busts and liberalization policies of different Indian governments. All the derivations and technical theory have been purposely left out because most of these are now programmed into the software. The important point is understanding how you can use the methods rather than the theory itself. Traders wanting to enhance knowledge can buy some of the other literature which discusses the theoretical aspects in great detail.

Now we get to what this book is all about.

This book is about using derivatives for the purposes of trading or speculation. Speculation is not a dirty word and neither is it gambling. Speculation is the art of making short term trading and investment decisions based on knowledge, research and trading philosophies. I would recommend that traders study at least a couple of basic books on technical analysis to get a better handle on the strategies used in the derivatives markets as the basis of making derivative trading decisions, is generally technical analysis.

This book starts with the first discussing the Indian economy, the Indian capital markets and the basics of derivatives instruments.

The second chapter discusses the concept of ADX which has been critical to my trading since it is one of the few indicators which helps a trader identify whether the market is trending or range bound. This is vital because only after this can a trader choose the tools and the methods appropriate for these two different market conditions.

The third chapter discusses a variety of technical tools, like the RSI, MACD, stochastics, moving averages, Fibonacci, etc. I have deliberately limited the number of technical tools since a lot of indicators provide essentially the same results. I have chosen to focus on two trading indicators and two trending indicators. Then I have discussed the Fibonacci methodology which helps in determining the price levels. It would do no harm to the trader to improve his knowledge on these subjects by reading more detailed books on technical analysis.

The fourth chapter pulls everything together, and shows the practical application of technical tools and methods discussed in chapters 2 and 3 in making derivative trading decisions.

The fifth chapter discusses day trading using intraday charts and provides the basic strategies for a day trader. Traders should remember that day trading remains one of the most difficult arts to master in trading.

The sixth chapter tackles cash and futures arbitrage and how idle cash can be deployed when there is no profitable trading opportunity available. This is a risk free strategy.

Chapter 6 thus concludes the discussion in trading futures.

The seventh chapter introduces the topic of options and discusses the various attributes of options and factors that affect option premiums. This chapter also discusses the calculation of implied volatility and how this can be used to judge whether an option is expensive or cheap.

The eighth chapter discusses the option strategies useful for Indian traders. At the end of this chapter you should be fairly comfortable with strategies that are useful in Indian markets.

The ninth chapter tackles covered call strategies. This strategy produces incredible returns in the Indian market as option premiums tend to be high in India. In good markets, this strategy can provide returns up to 5% per month on a portfolio.

The tenth chapter focuses on derivative techniques by which you can profit in special situations typical to India. This chapter discusses elections, company results, budget, etc.

The eleventh chapter deals with the crucial element of trading discipline and how it's important for a trader to develop a disciplined approach to trading and making trading decisions.

The twelfth and the final chapter deals with what I consider to be the most important aspect of this book and one that determines a trader's sustainability in this business — money management. This chapter discusses various methods you can use for limiting the amount of capital risked on every trade, and the consequences of over exposure relative to one's account size.

After finishing the book, novice traders should practice paper trading for a while and check the effectiveness of the various strategies and the best situations for implementing them. Subsequently in real life trading, keep your initial exposure small and increase it gradually as you develop a better understanding of the Indian derivatives market.

Finally, I must caution you that trading is one of the most difficult professions to master. Those who are able to master it, have huge rewards waiting for them. Here is wishing you good luck in mastering this wonderful art.

January 2005 ASHWANI GUJRAL

Chapter 1

The Indian Equity and Derivative Markets

When I began writing the first chapter of this book early in 2004, India appeared to be making rapid economic strides. The economy was being systematically unshackled and customs duties were being reduced to allow all comers freer access to the Indian consumer. Politicians were heard saying that they wanted to create a level playing field rather than thinking of protectionist ways. India was becoming the most favoured destination of outsourcing, from services to manufactured products. "Made in India" was slowly becoming a brand rather than a liability. A good monsoon ensured that agricultural growth was robust and rural incomes were on the rise. Interest rates stood at their lowest levels ever and the government was taking steps to reduce the fiscal deficit. On the geopolitical front, peace talks with Pakistan seemed ready to start.

Scarcely three months later, results of the 2004 Indian general election led to the unexpected fall of the Vajpayee-led NDA government. and everything seemed to change overnight. A new Left-supported dispensation was widely perceived set to reverse some deregulatory policies and slow others down. A nervous Indian stock market lost $22 billion in a single day — its fourth largest-ever one-day debacle.

Real-life often outdoes fiction in surprises, a lesson every trader needs to keep in mind.

The Indian Stock Market

India now has several home-grown multinationals listed on the stock market which have brought laurels to the country. India's stock markets have also made several structural changes to improve their security and efficacy. The days of Harshad Mehta and Ketan Parikh are over as the cash and derivative segments of the market have bee separated. Today, investors not only have equity shares but also their derivatives, such as futures and options, to hedge risk and trade. So from a situation where only a linear product was available till the 1990s, today there exist the new non-linear derivative products as well.

When trading derivatives, you are generally dealing with big stocks and these have the required fundamentals in place. They are unlikely to have abrupt shareholder-unfriendly moves. Smaller stocks which have limited institutional holdings are more prone to abrupt moves which cannot be explained either technically or fundamentally.

Myths About the Indian Stock Market

At this point it is pertinent for me to dispel some fears about the Indian stock market that new traders and investors may have based on past events. It is important to do so because all equity futures and options are derivatives either of stocks, or market indices; and are thus a part and parcel of trading in the stock market.

The Indian Market Can Have a Scam at Any Time

Indian investors and traders who have been in the market since 1990 have had to face a scam at some time or another. Actually, most of these were not stock market scams. Rather, they were scams in other financial institutions, but it was easier and more sensational to blame them on the stock market. In both Harshad Mehta and Ketan Parikh scams, financial institutions violated RBI guidelines to lend money to both these gentlemen which they used to inflate stock prices. Could charts have saved traders and investors from these scams? Absolutely. I believe most traders who followed charts did not get badly hurt because they had stop losses in place and it was clear that stocks were getting distributed.

In fact, nimble traders even made money by selling short in the ensuing bear market. Most bull markets worldwide end with scams. I look at it as footing the bill for the party that happens before the scam. The key is to recognise when it is that the market starts acting silly in paying valuations for companies. Charts play a very useful role in this as they give an indication of the market topping out. As readers would recall, the great bull market of the 1990s in the US ended with

WorldCom and Enron. Usually, scams trigger the end of bull markets. We in India are so used to secure assets that we tend to overreact to scams — and very emotionally at that. But investors and traders who take the time to study the market can hedge, and even trade profitably, through these scams with the help of derivatives now available.

Structurally, after ten years of reform, Indian markets today are probably among the safest in the world. The VAR (Value at Risk) system of margins on derivatives collects up to 50% of the total value of a transaction when markets become volatile. The chances of default by any of the exchanges or brokers are thus minimal. The Indian market regulator SEBI also has a lot more teeth today and is very vigilant to manipulation by any market player. I would like to point out here that insiders and manipulators are there in all markets. Equally, their activities are clearly visible on the charts. I would strongly urge all investors and traders to develop a feel for charting; it can help you save a lot of grief in the markets.

Also, in the last few years there has been consolidation of the regional exchanges and now there are really only two exchanges, BSE and NSE, which run the entire business of equities in India. Most regional exchanges either have no business or have taken broking tickets from these large exchanges, so the risk of a localised scam has also reduced.

Losses from Systemic Delays

There was a time when physical shares used to be traded on the Indian stock markets and there were a lot of hassles in getting them transferred; forms needed to be filled, there were cases of bad delivery, etc. (The process was so irritating that I almost left this business at one point.) But now things have totally changed. All shares and derivative products are traded in the electronic form and hence there is no procedural loss while trading them, and there is no paperwork at all. Today, Indian markets are one of the most sophisticated in terms of procedures and systems and are at the verge of explosive growth.

Lack of Trading Tools

The best trading software and trading tools are now easily available. Television channels such as CNBC and NDTV also serve to bring the stock markets close to traders.

Some of the good charting software available are Trade Station and Advanced GET*. People not wanting to invest a large amount can also buy Metastock. The price of the software does not determine success. Even a free software from the Internet can do the job. So the playing field is all set up, the tools are there and achieving trading success now depends on the individual trader. In many ways, the enemy of the trader lies within him and winning at trading, in a large part, is the outcome of a trader overcoming his own weaknesses.

Indian Economy Has Not Fulfilled Its Promise So Far

This is an issue that holds relevance for the investor but is not important for a trader. In fact most traders, including myself, enjoy going short on the market. This is because all markets fall faster than they rise. So a trader is not bothered about what is going on in the economy, or in the political establishment. He is able to find opportunities in all markets and under all circumstances. In fact, a trader should focus more on improving his trading skills and leave the worrying over the economy to economist and politicians. This aspect does not, and should not, affect trading results.

The Difference between a Trader and an Investor

In the Indian context, a trader is a person who buys and sells shares at relatively shorter intervals to earn a profit. The trader is not averse to going long or short on the market or individual stock derivatives. The trader could be:

- A day trader, who buys, sells and squares up his position during the same day;
- A swing trader who trades the various up and down swings, i.e. from one pivot to another; or
- A position trader who holds his long and short positions for periods ranging from several days to several weeks.

* Software providers: www.viratechindia.com; www.technicaltrends.com; www.trendwatchindia.com.

Most trading is done based on charting since that is possibly the only consistent method of making money. Traders are active participants in the market. They risk a certain amount based on chart patterns and indicators and try to earn several times their risk.

Then there are the investors who buy and hold stocks for years. These investors generally do not trade the swings of the market and make buying decisions based on fundamentals and market news. In my experience, investors generally lose except when there are secular bull markets for several years, or if they can get multi-baggers. But such bull markets are so few and far between that I have not found it worth waiting for one. When the market moves in smaller swings, however, these investors often lose 80 to 90% of their investment because they often buy at market peaks. To my mind, long-term investors are the people who finance the traders' profit. Basically, I would characterise anyone holding positions for less than a year as a trader, and the others as investors.

Derivatives

Derivatives, as the name suggests, are financial instruments whose value is dependent on another underlying asset. The underlying security in the case of equity derivatives is an equity share, or the widely followed Nifty and Sensex indices. A share of equity can only provide an unhedged position whether long or short, and the entire risk of the transaction lies with the trader or investor.

There are two types of derivatives. One is the futures product and the other is the options product and trading strategies can be created using them individually or in combination. Derivatives add a lot of flexibility to a trader's tools. They can be used for two purposes, namely speculation and hedging.

Speculation

Contrary to what many people believe, speculation is not gambling. Speculation is the skill of analysing data and taking positions on the various market situations to profit from favourable price movements. In the stock market arena, this activity is also called trading. Throughout the remainder of this book, speculation in the stock market will be referred to as trading, which includes going both long and short on the market. Also, contrary to popular opinion, trading is neither about predicting the direction of the stock market nor is it about predicting prices. The most important aspect of trading is money management. There is a complete chapter later in this book which deals with the issue of money management (Chapter 12).

Briefly, money management involves risking a particular amount of money to make several times the amount risked. There are various situations, called setups on the technical charts, which increase the probability of successful trades. But, and I want to state this loud and clear, since no one can predict the stock market, the key to making money in trading on a sustained basis is to make big profits when you are right and limit your losses when you go wrong. Also important is the size of your trading positions in proportion to the overall size of your trading capital; correct position sizes enable you to stay in the game for the longest possible time and hence increase the chances of making money.

Anyone who has bought this book in the hope of making easy money can stop reading it right now. Trading is a skill that is learnt over a period of time. No one is born with this talent. No one has a holy grail which can predict stock prices consistently over any length of time. This is the most important lesson of this book. Once you stop chasing the impossible dream of predicting prices, you will save all the time otherwise wasted in trying to find the perfect system. I often see people predicting prices in the media which can lead novice traders to believe that this is a skill which can be acquired. I will only say that if these experts had any such magical knowledge, they would not be sharing it on television with the rest of us for free but, instead, be sitting on a beach in California.

Trading, in fact, is a skill that can be learnt and, once learnt, you can make huge amounts of money. To do so traders should get used to the notion of losses at the very outset. Trading is both about profits and losses. The key is to keep losses small and profits big.

Hedging

The idea of hedging is more important in the commodities and currency markets. In the equity market, hedging can be an expensive exercise. Often people think they will be fully protected if they take a position which profits if the market starts moving in the reverse direction. True they will protect themselves but not totally because hedging comes at a cost, for while hedging can reduce losses but it also lowers your profits. In my experience, it is not worthwhile for traders to hedge their positions. Instead, when a trade starts moving contrary to the expected direction, you need to quickly get out. Often in the media we hear recommendations about buying stock futures and hedging it by buying a put. This strategy sounds great but the put comes at a cost which is deductible from the profits that you earn on futures, assuming that the profit on your futures position is higher than the cost of the put. More on this in later chapters.

Futures

An equity futures product is a derivative of either an underlying stock, or a stock index. In other words, the value of futures depends on that of its underlying stock or index, as the case may be.

During the rest of this book we will distinguish the stock market consisting of all the listed stocks by calling it the cash market. The term derivatives market, or futures market, will be used to refer to the futures and options market.

Here, it is important to understand how a futures contract is different from the underlying stock:

- When you buy a stock you pay the full value of the transaction (i.e the number of shares multiplied by market price of each share).
- There is no time component, you own the stock for all times to come.
- You make a loss or profit only when you sell the shares you own.
- You may or may not have a long-term view on the stock.
- You can go long on a stock only if you own it (because of rolling settlement). You cannot short sell unless you borrow the stock, something which is neither cheap nor convenient.
- There is no way of taking a position on the index through the cash market.
- The cash market has a market lot of one, i.e. you can buy any stock in the multiples of one unit.

When you trade futures:

- Long is the equivalent of initiating a futures position by buying a futures contract and then squaring up by selling it.

- Short is the equivalent of initiating the position by first selling a futures contract and then squaring up by buying it back.
- You pay only the margin which is a fractional portion of the total transaction value, generally about 15% in the case of index futures, and up to 50% in the case of individual stock futures.
- All futures contracts are dated. For example, Indian futures and options settlements currently take place on the last Thursday of every month. So the current month's futures expire on the month's last Thursday. If a trader has to carry his position to the next month, he has to shift his position to the next month's futures.
- Futures are generally traded using technical analysis because the product facilitates speculation; futures are not an investment product.
- You can go long or short on the futures depending on your short-term view of the market, or a particular stock.
- The futures market helps you take a variety of views on the market and a particular stock.
- A futures contract is the smallest unit which you can trade in the futures market. A contract consists of different numbers of shares for each underlying stock. The futures market lots are decided on the basis that the minimum market lot should be worth at least Rs. 2 lakh. For example, one contract of Reliance futures is worth 600 shares. When you trade Reliance futures, you can do so only in lots of 600 shares of Reliance, which is one futures contract.

Theoretically,

Futures Price = Cash Price + (Monthly) Cost of Carry

In theory, the cost of carry should always be positive because a futures trade is really a carry forward product similar to the erstwhile *badla*. But just as *badla* rates sometimes became negative when the market sentiment was bearish, the cost of carry can also similarly be negative when the sentiment is poor.

Presently, in India the current month's stock or index futures are the only futures products which can really be traded. Futures for the succeeding months are usually not liquid enough for trading.

For example, during January, only the January futures would be liquid enough to be traded during most of the month. The February and March futures are unlikely to be liquid for active trading for most of January. Only in the last week of January might the February futures become liquid. This is because the futures and options settlement takes place on the last Thursday of January.

Henceforth in this book, which is about derivatives, whenever we talk of trading we will be talking about trading futures or options. Trading otherwise is a term also used in the context of stocks of individual companies — but not so in this book.

Options

Options are the second type of derivative instrument. An option is available in its most basic forms in two versions, namely:

- Call option, and
- Put option.

Call option is the right to buy a certain asset at an agreed price, and before a certain date, by paying a premium.

Put option is the right to sell a certain asset at an agreed price, on or before a certain date, by paying a premium.

A lot of Indian investors will relate to options as being akin to the advance or *bayana* given or received at the time of sale or purchase of a property. A better understanding of options is gained by seeing how these differ from futures:

- An option is a non-linear product where the loss is limited and the profit is unlimited. A future is a linear product where profits and losses are both unlimited.
- An option has two components built into its premium, a time component and an intrinsic value component. The value of a future is the cash price added to the cost of carry per month.
- Once an option is bought, the only loss can be the premium. In the case of futures, mark to market losses need to be paid at the end of each trading session.
- Options depend more on the availability of a buyer and a seller and are not necessarily liquid at every price point. Most futures contracts are liquid enough to ensure excellent price discovery. We shall talk much more about options in Chapter 7.

Myths About Trading Derivatives

Now let's tackle some of the myths about trading derivatives.

It's Too Risky

I would reckon that trading derivatives is about as risky as doing anything else that you do not have knowledge about, such as driving a car or flying an aircraft. And until you equip yourself with appropriate knowledge, you have no business to be trading anyway. It is important to understand that successful trading requires behaviour completely opposite to how we normally behave. For example, being a contrarian is one of the most successful strategies in trading. In most situations in life, on the other hand, there is comfort in being part of a group. Averaging downwards, for instance, is a wrong strategy that traders commonly use. Booking losses is yet another difficult area that traders must contend with, something we instinctively shun from.

It's Only for the Experts

It can be categorically stated that none of the experts are perfect in predicting either the stock trends or prices. Any lay person with some practice, hard work, and by learning good money management is at par with the Dalal Street experts who talk so intelligently on television. Talking and trading are as different as taking a shower and swimming. A one-line description of trading is: trend following and money management. If you can master these two, you can make a better living than most others out there. There are no secret or hidden strategies. The point of trading is to try to get on to a trend, and if the market goes against you, to limit your losses to only a small percentage of your equity.

You Can Lose All Your Money

Yes, you can. But so can you lose your life while driving, or for that matter while playing cricket, or even just walking down the road. The most critical aspects which determine a trader's survival are the use of proper position sizing and money management techniques. When you are driving your car at a speed at 100 kmph, the chances of a fatal accident are at least 50% higher than when driving at 50 kmph. Similarly, in trading it is important to use leverage in a manner that does not border on the dangerous. It's important to remember that big money is made by having a number of big-win trades. This number does not have to be larger than the number of losing trades; the key is that the quantum of each winning trade should be several times each losing trade. The goal of this book is to help you achieve this objective. Anyone who says there is another secret to making money in trading is just taking you for a ride.

Derivative Markets Are Manipulated

Most markets of the world are manipulated, including the mother of all markets, the US market. So, this is generally an excuse trotted out by losing traders. I believe that through a system of proper money management and a working knowledge of charting, investors and traders can see what is going on in the markets. Whether or not the markets are manipulated should not affect the trader. He should have his defined set of rules by which he plays.

Aspects of Successful Trading

Successful trading consists of the following three aspects:

- Charting and entry techniques;
- Money management; and
- Psychology.

In Figure 1.1, you can also see the relative importance of each of these three aspects of successful trading. Most traders go bust even while learning the first aspect, namely charting and entry, which actually happens to be the least important of the three. Novices often start trading without understanding the far greater importance of money management and psychology, and it takes them years to do so. Most books and seminars focus chiefly on charting and entry techniques which are the least important though the most glamorous. I know enough entry techniques to fill up an entire book and it will sell by the millions because most people just want to know that one magic technique which will lead them to riches. The fact is that charting and entry techniques are relatively less important. Once you can understand this, you will save yourself a lot of time, money and heartburn. Trust me, I have been there.

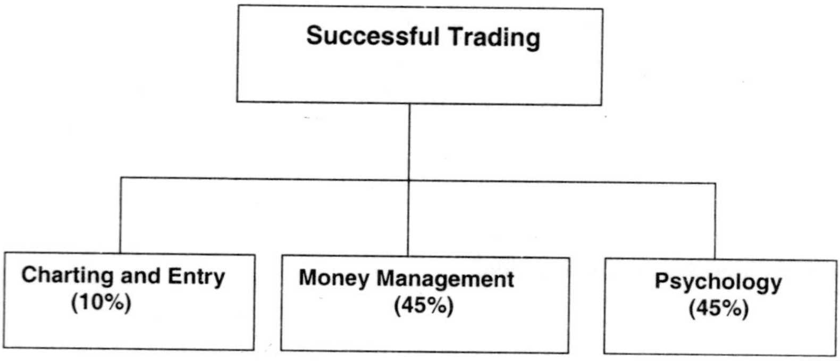

Figure 1.1

As for charting, all we can realistically do is label patterns which have a higher probability of working out. But in real life trading patterns fail as well. Also, most times they do not work out in the picture perfect manner in which they are shown in books. A trader should therefore never risk more than his usual risk capital and should use position size according to the money management technique he has chosen to follow. The key to successful trading, as I have noted earlier, is to get a few big winners and keeping losses small. Although I am chartist, but I am aware of its limitations. There are a number of times when chart patterns do not work at all, or as well as they are supposed to. The key is to capture those 5-, 6-, 7-bagger profits when the patterns do work out, and exit at breakeven or at small losses all the other times that the patterns do not work out. As we will see throughout the book, money can only be made if the same amount is risked every time, and the patterns are traded a number of times. The focus should be on protecting one's capital, not risking it. The average position size should not be increased just because a favourable pattern is shaping up. This should be done only when the size of your trading account grows to be large enough to add more contracts. The methods of doing so are described in the chapter on money management (Chapter 12). This is the reason why it is extremely difficult to find consistently successful day traders; they cannot have huge winners because they need to square up at the end of each day.

Last, but by not the means the least, is psychology. There is nothing more powerful than the mind. The human brain can process lots of information simultaneously. The human mind can also get fearful and greedly depending on situations. The logical mind avoids being a contrarian. It is precisely these aspects of human psychology that work against the trader. If traders can avoid being led astray by the behaviour of others, they will make consistent profits. Successful traders try to make all their buying and selling decisions as mechanical as possible, and eliminating all emotion so far as possible. While watching the stock ticker on television, I keep the volume at mute. I do not want to hear what other people are saying about the market. Trading is not about arriving at a consensus. Trading is about getting on to big trends as often as possible — and keeping your losses small when you can't. During the course of this book I will repeat this mantra so many times that you would be better off writing it on a piece of paper and sticking it on your table.

Successful traders also try to buy a market on retracement because that reduces the risk in the trade. They do not chase the market but wait for the shorter trend to move contrary to the main trend to make their entries. They remember that the markets get stronger with each successive fall, and weaker with each rise. They avoid making entries into agitated or violent markets. They avoid making trades during the first hour of trading.

Most important, they are not afraid of losses. They understand that not only are losses inevitable, but that losses are the price of gaining entries into big rends. The one thing they do understand is that losses need to be kept to a minimum and should only be used as an entry ticket. They understand which phase the market is in — whether it is trading or trending. They know it's time to keep out of the market when the market is trendless and moving only in very small swings. There is no point trying to win in a market which is totally trendless. A complete chapter later in the book discuses the finer points of psychology (Chapter 11).

At the end of this book, a trader should have answers to the following key points:

- What is the trend of the market.
- What are the setups with which you are the most comfortable for an entry in the market.
- What is the size of the position you should take based on sound money management principles.
- What stop loss to place that would not only protect your capital but also keep out the market's daily noise.

- When should you keep out of the market because the market shows a very weak trend, whether up or down.
- At what point, depending your account size, should you increase your position size.
- Also, when should you exit your trading positions.

Chapter 2

ADX — The Anatomy of a Trend

Technical Analysis

Technical analysis is the most useful and consistent approach to trading the markets. Although this is not a book on technical analysis, but it is critical that a trader be a good technician in order to trade futures profitably.

Simply put, technical analysis is the art and science of putting stock information on a chart in the form of various kinds of bars and detecting different patterns and indicators to assess the market's direction. While a lot of people know at least a little about technical analysis, very few really know how to use it. Technical analysis is not an astrological science for predicting prices and market direction. The main function of technical analysis is to show the current demand-supply position of the market, or a particular stock, define risk and reward of each particular trade, and help in following market trends. Technical analysis is not an end in itself; the end is its effective use for profitable trading. After having spent many years trying to learn every available technical technique under the sun, I am also of the opinion that people should use only those techniques which suit their style, instead of trying to apply too many of them. Making serious money has no correlation with the number of technical theories that you may have mastered. There are plenty of people who run down technical analysis. Well, more the people who do so, and more the people who disregard it, the happier I am because it ensures that the technical techniques will keep working for a longer period of time.

The basis of technical analysis is the trend following system. Trends can be identified by using simple indicators in any technical analysis software. A lot of people have introduced many complicated patterns and methodologies to take advantage of very short term mispricings. Personally, I prefer position and swing trading which includes holding positions from 3-4 days to several weeks.

Computers and Technical Analysis

The advent of computers has revolutionised the use of technical analysis. The availability of huge computing power at an affordable cost has eliminated the grind of manually making technical analysis-charts. Stock market data is now available in both intraday and end-of day formats. Computerised analysis allows a trader to track many markets simultaneously and also allows him to focus on the skills and judgement required in trading rather than getting drowned in its mechanics. It also enables the technical analyst to look at charts in more than one time frames, allowing him to make better entries and money management decisions.

In my experience, a software that allows for charting of data and has standard indicators is good enough for beginner and intermediate technical analysts. As your skills grow, you can start building custom indicators and also use back-testing strategies.

I must however caution at this point that technical analysis is more about how an analyst uses the software, rather than about the software itself. There is no software which can take the hard work out of detailed analysis, or which can be a substitute for human judgement. Although there are many softwares that claim a lot of things, the fact is that no software or trading system can adapt to changing market conditions as well as the human mind can. I would like to advise all readers of this book to go through at least two basic books* on this subject in order to gain full advantage of the technical analysis-related chapters of this book (chapters 3 and 4). Also, all readers should have access to a basic charting software so that they can test what they read in this book.

---

* *Technical Analysis of Stock Trends* by Robert D. Edwards & Magee and *Martin Pring on Market Momentum* by Martin Pring, both published by Vision Books, are two fine books you could consult. (www.visionbooksindia.com).

Types of Trading

There are three types of trading, differentiated mainly by the time frame involved. These are:

1. Swing Trading

Swing trading is the method which allows trading of tradable swings, up and down. The length of time the trade is held could be from 3 to 4 days, to a couple of weeks.

2. Position Trading

Position trading is used by traders who tend to hold trades over multiple swings, not ending their trades on intermittent corrections. They could be holding trades anywhere from a couple of weeks to many months.

3. Day Trading

Day traders trade within the course of a day. They generally do not carry overnight positions. Day trading, in particular, remains one of the most difficult forms of trading to master.

There are successful traders of all three types. Choosing the type of trading approach appropriate for you is a function of many things, but most successful traders tend to adopt, and try and master, any one of the three. The factors affecting your choice could be the size of your trading equity, your personality, and probably the development of your own niche which a trader discovers after many years in trading.

Based on my style of trading, I like to consider myself a swing trader, and in extraordinary circumstances of a strong weekly trend, a position trader. The way I use technical analysis is:

- Identify the trend of the market.
- Measure the strength of that trend.
- Look for a low-risk entry into that trend.
- Use money management to determine the size of any position.
- Use an appropriate stop loss.

- Keep following the trend till the market proves it has reversed.
- Keep out of the market when the market is not showing any significant trend one way or the other.

I hope by the time you finish reading this book, you would be able to do all of the above effectively.

The Anatomy of a Bar

A bar is the most basic component of a chart just as an atom is the most basic component in all living and non-living matter. The bar contains very useful information provided the trader picks it up early enough. The normal bar on a chart consists of the open, high, low and close prices.

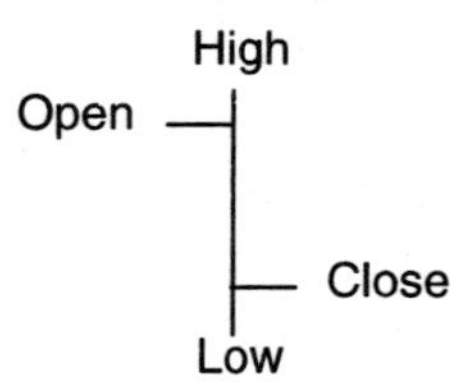

The open belongs to the amateurs; the high of any bar belongs to the bulls and depicts how much force they had; the low shows the maximum power of the bears; and the closing action is set up by the professional investors. Since most major movements in the market are determined by the professionals, it pays to follow them. I am not at all suggesting that traders should blindly follow what they perceive professionals to be doing. But just waiting till the last one hour can sometimes help you avoid taking false trades that you might otherwise get into. During the day the market gyrates in both directions, i.e. up and down, trapping players in both directions and then finally moves in one direction, either rewarding one set of players or closing in a narrow range. In either case, my experience is that out of the hundred trades I might have taken in the beginning of the trading session, I would have avoided taking at least sixty had I waited for the last half-hour. This makes a huge difference to your trading equity; you not only avoid overtrading, but this also allows you to follow the market in its truest sense without having to base your trades on predictions.

And, believe me, trading is both about reducing losses and increasing profits. The same applies even to weekly bars.

Trends

Contrary to what a lot of people think, technical analysis is the art of trend following rather than one of predicting prices and turning points. Trend following remains the single most effective strategy for making big trading profits in the stock markets:

- A trend is a series of rising or declining prices over any length of time.
- An uptrend is a market which seeks consistently higher prices over time.
- A downtrend is a market which seeks consistently lower prices over time.
- At any given time the market is comprised of three trends, namely the primary, secondary and minor trends.
- Primary trend can be either a series of rising or declining prices. Primary trends can last from one to several years.
- Secondary trends are intermediate corrective trends to the primary trend. These reactions generally last from one to three months and retrace one-third to two-thirds of the primary trend.
- Minor trends are short term movements lasting from one day to three weeks.

The Big Question: Is the Market Trending or Trading?

Market movements can be characterised by two distinct types of phases. In one phase, the market shows trending movements either up or down. Trending movements have a direction bias over a period of time.

In the second phase, the market shows trading range movements or consolidation, where the market shows no consistent directional bias and moves between two levels.

These two different phases of the market require the use of different types of technical indicators:

- Trending markets need the use of trend following indicators, such as the moving averages, MACD, etc.
- Trading range markets, on the other hand, need the use of oscillators, like the RSI, stochastic, etc. which use overbought and oversold levels.

So identifying the phase of the market is extremely critical, for that would decide the methodology a trader needs to follow.

ADX: Answering the Big Question

The ADX, or the Average Directional Movement Index, fills this need for identifying whether market is in the trending or the trading phase. Welles Wilder developed the ADX, which to my mind is his most useful but least understood innovation.

The concept of trends is central to the idea of ADX. The ADX can tell the strength of the move that a market may be in and thus help keep you out of a whipsawing market, or keep you in long enough during a trending market to make huge profits.

ADX forms the core of my trading style since my trading is based on trend following. The ADX is a standard indicator available in all technical analysis software. Traders would do well to incorporate the key aspects of ADX in their trading style.

ADX defines the degree — or strength — of the directional movement and not its direction.

The directional movement system is a trading system based on the use of ADX, and gives timing information based on the strength of the underlying trend. We will now discuss the interpretations of ADX reading, and timing signals provided to the trader by the Directional Movement System.

Directional Movement

Directional movement is defined as the difference between the high and the low of a particular bar on a chart that falls outside the range of a previous bar. In terms of a daily chart, price action above the previous day's high is positive directional movement (+DM), while anything below the previous day's low is negative directional movement (-DM). This analysis can be equally applied to monthly, weekly, daily or intra-day data.

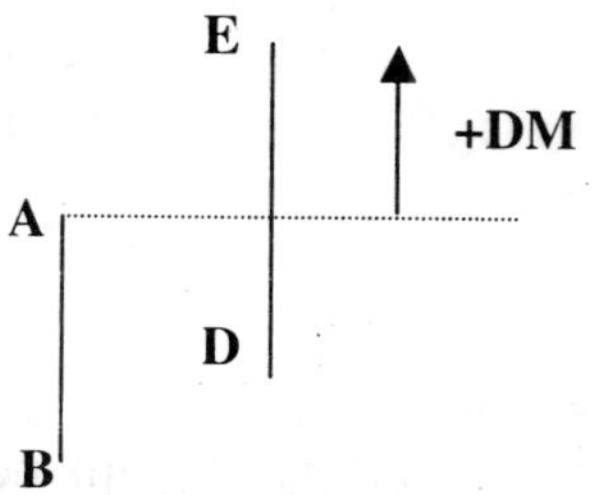

Figure 2.1: **Positive Directional Movement**

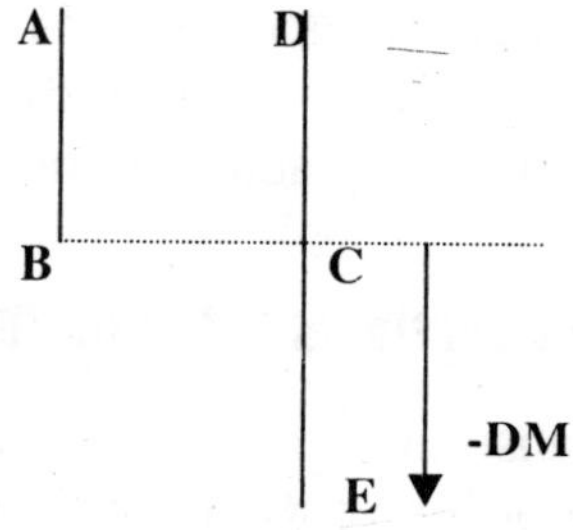

Figure 2.2: **Negative Directional Movement**

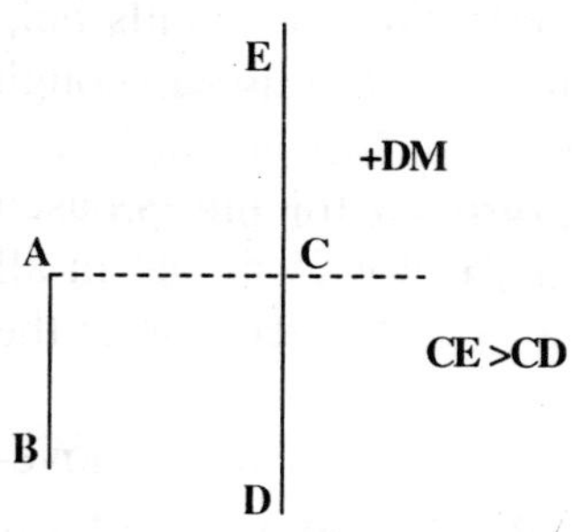

Figure 2.3: **Outside day — directional movement taken as the greater of CD and CE, namely CE**

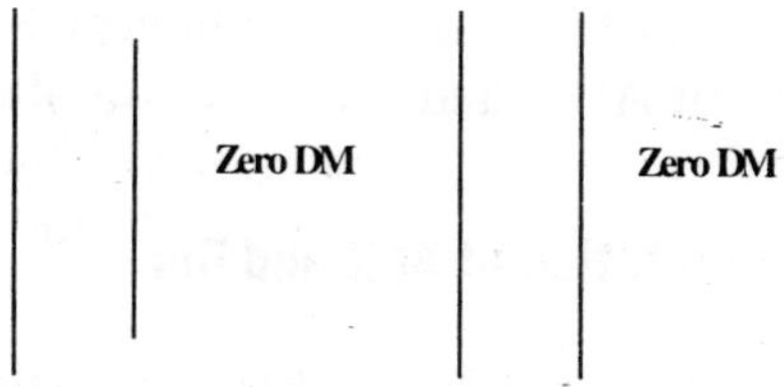

Figure 2.4: **Inside day — the DM is considered zero as there is no directional movement**

Figures 2.1 to 2.4 show movements across two trading days highlighting positive directional movement (+DM), negative directional movement (–DM), and zero directional movement.

In Figure 2.1, the portion EA on the second day, which lies above the range of the first day, is defined as positive directional movement (+DM).

In Figure 2.2, the part CE that lies below the range of the second day is known as negative directional movement (-DM).

Figure 2.3 shows an outside day, which is a day whose range encompasses all of the movement of the previous day. In this case both CD and CE exceed AB so the greater of the two, namely CE, defines the directional movement index, i.e. +DM.

Figure 2.4 shows an inside day where the range of the first day encompasses the entire movement of the second day. As there is no directional bias achieved on this day, there is zero DM.

The Directional Indicator (DI)

As absolute difference in price movement fails to take into account the proportion of the movement, Welles Wilder developed the directional indicator (DI). To make the DMs consistent across all stock prices, Wilder decided that price movements are best described as ratios rather than absolute numbers. Accordingly, Wilder decided to divide the directional movements (+DM) and (-DM) by the market's true range. Since no trend is determined in a day, so the DIs are calculated over a number of days. Wilder decided to use 14 days for this purpose. The DIs provide the timing signals in the Directional Movement System, and their understanding provides the background for interpretations of ADX and effective use of its timing signals.

Interpretation of ADX and DIs

ADX was developed from the DIs, and we will move straight to the use of this indicator without going into any more calculations. This indicator has been programmed into most popular technical analysis software.

The first step in using ADX is to identify a security with a high ADX since that would offer enough directional movement to allow trend following trades:

- A high ADX value defines a strong trend; the trend could be either up or down.
- A low ADX shows a consolidation, such markets are generally difficult to trade.

In general, the following rules may be followed with regard to interpreting the ADX:

ADX Interpretations

1)	ADX less than 20 is interpreted as a weak trend or consolidation.	Indicating the use of oscillators.
2)	ADX rising from 15 to 25 from lower levels means the trend is strengthening.	Use trend following systems.
3)	ADX above 30 is interpreted as a strong trend.	Use trend following systems.
4)	ADX at an extremely high level of 45 or above is interpreted as a market in a strong trend with a consolidation expected anytime.	Start booking profits if the ADX makes a top or flattens out.
5)	ADX declining below 30 is interpreted as a consolidation after a trending move.	Use oscillators or credit spreads to trade thee consolidations. If bearish patterns develop and breakdown, look for ADX to move higher, this time indicating a trending move on the downside.

DI Timing Signals

DIs, on the other hand, can be used as timing devices:

- Long trades can be entered when +DI moves over-DIs, and
- Short trades are entered when –DI moves below +DI.

The success of this timing methodology depends on the strength of the trend determined by the ADX. The greater the strength of the trend, the greater is the directional movement. The stronger the trend, the fewer the whipsaws given by the DIs.

Wilder noted that important turns are indicated when ADX reverses direction after it has moved above both the DIs. Divergence between the ADX and the price is an important indicator of an impending reversal. Profits should be booked at every level once the ADX tops out. DI signals may occur with lagging effect. ADX should be used to filter the DI signals, taking only the ones occurring when ADX indicates trending.

Conversely, when the ADX is at very low levels, Wilder recommended not using trend following systems.

Let's go through some examples and see how we can best use this wonderful trading system.

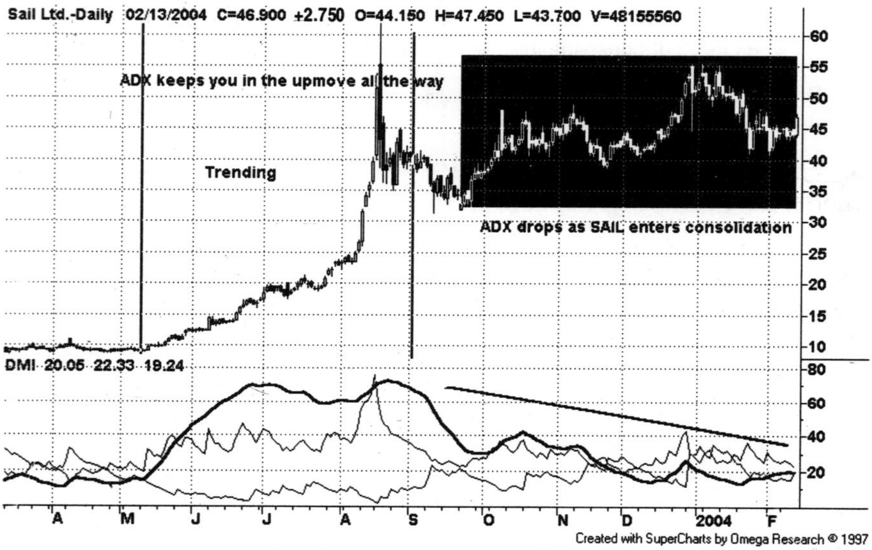

Figure 2.5

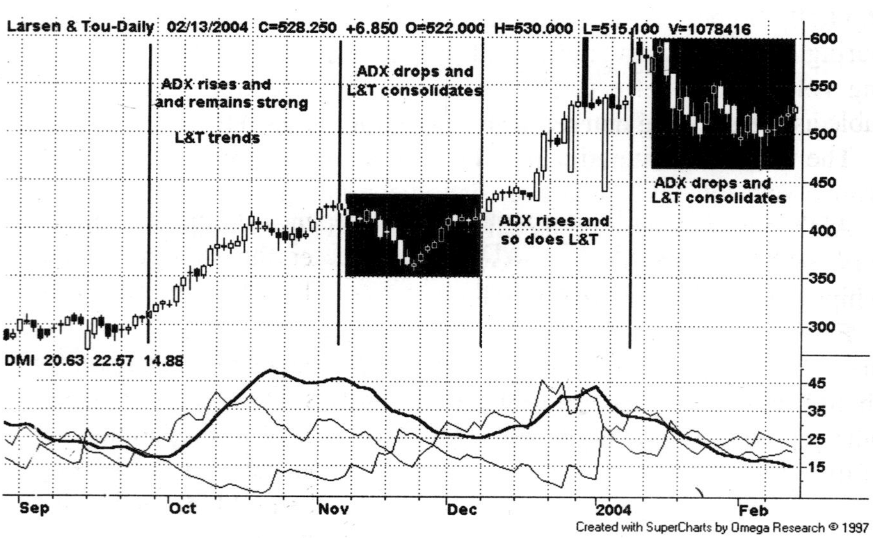

Figure 2.6

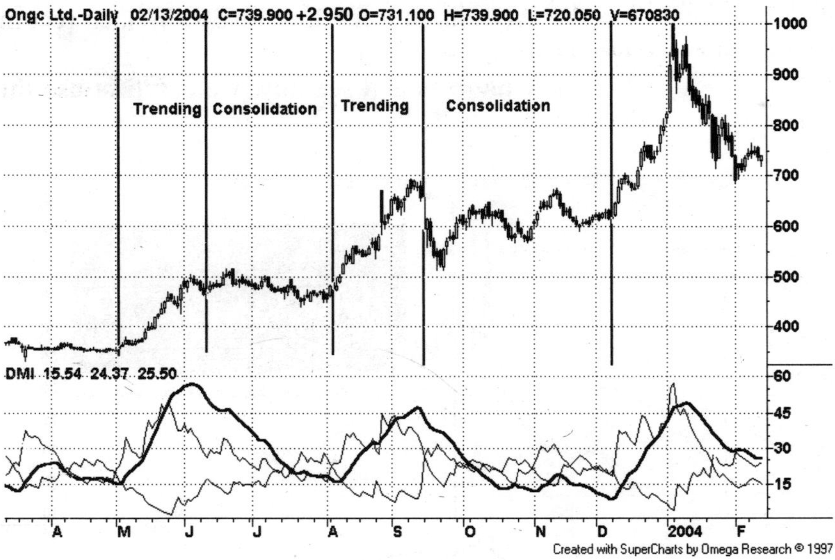

Figure 2.7

As can be seen from Figures 2.5, 2.6 and 2.7, the ADX keeps you in the trending moves, while indicating consolidations. The way I use the ADX is that I trade lighter volumes during consolidations and substantially higher volumes during trending moves. The drop in volume during consolidations could be of the order of two-thirds of the trending volume. This effectively means taking substantial profits off the table as the trending market turns into a trading market.

The most effective signals from ADX are received when it rises from a very low level to above 15, and continues on beyond 30.

ADX can also be used as filter for various trend-following indicators, such as MACD and moving averages which otherwise give whipsaws in consolidating markets.

Figures 2.8 and 2.9 illustrate examples of trading markets and how they can be traded using oscillators. RSI (7) and Stochastics (7,10) should be used to trade consolidating markets with a low ADX. Another option is to use credit spreads or covered calls to take advantage of time decay.

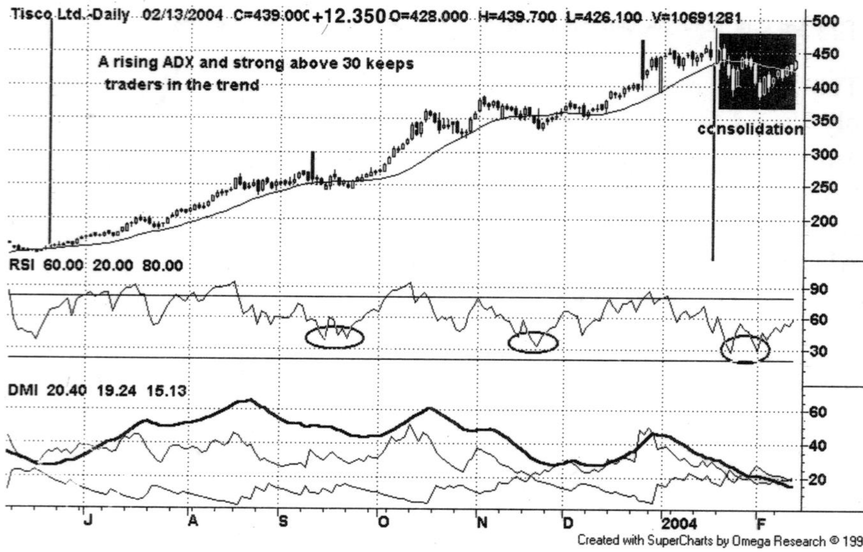

Figures 2.8

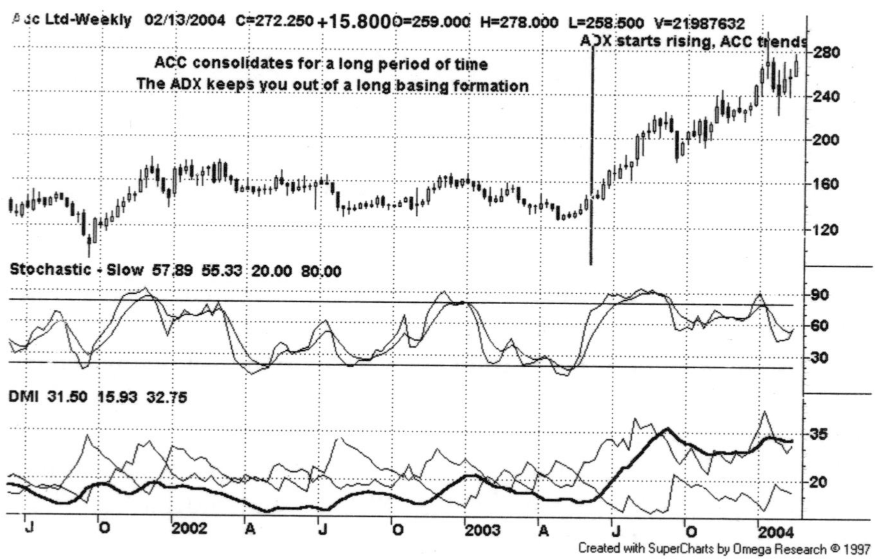

Figure 2.9

The ADX Works on All Time Frames

The ADX indicator and the directional movement systems are possibly the most useful tools in technical analysis. The most important aspect of the ADX and the DIs is that they keep you in the trend. I believe that technical analysis always works best when there is a confluence of indicators and patterns. I would advise all traders to use ADX in conjunction with other technical patterns and indicators.

Chapter 3

Technical Methods

Indicators

As technical analysis has become more and more computerised, several indicators have become fairly popular. Indicators like the MACD, stochastics, RSI, and momentum are now commonly used. I find it useful to divide technical indicators into two categories, namely:

- Trend following indicators, and
- Oscillators.

Also, more than the nuances of various indicators, what is important is to understand when to use these indicators.

Trend following indicators are used in trending markets — and oscillators are used in trading markets.

MACD and moving averages form part of the trending indicators while stochastics, RSI, momentum, etc. are some of the trading indicators. Typically, I use trend following indicators such as the MACD and moving averages when the ADX is rising over 16 to 20 which indicates a trending market — and oscillators when the ADX is declining, thus indicating consolidation. Using either type of indicator in the wrong market context can be lethal as described in the previous chapter on ADX.

MACD (Moving Average Convergence Divergence)

Traders should remember that MACD is a trending market indicator and thus gives the best signals only when the market is trending. MACD indicator, developed by Gerald Appel, is a more advanced version of the moving averages.

MACD consists of two lines, the MACD line (fast line) and the signal line (smoothed average). Buy and sell signals are given when the MACD line crosses above or below the signal line. The MACD line is the difference of the 26-day EMA and the 12-day EMA which is smoothed by a 9-day EMA of the MACD line. My preferred MACD settings are 3,10,16. This is the slow signal line.

Most novice traders make the mistake of using MACD in all types of market conditions. Whether the market is trending or not can be ascertained by using ADX as described earlier. In trading range-bound markets, MACD is likely to give many whipsaws and frustrate the trader.

MACD Trading Rules

- Go long when the shorter term moving average moves above the longer term moving average. (*See* Figure 3.1)
- Go short when the shorter term moving average moves below the longer term moving average.

MACD Histogram

The MACD histogram offers deeper insight into the balance of power between the bulls and bears than does the original MACD. It not only

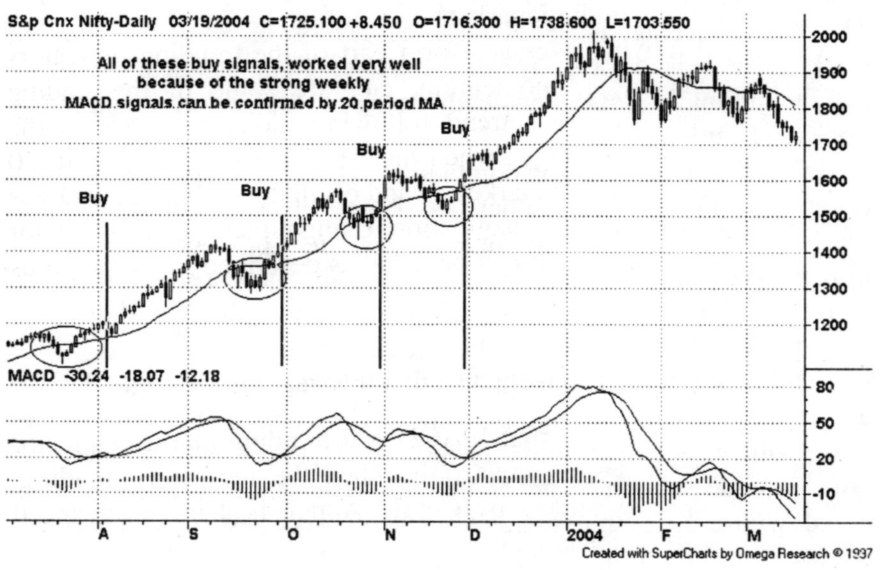

Figure 3.1

shows whether it is the bulls or bears who are in control but also whether they are growing stronger or weaker.

If the fast line is above the slow line, the MACD histogram is positive and is plotted above the zero line. Conversely, when the fast line is below the slow, the histogram is plotted below the zero line (*See* Figure 3.1).

[MACD Histogram = MACD Line — Signal Line]

The MACD histogram measures the difference between the MACD and the signal lines, plotted as a histogram. When the spread between the MACD and the signal line increases, MACD histogram becomes taller (deeper). When the two lines are closer together, MACD histogram becomes smaller (shallower).

The slope of the MACD identifies the dominant market group. A rising MACD shows that the bulls are becoming stronger. A falling MACD shows that the bears are becoming stronger.

The MACD histogram confirms a trend when, together with prices, it reaches new highs or lows.

Moving Averages

A moving average is the average of a pre-decided number of data points, where with each new data point the first data point is rejected. The moving average is an indicator that is most effective in a trending market. The reason for using a moving average in technical analysis is that it eliminates noise and tends to show the underlying trend of prices indicators.

One of the most common complaints against moving average is that it gets you into the trend rather late. I have always found this charge funny. Except in the case of bigger time frames, or a very large-period moving average, a moving average can only show a trend once it is there; it cannot predict trends, in fact nothing can. The shorter the moving average, the shorter is the trend it's able to show.

There is no perfect number to use for a moving average. Traders use moving averages ranging from 10 DMA to 200 DMA and the same with weekly and monthly moving averages. Moving averages often provide support to prices in an uptrend and resistance to prices in a downtrend. The moving average that works best for you can only be discovered by trying it out often; it also depends on the time frame you want to trade. It's like buying a shirt; the same shirt does not fit everyone.

I prefer to use the 30-day and 200-day moving averages to get a feel of the broad long term trend. If the shorter moving average is above the longer moving average, the trend is up. Conversely, when the longer moving average is above the shorter moving average, the trend is down. These are two of the most important moving averages, and a stock or the market closing below the 30 DMA often signals the beginning of a larger correction in an uptrend. Closing below the 200 DMA is the beginning of a downtrend. No long positions should be held once a stock or a market closes below its 200 DMA. Conversely, closing above the 200 DMA signifies the beginning of an uptrend. Another way I use the 30-day and 200-day moving averages is using the turnings of the moving average — from down to up, or up to down — to book profit or to change my view from bullish to sideways or bearish to sideways, respectively. I have always found moving average crossovers leading to large moves in the direction of the crossover (Figure 3.2).

Shorter term trends can be determined by using shorter term averages such as the 30 DMA or 50 DMA. The number used for the moving average is not important here. That is because it would not make a

Figure 3.2

Figure 3.3

huge difference whether 35 DMA or 55 DMA is used as both would give information similar to the 30 DMA or 50 DMA. Again, prices above the 30 and 50 DMA show an uptrend, and below the 30 and 50 DMA show a downtrend (Figure 3.3).

Sometimes two moving averages are used for the purpose of short term trading, the averages selected would depend on the time frame of trading. For example, for short term trading it could be 10 and 50 DMAs. For longer term trading, it could be 30 and 200 DMAs. When the shorter term moving average moves above the longer term one, traders can go long. Conversely, when the longer term moving average goes below the shorter term moving average, traders can go short. Another combination to achieve the same result could be 13 and 30 DMAs. Again these combinations are not important, almost any two moving averages will do.

Moving averages do an excellent job of providing support and resistance so they should be used to put stops. Any decisive close below a moving average should be taken as a breach of that support. Similarly, any decisive close above a certain moving average should be taken as breach of resistance.

I also like to use a 20-period moving average on all time frames that I look at because it provides the relative position of the market at that point. The 20-period moving average indicates the prevailing bias of the market, particularly in shorter time frames, such as the 30-minute chart. It also provides great entries into existing trends in all time frames and buying options once the price goes below the 20-period moving average and then comes back above it, signifying that a reaction in an uptrend may be over. This is one of my favourite entry methods. Also, the number of bars above and below the 20-period moving average give a fair indication of both the prevailing intraday trend and also when it starts changing [Figure 3.4 (a & b)].

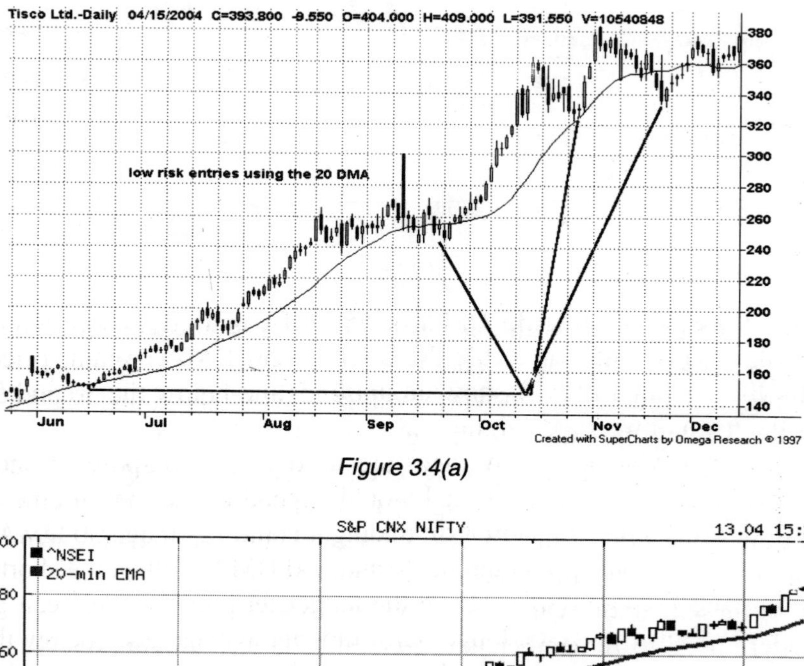

Figure 3.4(a)

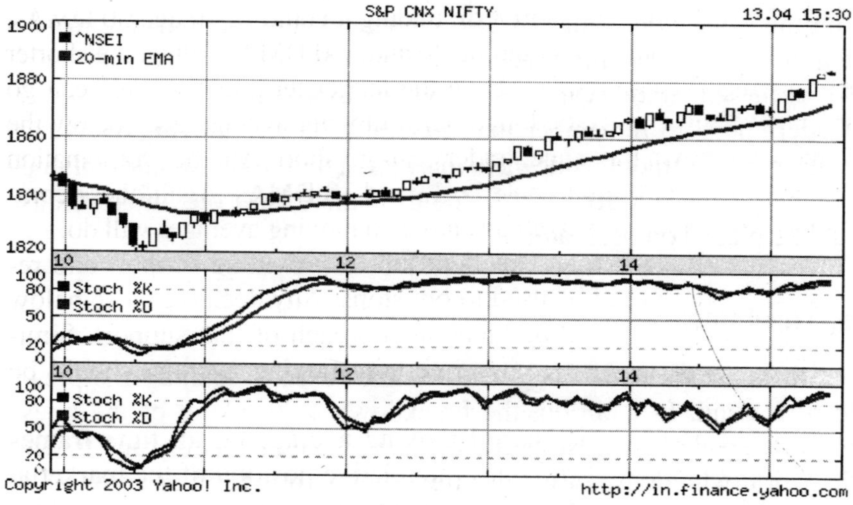

Figure 3.4(b)

Figure 3.5

One of the problems with this system is that it gives whipsaws in a sideways market. This can be addressed using three moving averages, involving 5, 8 and 13-day moving averages. When the 5 and 8 DMA cross the 13-day moving average, go long. When the 5-day average crosses back below the 8-day average, you get an exit signal. However, you don't get a new entry signal until both the 5 and the 8 DMA are on the same side of the 13-day average. These methods are available in most technical analysis books (Figure 3.5).

All of these methods can be used on any time frame.

Traders need to remember that both MACD and moving averages fail miserably in trading sideways markets. These tools should only be used when there is a discernable trend. If there isn't one, more focus should be placed on oscillators.

Using Trend Lines

Trend lines, as the name suggests, are lines used to identify the presence of a trend. In addition, the breakdown or breakout of the lines suggest reversal of an existing trend. There would be hardly any trader in the world who does not use the trend line in one form or another. It is critical to grasp the essence of a trend line in order to use it in more innovative ways. This is a very simple and very handy tool which if applied correctly makes a trader's life very easy. A trend line can be used on any chart starting from yearly, quarterly, monthly, weekly, daily, 60-minute, 5-minute, etc., and for any market that is chartable.

Support Line

A line running under the prices and connecting three non-consecutive turning points on a bar chart, and which is either horizontal or slanting upward.

Resistance Line

A line running above the prices on a bar chart connecting three non-consecutive turning points and which is either sloping downwards or is horizontal.

Interpreting Trend Lines

However there are certain rules to be followed while drawing trend lines and in interpreting the signals they throw up:

1. There should be at least three non-consecutive points joined by the trend line and a trend line should not be "forced" upon a chart. There should actually be a line which shows a trend, the breakdown or breakout of which should show some kind of reversal. Remember, at least three non-consecutive points should be joined to form a valid trend line.
2. The longer a trend line, the more will be the consequences of its breakdown. In fact, the length of a trend line is critical in determining its significance. For example, a two-year trend line is more significant than a two-month trend line, and a two-month trend line far more significant than a two-day trend line.
3. The flatter the trend line, the more significant is its breakdown. Trend lines with higher slopes are known to be broken easily. So a breakdown or breakout of a flatter trend line is much more significant as it would show huge selling or buying having taken place at that level.
4. The more tested a trend line is, the greater is its significance. A trend line which has provided support or resistance in the past needs to be respected. Not only is it likely to provide support again, its breakout or breakdown provides a tradable move in that direction.

5. Another important application of the trend line is that it provides a reference for placing stops. A stop should be placed at least 3% after a breakdown or breakout occurs.
6. Traders should use only closing prices to assess if a trend line has been broken. Often the breakout or breakdown of trend lines are at well-advertised levels. Media analysts repeat those levels often enough. Contrary to what they think, however, this is not a service to the trader; in fact, it works to his detriment. This is because the large traders and institutional investors create the particular intra-day breakout or breakdown, leading other investors and traders to believe that a significant change has occurred. When individual traders take positions, the market is conveniently reversed and such a breakdown or breakout is called false. At the end of the day the market closes at a level higher than the trend line, and the trend line still remains valid. This is most likely to happen in illiquid and small stocks. Traders should not pre-empt a breakdown or breakout till it actually occurs and the closing prices confirm it for at least a couple of sessions.
7. Trend line breakdowns should occur with volume. A warning that a particular breakdown or breakout is false is the kind of volume that accompanies it because breakdowns generally occur when a much higher than average volume is traded. I would be very cautious on a breakout or breakdown that occurs on low volumes.
8. Trend lines should be extended into the future. All trend lines should be extended into the future as they often continue to provide support and resistance at those levels even at a future date.

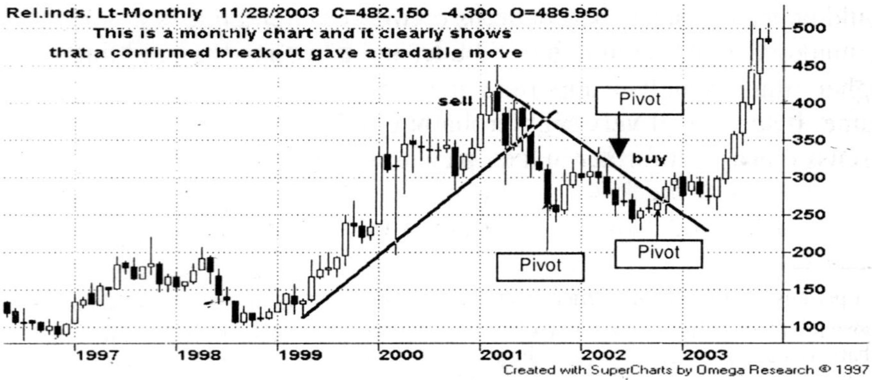

Figure 3.6

Now some personal notes on trend line signals that I have observed in my experience of trading.

Trend lines work beautifully on intraday charts for all those interested in day trading, and it is the one technique which is consistently proven. In real life, it is not only critical that a trend line break occurs and is supported by volume, it is also important for the market to show strength in the direction of the break. I identify pivots* on a chart and would like to see these too violated along with the trend line violation and volume breakout (*See* Figures 3.6 and 3.7). Generally, two of the above conditions are sufficient to enter the trade. It is also advisable to enter the trade in the direction of a trend identified in the higher time frame. This further increases the probability of a successful trade. The procedure for entering a trend line breakout trade is to take the trade as prices break a trend line and close on the other side. Sometimes there is a pullback to the trend line, and some people like to buy or sell the pullback. A stop can be placed on the valid side of the trend line. Once in the trade, traders should draw a fresh trend line and continue to hold the trade till the new trend line is broken. You will be amazed how many big trends you can catch using this method. Trend lines can also be used by traders to scale their position. This means you can keep adding a certain quantity of stock as more downward sloping trend lines are broken in a rally or *vice-versa* (see, for example, the accompanying intraday Satyam Charts: Figures 3.8 and 3.9). Scaling in would further help manage risk, as positions will get added as the market gains strength.

However good a trend line appears, I still like to look for additional information that would substantiate the beginning of a new trend. It could be the classical chart patterns on the current time frame. It could be market action on the higher time frame. If the market action on the higher time frame is supporting market action on the current time frame, it suggests a very high probability of profitable trade. We will discuss this aspect further in later pages.

---

* A pivot is a bar on any time frame which is a turning point on a chart, also called the swing high or swing low. For example, an upward pivot bar will have the two adjoining bars with highs below the high of the pivot bar. A downward pivot bar, will have two adjoining bars with lows higher than the low of the pivot bar (*See* charts in Figures 3.6, 3.7, 3.8 and 3.9).

Figure 3.7

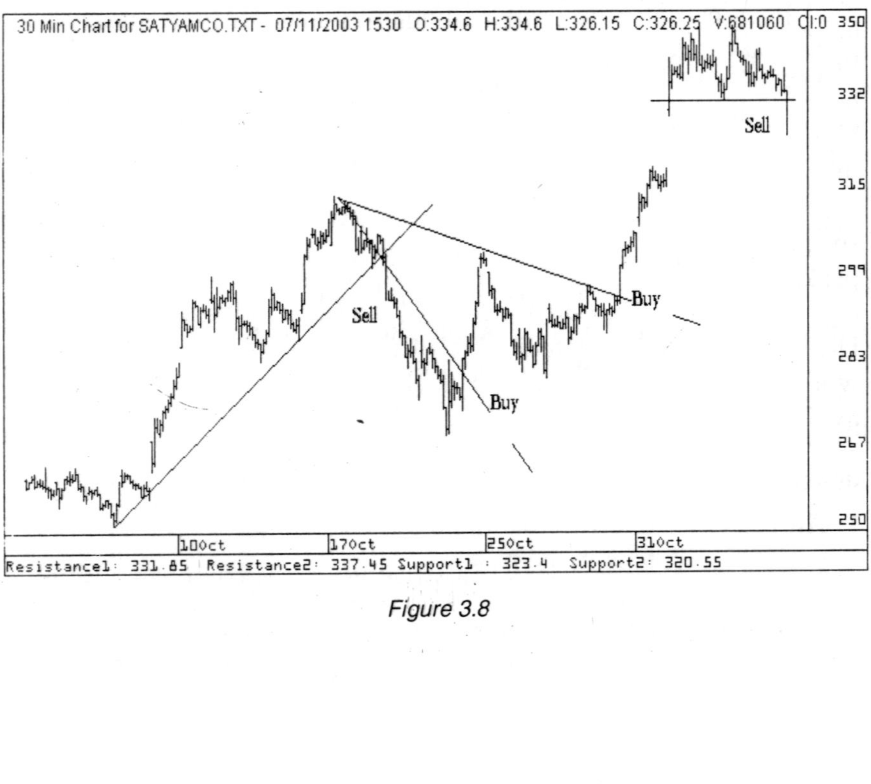

Figure 3.8

Figure 3.9

Oscillators (or Momentum Oscillators)

Oscillators identify the emotional extremes of market crowds. They help in determining unsustainable levels of optimism and pessimism. Professionals trade these extremes by betting against them, i.e. they bet on a return to normalcy. So long as oscillators keep making new highs, it is safe to hold long positions. Correspondingly, so long as they keep touching new lows, it is safe to hold short positions. When an oscillator reaches a new high, it shows that an uptrend is gaining speed and is likely to continue. When an oscillator traces a lower peak, it means that the trend has stopped accelerating and a reversal can be expected from there, much like a car slowing down to make a U-turn. The two oscillators which I use most extensively, and which work well, are the RSI and the stochastics. There are other indicators available but those too provide the same information.

Overbought and Oversold

- An oscillator becomes overbought when it reaches a high level associated with tops in the past.
- An oscillator becomes oversold when it reaches a low level associated with bottoms in the past.

When an oscillator rises or falls beyond its reference line, it helps a trader to pick a top and a bottom. Oscillators work splendidly in a trading range, but they give premature and dangerous trading signals when a new trend erupts from a range.

An oscillator can stay overbought for weeks at a time when a new, strong uptrend begins, giving buy signals. It can also stay oversold for weeks in a steep downtrend, giving premature buy signals.

Types of Divergences

There are three types of divergences as defined by Dr. Alexander Elder in his book, *Trading for a Living*.

Class A divergences identify important turning points and are the best trading opportunities. Class B divergences are less strong, and Class C divergences are the least important. (*See:* Figures 3.10, 3.11 and 3.12).

My experience with divergences is that they work very well in retrospect but trades should be taken based on price action. Divergences can take weeks to work out, and sometimes they do not work out at all; remember, there is no holy grail in technical analysis. These

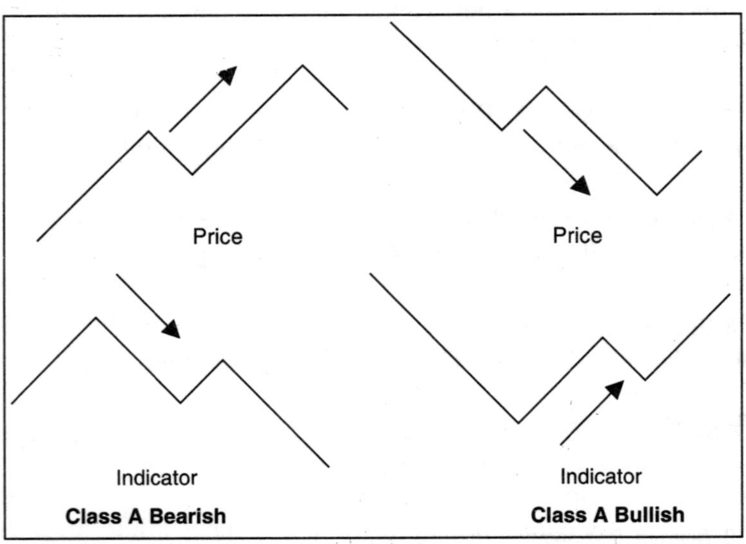

Figure 3.10: **Class A Divergence**

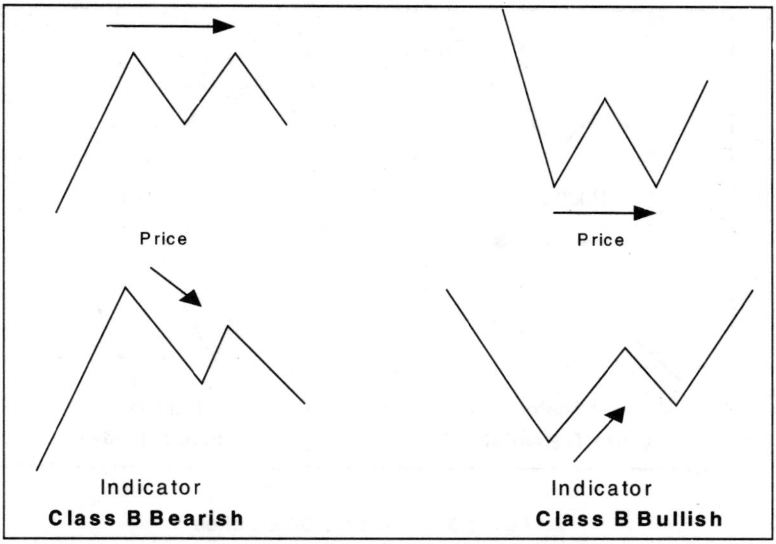

Figure 3.11: **Class B Divergence**

divergences serve as excellent points to tighten stops and take some profits off the table. Divergences should not be used as buy or sell signals but, instead, as a "get ready" signal — but you must hold your shot till you see the target. Remember, momentum measures trend acceleration, i.e. any gain or loss of speed.

Class A Bearish Divergence: Prices reach a new peak while an indicator reaches a lower bottom. This is the strongest sell signal.

Class A Bullish Divergence: Prices fall to a new low while an indicator is corrected above the earlier low. This is the strongest buy signal.

Class B Bearish Divergence: Prices trace a double top while an indicator reaches only a lower peak. This is the second strongest sell signal.

Class B Bullish Divergence: Prices trace a double bottom while an indicator traces a higher bottom. This is the second strongest buy signal.

Class C Bearing Divergence: Prices reach a new peak while an indicator traces a double top. This is the weakest bearish divergence.

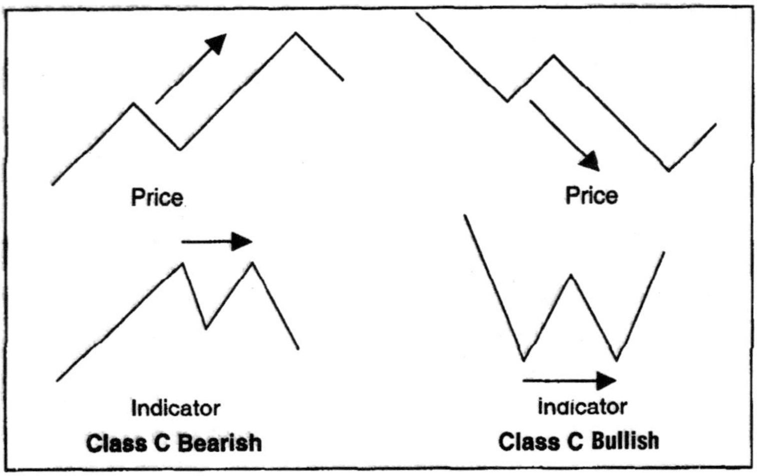

Figure 3.12: **Class C Divergence**

Class C Bullish Divergence: Prices fall to a new low while an indicator makes a double bottom. This is the weakest bullish divergence.

Class A divergences often identify good trades. Class B and C divergences lead to whipsaws, and are best ignored.

Triple Bullish or Bearish Divergences

These consist of three price tops and three oscillator tops, or three price bottoms and three oscillator bottoms. They are even stronger than the regular divergences. But again, do not buy based on divergence alone.

Relative Strength Indicatorn (RSI)

There are some myths about RSI which I would first like to dispel.

Myth: Bullish and Bearish Divergences Give the Strongest Buy Signals: Divergences between RSI and prices do not give the strongest buy and sell signals although these tend to occur at major tops and bottoms. They show up when the trend is weak and ready to reverse. While this is theoretically true, in actual fact it is very difficult to trade divergences. The reason for this is that the market continues to move up long after the bearish divergence is visible on the charts. So, too, is the case with a bullish divergence. What these divergences help in is providing a warning signal that the trend is weakening. Accordingly, at such times stops need to be tightened and profits protected.

Myth: Overbought and Oversold Levels Can be Used to Buy and Sell: Overbought and oversold levels cannot be used to buy and sell under all circumstances. In trending markets, RSI tends to become overbought and oversold for long periods of time. Using it make buy and sell decisions can be disastrous in such markets. Even when trading range-bound markets, RSI can be prone to whipsaws and trading volumes should be reduced while using it in such markets. These levels should be used for the range-bound market and for re-testing trades.

Nevertheless, RSI remains one of the most popular indicators in technical analysis and can be used in a variety of useful ways as described below.

Charting Patterns

Chart patterns like head and shoulders breakouts, trendline breakouts, support and resistances work well with RSI which often completes these patterns in advance of prices, thus providing hints of likely trend changes.

Zone Shift

Since RSI indicator is based on closing prices of a security or an indicator, it tends to travel between the bullish and the bearish zones. It can be used to assess the trend of the market as this zone shift takes place. Notice how the RSI holds the 50 level in the main uptrend and at the same time finds resistance at the 50 level during the intermediate downtrend (Figure 3.13).

RSI is also used as a contra indicator. This means that once the weekly trend is identified, whether up or down, the daily RSI is used to enter trades in the direction of the weekly trend. When the weekly trend is up, an oversold level of daily RSI is used to enter long trades. When the weekly trend is down, an overbought level of daily RSI is used to enter short trades. Profits can be taken when the daily RSI moves to the other extreme, i.e. when RSI moves from oversold to overbought — or overbought to oversold. This technique is used in

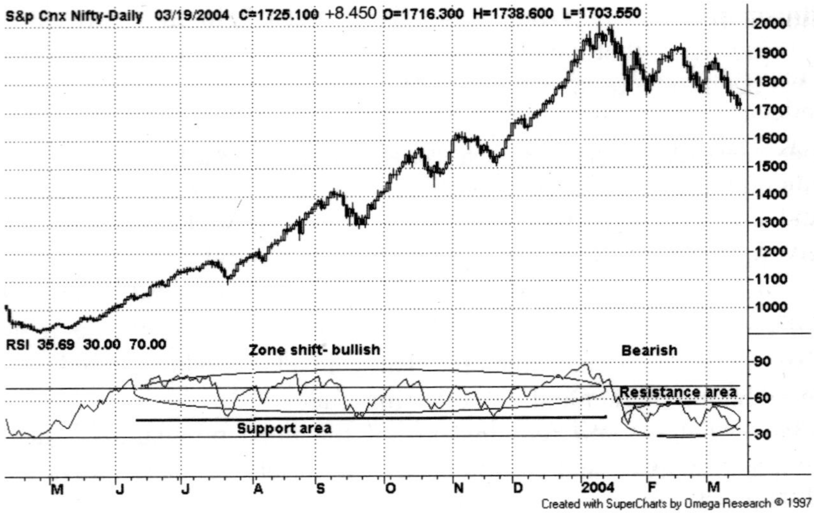

Figure 3.13

conjunction with either the Fibonacci levels, stochastics, and/or the 20-period moving average. Perfect levels of entry are impossible to predict but generally an oversold or overbought region can be identified. Actual trading signals are taken when a significant pivot is broken. I like to use the 7-day RSI as shown in Figure 3.14, which does a good job of identifying decent entry points.

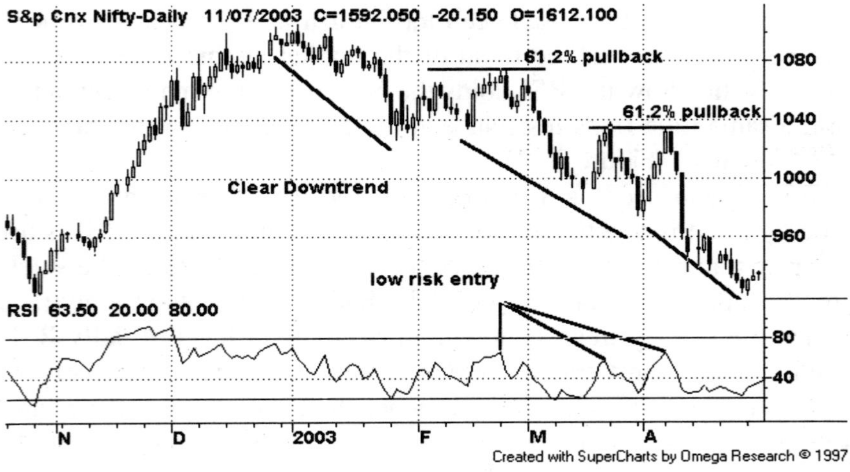

Figure 3.14

Stochastics

Stochastics is the other popular oscillator which can either be used or independently in conjunction with RSI. It consists of two lines, the %K (fast line) and the %D (slow line). The slow %D line is a smoothed version of the fast line. My preferred setting for %K is 7 and that for %D is 10. %K crosses over %D when a buy signal is given and %D crosses over %K when a sell signal is given.

There are two varieties of stochastics, the fast and the slow version. The fast version is a very sensitive oscillator and has the tendency of giving whipsaws. Some traders prefer to use the slow stochastic which is constructed by using %D of the fast stochastic as %K of the slow stochastic. This is then smoothed over a given period to find the %D of the slow stochastic. This oscillator can also be used as a contra indicator similar to the RSI. Stochastics has the tendency to stay overbought and oversold in highly trending markets (Figure 3.15).

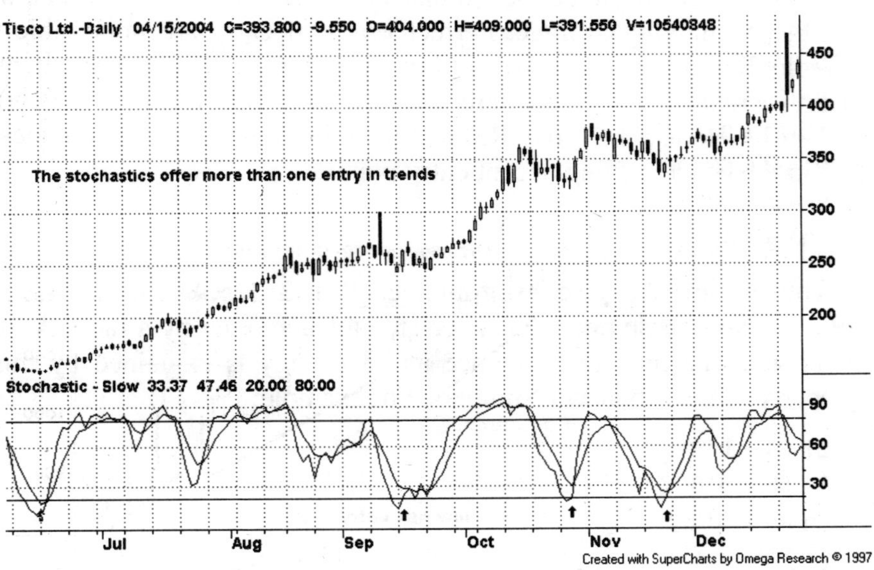

Figure 3.15

Fibonacci Methods

One of the enduring goals of traders is to find a meaning in the maze that is the stock market. They have used astrology, rocket science, fundamental analysis, and technical analysis, etc. to try and achieve this goal. Fibonacci methods is one such attempt at unravelling the mysteries of the stock market by relating its movements to the Fibonacci Series. Fibonacci Series was discovered long before there were stock markets and but, amazingly, it works very well in the stock markets as it does with many other natural phenomena.

Leonardo Fibonacci is credited with the creation of Fibonacci Series. The series has its first two number as 0 and 1. The other numbers are arrived at by adding the previous two numbers. For example:

0+1 = 1
1+1 = 2
1+2 = 3
2+3 = 5
3+5 = 8
5+8 = 13
8+13 = 21
13+21 = 34
21+34 = 55
34+55 = 89,
and so on.

Thus we arrive at a series of numbers 0, 1, 2, 3, 5, 8, 13, 21, 34, 55, 89 . . . . Now these numbers are related to each other by a ratio. A lot of phenomena in nature, science and astrology is explained by this property of the Fibonacci Numbers. For example:

21□34 = .618
34□55 = .618
55□89 = .618

Similarly,

34□21 = 1.618,
55□34 = 1.618,
89□55 = 1.618

This ratio is known as the Golden Ratio and forms the basis of the Fibonacci Methods in technical analysis.

The other two fractions most commonly used in technical analysis — 0.382 and 0.5 — are calculated as follows:

(1–0.618) = 0.382, and
0.5 is the mean of 0.382 and 0.618

Fibonacci Retracements

Figure 3.16(a) shows Fibonacci retracements in an uptrend and Figure 3.16(b) shows Fibonacci retracements in a downtrend.

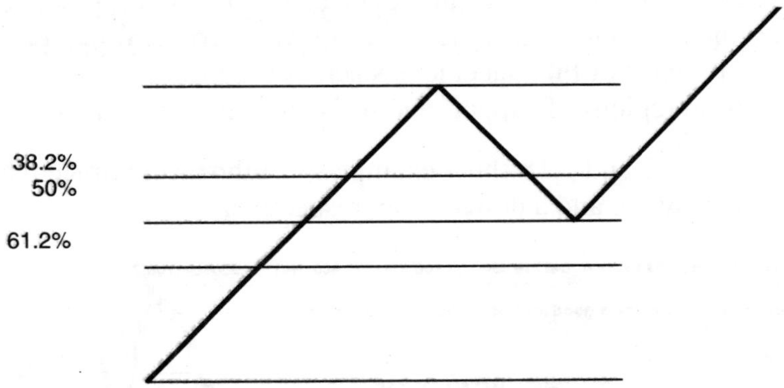

Figure 3.16(a): **Fibonacci Retracements in an uptrend**

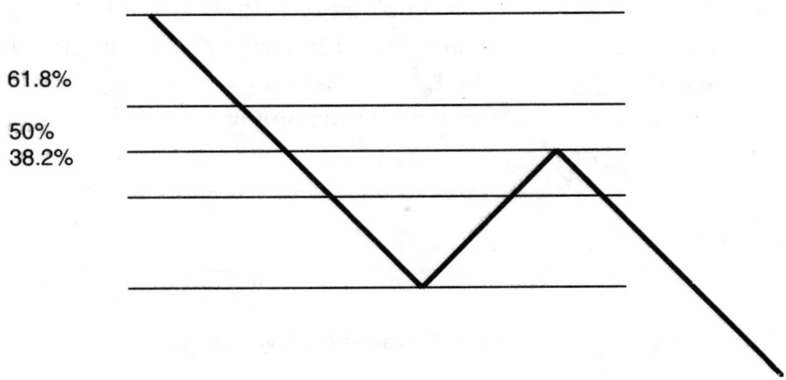

Figure 3.16(b): **Fibonacci Retracements in a downtrend**

Here are the rules for using the Fibonacci retracement tool:

- Identify a swing high and a swing low in the price action;
- Generally 38.2%, 50% and 61.8% values are used;
- 25% and 75% can also be used in case the above values do not hold.
- In very strong bull and bear markets, prices usually do not retrace more than 25% to 38.2%. In moderately bullish and bearish markets, they can retrace up to 50% to 61.8%.
- If the prices start breaking the 61.8% to 75% retracement, the main trend may be under threat.
- Always look for supporting evidence along with Fibonacci retracements, such as extreme values in short term RSI or stochastics, or confluence of Fibonacci levels across time frames.
- Focus on regions of support and resistance instead of actual values.

Figures 3.17 and 3.18 show examples of Fibonacci retracement levels in an upswing and a downswing, respectively.

Figure 3.17: **Fibonacci Retracement levels in an upswing**

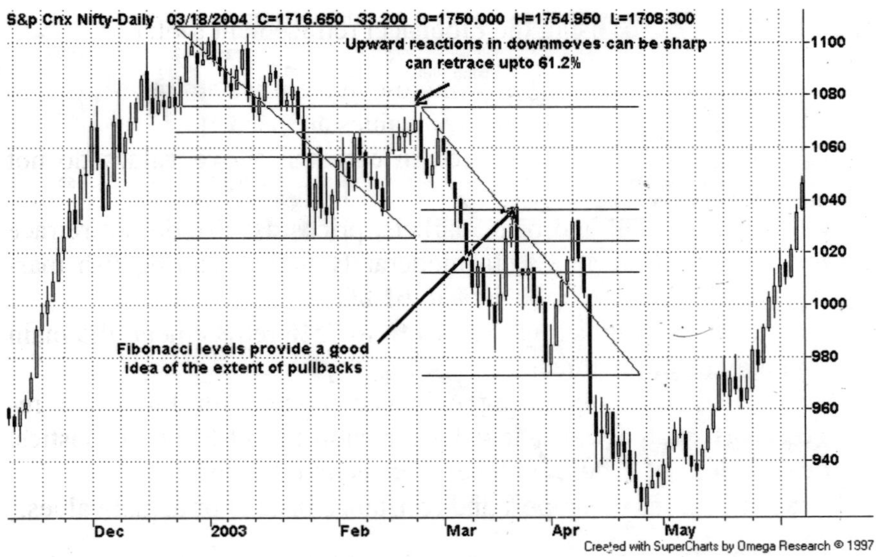

Figure 3.18: **Fibonacci Retracement levels in a downswing**

Confluence of Fibonacci Levels

With almost five Fibonacci levels to contend with, traders can often be left wondering which one of the levels is most likely to hold. In such cases:

- Confluence of two Fibonacci levels measured from two different swing lows to the same swing high in an upswing is considered the most significant support level.

- On the other hand, confluence of two Fibonacci levels measured from two different swing highs to the same swing low is considered to be the most significant resistance level.
- When the stock gets close to a confluence level, traders need to be on their toes and look for supporting evidence in order to act. Fibonacci levels like other indicators cannot be acted upon in isolation.

Examples of confluences of Fibonacci levels are illustrated in Figures 3.19 and 3.20.

Figure 3.19

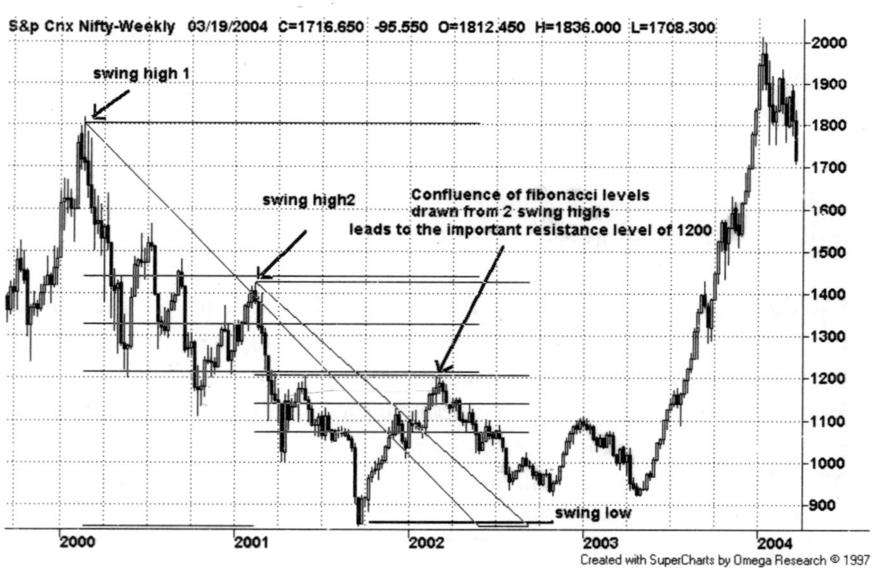

Figure 3.20

Candlestick Charting

Originally developed in 17th century Japan for rice trading, candlestick charting consists of depicting price information in terms of hollow or white bodies, and filled or black bodies, with wicks at both ends. A white body indicates the opening price of the session being below the closing price; and the black body shows the opening price of the session being above the closing price of the session. The wicks at the top and bottom of the real bodies depict the high and low of the day.

The major difference between the Western technical charts and the candlestick method is that the candlesticks give a clear view of market behaviour both in terms of buying and selling activity in the market, and whether the trend is indecisiveness or clear. Candlestick patterns often provide the trigger for a buy or sell decision once the Western technical indicators move to extreme overbought and oversold conditions. Candlesticks is nowadays a standard formatting option in most technical analysis software. A brief overview is presented here to give you its flavour. Excellent books on the subject are available which go into the details.*

Bearish Candle **Bullish Candle**

The doji occurs when the open and the close for the day are the same. It depicts indecision and can often mean impending weakness in an uptrend.

---

* *Candlestick Charting Explained* by Gregory L. Marris, published by Vision Books is a book you could consult.

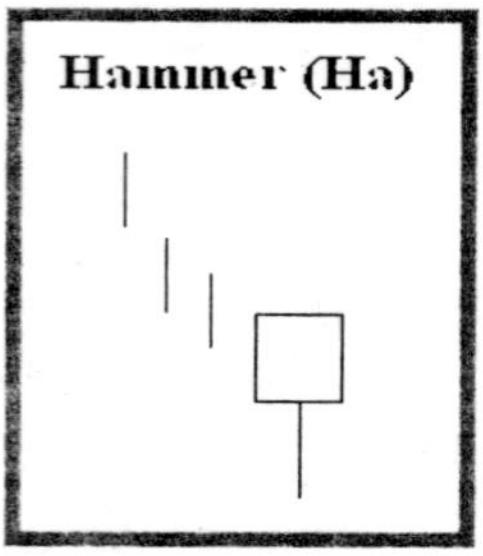

The real body is small and at the upper end of the range; the color is not important. The lower wick should be longer than the upper body; generally bullish.

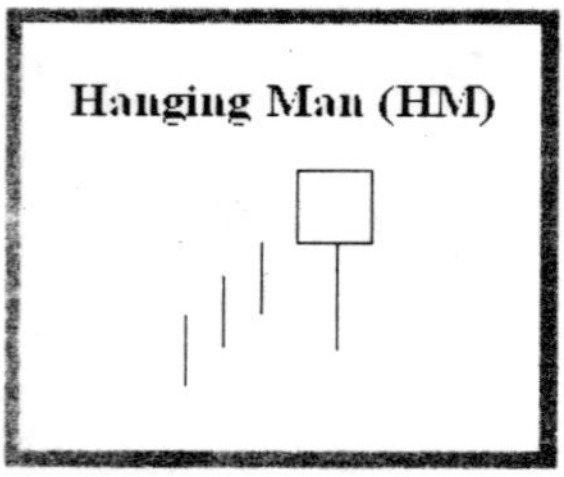

The hanging man is considered bullish because of the uptrend. The color is not important; could be bearish if the body is black and the next day opens lower.

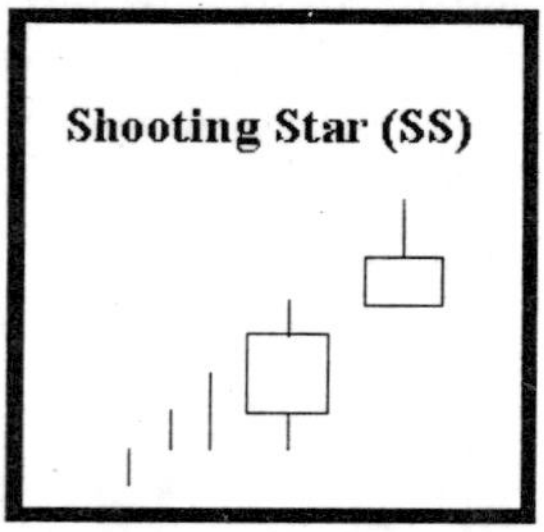

The shooting star indicates an end to the upmove. The body of the shooting star does gap up over the previous day.

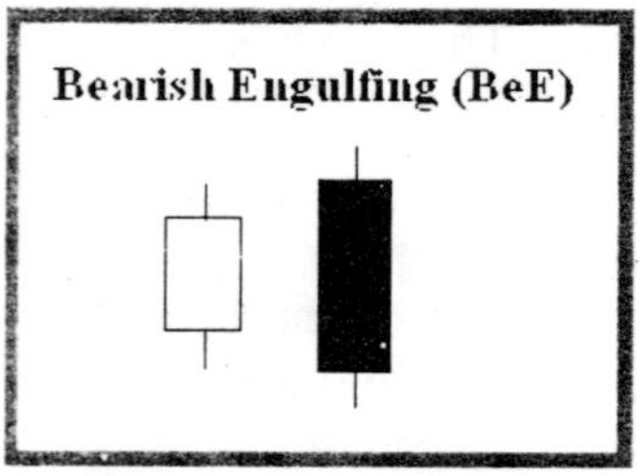

In an uptrend, on one day a small white body occurs. The next day prices open at new highs and quickly sell off, closing below the open of the previous day.

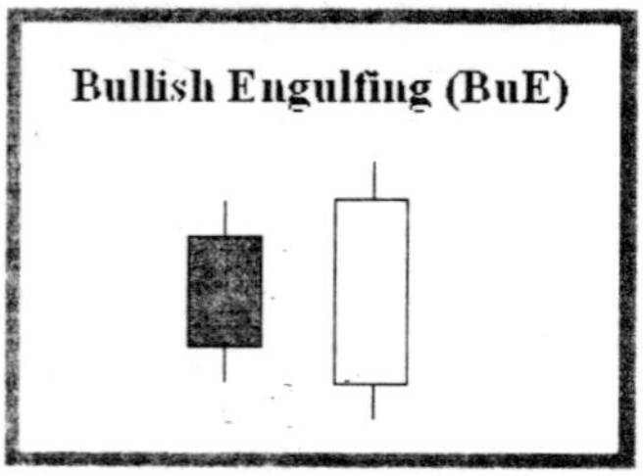

In a downtrend, a small black body occurs. The next day prices open at new lows and then quickly rally to close above the close of the previous day.

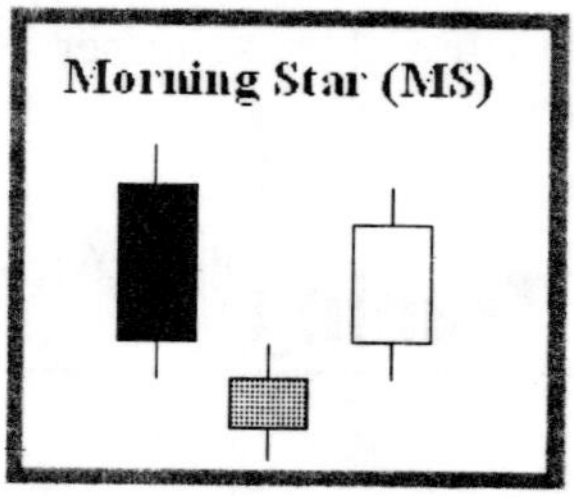

The morning star is a bullish reversal pattern. Ideal morning stars have gaps before and after the middle day's body.

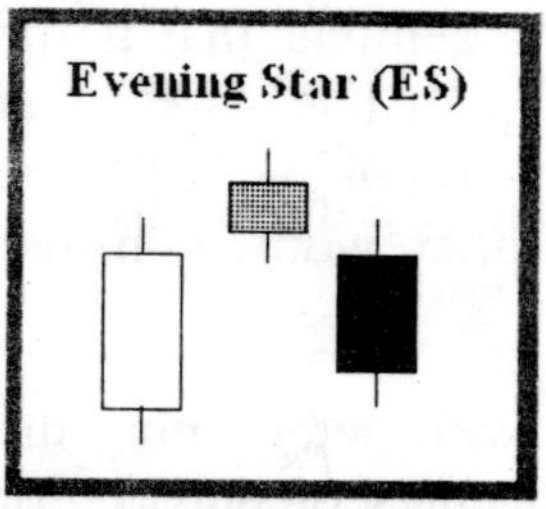

Evening star is a bearish reversal pattern. It occurs after an uptrend and should have gaps before and after the middle day's body.

The real body is small and at the upper end of the range; the colour is not important. The lower wick should be longer than the upper body; generally bullish.

In an uptrend, on one day a small white body occurs. The next day prices open at new highs and quickly sell off, closing below the open of the previous day.

In a downtrend, a small black body occurs. The next day prices open at new lows and then quickly rally to close above the close of the previous day.

Chapter 4

Applying Technicals to Trading

Ed Sekyota, a millionaire trader, once said at a seminar that if the trend of a market was up, he would take a chart of the market and hang it on a wall and walk to the other side of the room and then turn back. If the trend of the market still appeared up, he would consider the market.

The foundation of the trading process starts with determining the main trend of the market. To profitably trade futures or options, or even a stock for that matter, it is important that we establish the trend of the underlying security. Using a cricketing analogy, youngsters are always taught never to hit across the line of a ball, or never to hit the ball against the spin. To take a boat against the tide is much more difficult than rowing downstream. The human ego seems to get extreme satisfaction from trying to predict future events, particularly so in India. Also, people generally like to be thought of as trendsetters rather than trend followers. It is this kind of behaviour that the market seeks to punish. If there is nothing else you gain from this book and just remember that "the trend is your friend", this book would have done its job.

In the Indian bull market of 2003, for example, far too many individual investors and experts actually missed the big upward move because they were too busy predicting corrections.

When a market takes a particular direction, you don't ask questions — you simply enter in the direction of the trend at the first opportunity. You do not try to figure out the reasons, or the growth rate of the companies, or the health of the Indian economy, etc. The truth really is that the market needs people who are far less sophisticated and smart than those who come to it. The more mechanical you make the process of finding the trend, the fewer mistakes you will make.

Swing Trading

Swing trading is the most consistently profitable strategy that you can use in the futures market. It involves taking positions for about 3-4 trading sessions and capitalising on short term up and down swings in the market. Swing trading banks on catching the largest part of the swing by three main methods:

1. Entering trends on reaction;
2. Successful retests of highs or lows; and
3. Buying or selling breakouts or breakdowns from flag patterns.

Entering Trends on Reaction

The most effective futures swing trading strategy is determining the trend in the higher time frame, and then looking for low risk overbought or oversold conditions within that trend.

For example, if the time frame to be traded is daily, then the trend of the weekly charts needs first to be determined. If the time frame to be traded is intraday, then the trend of the daily chart needs to be determined, and so on.

There are several different ways of determining trends. Traders should remember that they can only determine a trend if there is one. They should not "force" a trend where there is none.

Obviously, entering trends on reaction is a methodology which can only be used in trending markets. For ease of explanation, we will use the weekly and daily time frames. The techniques, though, are applicable for all time frames.

1. The trend on the larger time frame can be determined by using either the moving averages or the MACD.
2. The strength of the trend should be determined by using ADX as already described in Chapter 2.
3. Now, on the smaller time frame entries can be made using:

   - 20 DMA;
   - RSI; or
   - Stochastics

4. Also on the smaller time frame traders should draw lines at significant support and resistance areas, so that a roadmap for a trade is drawn.
5. Use trailing stop losses once the market moves in the appropriate direction. I generally advise against strict adherence to predetermined target for moves, as markets tend to overshoot such targets. Traders should hold on to positions so long the market is acting as anticipated.

What is a Trend?

A trend is a series of rising or declining prices over any length of time. Thus, uptrend is a market which sees consistently higher prices over a period of time. A downtrend, on the other hand, is a market, which sees consistently lower prices over a period of time.

Trends could be classified as short term, medium term and long term.

A short term trend could last for 1 to 2 weeks, a medium term trend from 10 to 12 weeks, and a long term trend could be one lasting 12 to 15 months.

A trend is assumed to be in force till there is evidence that it has reversed. Traders should avoid the temptation of assuming trend reversals before they actually happen. Once a trader discovers a bias in the market, he can then use entry setups to find those with the lowest risk for trading futures or applying option strategies.

The Ed Sekyota incident cited at the start of this chapter shows that there are no hidden formulas to finding the market trend. In this chapter we will consider the methods for determining the main trend of the market and determine whether it's a trading or a trending market. Once we have established the market's trend, we can then look at entry setups in the direction of the main trend. Looking for entry setups in the direction of the trend enhances the chances of successful trades.

Methods of Trend Determination

There are three methods of trend determination which are easiest and that I use most. There are lots of other methods of doing so as well and these can be found in books on technical analysis. Since this is a book on derivatives, I am discussing only a limited number of methods of technical analysis.

Thus, three of the easiest methods are:

1. Visual inspection.
2. Moving averages.
3. MACD.

Visual Inspection of Charts

A visual inspection of the market chart is usually enough to determine its trend. In the market, as in life, if something is visually clear, it is generally pure. As far as I am concerned if it takes more than a minute to tell the trend of any stock chart, then it probably is not worth trading because it's not likely to be a trending market.

One drawback of this method is that it might not help in identifying smaller trends. Nonetheless, it is very useful in filtering charts for beginner users. Let's go over some examples of visual inspection from the Indian stock market. Skeptics might call these "well chosen examples" but my response is why not trade the "well chosen" examples? Why go looking for trends where there are none? When a trend is there, one glance is sufficient, as in Figures 4.1 and 4.2.

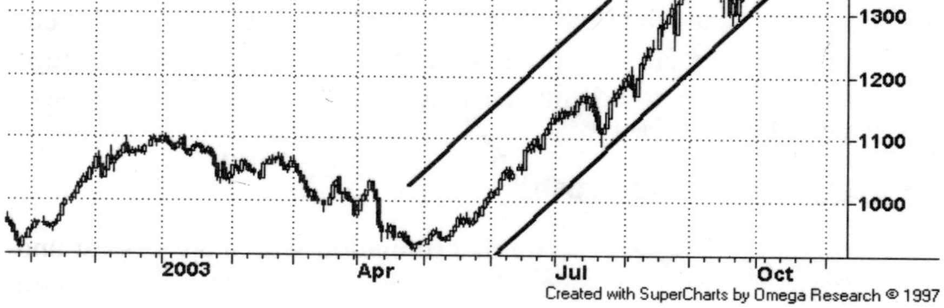

Figure 4.1

Figure 4.2

Moving Averages

When looking at a chart, I would like to know if it's in a long term up or down trend. This is done by using the 200 DMA to develop a bias on the stock or the market. A price chart over its 200 DMA is in an uptrend, and when below its 200 DMA it is in a downtrend (Figure 4.3).

Figure 4.3

MACD

On the weekly chart:

- Look for a strong up or downtrend based on the ADX.

On the daily chart:

- When the fast MACD line crosses over the slow signal line, it gives a buy signal. Go long and place a protective stop below the latest minor low.
- When the fast line crosses below the slow line, it gives a sell signal. Go short and place a stop above the latest minor high.
- In the absence of a strong weekly trend, this same technique will give many whipsaws to traders.
- The default specifications for the MACD are 12, 26, 9 although I prefer to use 3, 10, 16.
- As explained in Chapter 3, the MACD signal may be a little delayed. Using the upward sloping MACD histogram as the market rallies again after a correction is a leading signal. Similarly the declining slope of the MACD histogram can indicate resumption of a downtrend after an upward reaction (Figure 4.4).

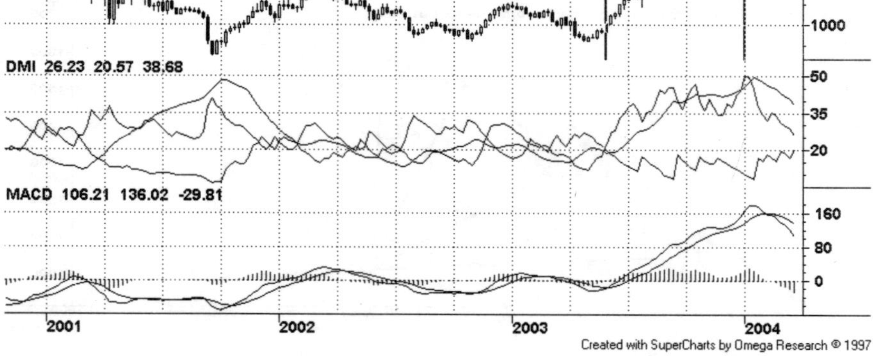

Figure 4.4

Low Risk Entries

Once the trend has been determined, the next step is to get low risk entries into the trend. The best entries are ones which occur after a contra trend reaction since entering after a correction allows for a stronger move and reduces the risk of correction. There are several techniques to accomplish this:

- Use of a 20 DMA in the case of a daily chart;
- Use of a 7 day RSI;
- Use of stochastics (7,10).

Use of 20 DMA

The 20 DMA is the most effective tool for entering the weekly trend on correction in the daily chart. Once the price corrects below the 20 DMA and moves back over it, the correction is deemed to be over and the market is expected to resume its uptrend again. Thus as the market moves back over the 20 DMA, traders can go long. If the weekly trend is down, a price move over the 20 DMA signifies a pullback rally in a downtrend (Figure 4.5). This downtrend is resumed as prices again move below the 20 DMA. The 20-period moving average can be used as a very effective tool in all time frames.

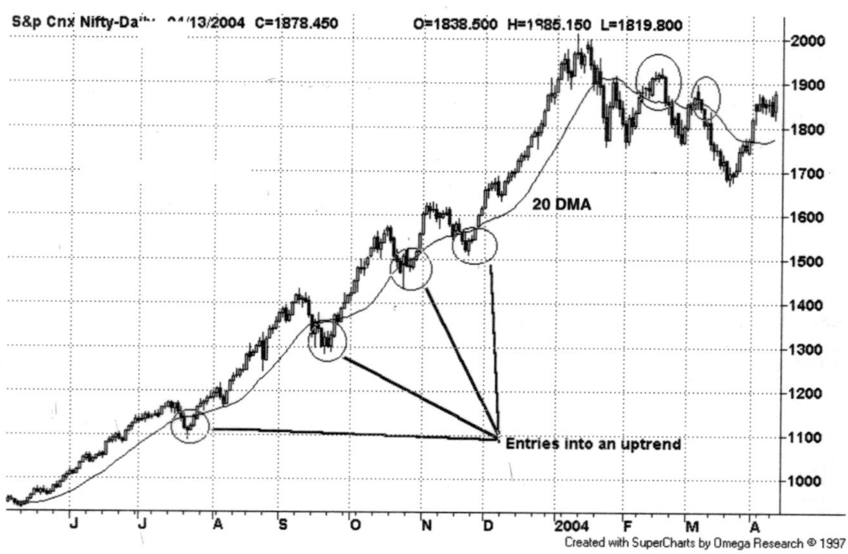

Figure 4.5

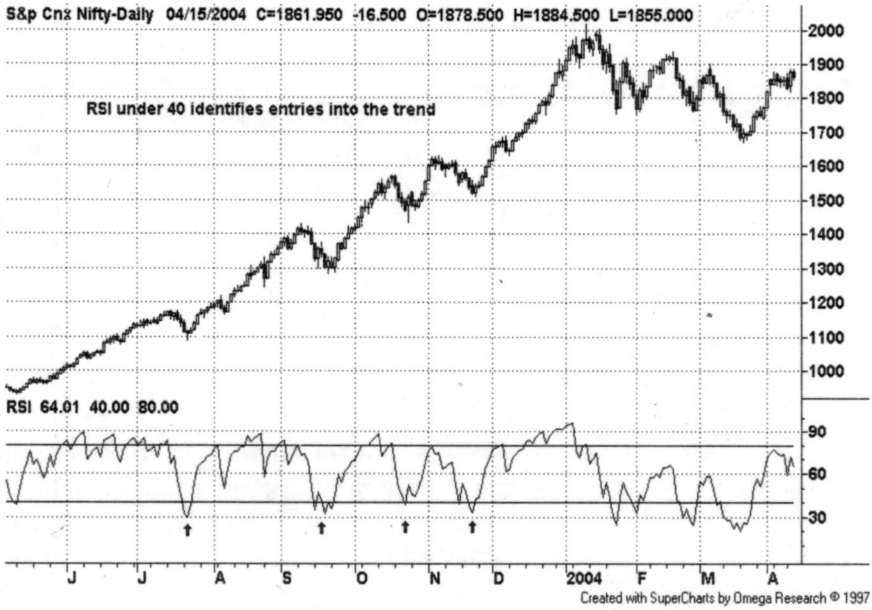

Figure 4.6

Use of 7 Day RSI

The daily RSI (7) identifies entry points as it moves below the 40 level and then turns back upwards. These points are marked with the dotted arrows on the chart. Traders need to note that there are other times as well when the RSI goes below 40 but the weekly trend is not up in those cases.

A similar procedure can be used in downtrends where an RSI level of 60 can be chosen as the benchmark. In this case a downtrend can be taken to have resumed as the RSI declines after going over the 60 level (Figure 4.6).

Use of Stochastics (7,10)

The daily stochastics (7,10) can also identify low risk entries into a trend. The stochastics going below the 20 level during a weekly uptrend, and then turning upward, signifies the resumption of the daily uptrend. Similarly, the stochastics going above the 80 level and then turning down during a weekly downtrend signifies resumption of the daily downtrend (Figure 4.7).

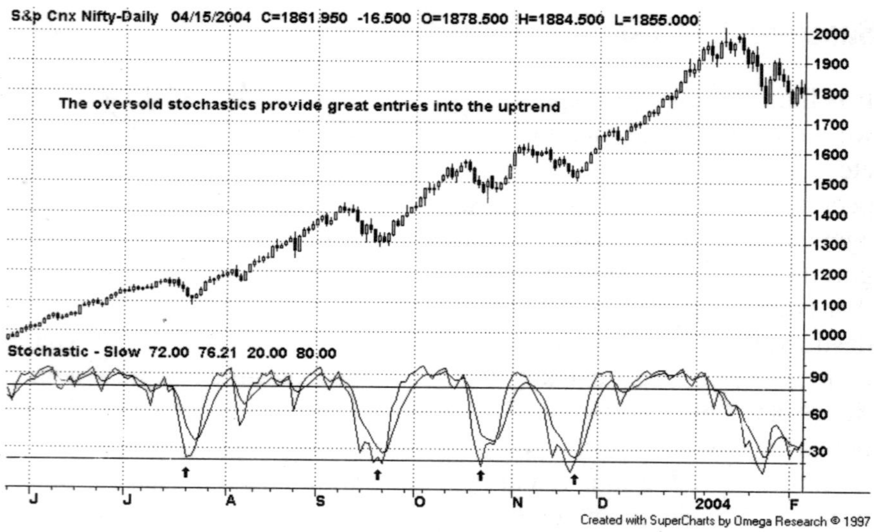

Figure 4.7

Using All Three Techniques Together

Using the RSI, stochastics and the 20 DMA together as a confluence of indicators, entries can be timed nearly to perfection. When all these three indicators are in agreement, traders can take that as a confirmed signal (Figure 4.8).

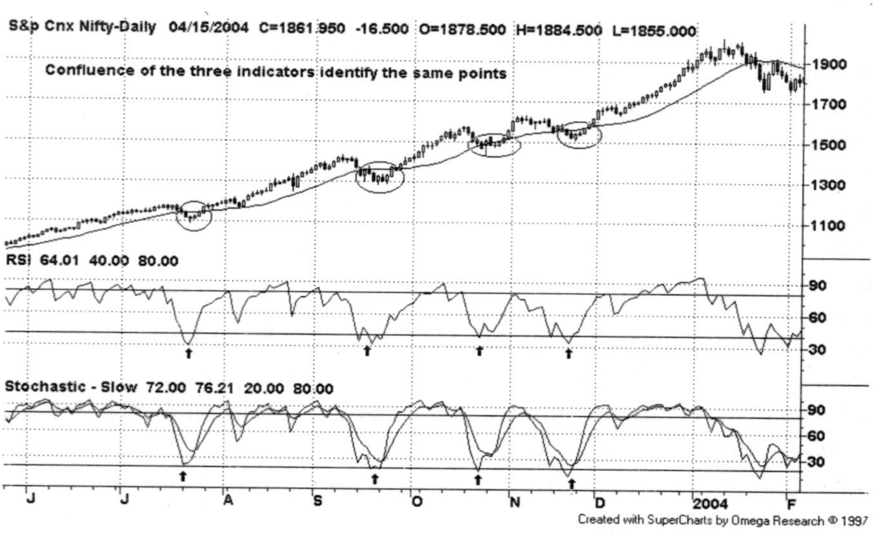

Figure 4.8

Successful Retest

It is human nature to respect things that are complicated. As children, we were taught that making money is difficult — "no pain, no gain", etc. I would like to say that in my ten years of trading, the easiest aspect has been looking for entry setups. The more difficult part is management of a trade, and a profitable exit. At this point I would categorically state that simple methods work best. Anyone who believes that charting or trading can be profitable by making it complicated is destined for failure. Beginner traders often make the mistake of trying to look for the magical key that will open the door to tremendous riches, and keep buying all kinds of hyped and expensive software and books.

Let us now turn to a visual technique which can be used for determining an entry setup for both cash and derivatives market. It has been around since the time stock markets were invented but is often forgotten because it is not complicated enough to be respected. Any market which makes a higher top during the course of a rally, pulls back, and is then unable to cross the previous top is said to have successfully retested the previous top. Conversely, any market in a downtrend which makes a new low, pulls back up, and then is unable to pierce the previous low is said to have successfully retested the bottom.

These days as technical analysis becomes more popular, prices momentarily go past previous significant highs or lows, and then there is a sharp decline or a rally, respectively, after getting the retail investors to go long or short on the market. In fact, up to 70% of the time these highs or lows are tested and the market comes back without being able to pierce them. So, generally speaking, whenever a significant high or low is getting tested, it's useful to take a long or a short position with a small stop loss and this often turns out to be a high percentage trade. In case the market successfully takes the high out, the opposite position can be taken once the previous stop is hit. Traders should practice these trades because these are very effective trades in a range-bound market, which is what the market is most of the time.

The failure to pierce previous extreme levels is a signal that the trend is reversing. Even if the trend is not reversing, these conditions provide potentially powerful moves as lots of participants need to reverse positions. These patterns have a higher than 90% probability of success. In calculating this percentage, I am including all the three following scenarios:

1. The price makes a higher bottom, or a lower top, after a decline or a rally, respectively.
2. The price touches the exact same bottom, or top, and then rallies or declines, respectively.
3. The price momentarily pierces previous top or bottom, only to reverse course again.

The third situation gives the most powerful moves. But just a higher bottom or a lower top by itself would be a premature signal for taking positions in the opposite direction. I prefer to use these signs to lighten up longs in an uptrend and shorts in a downtrend. Breaking of a previous pivot in the opposite direction can conclude the confirmation of a reversal. Breaking of a down pivot in an uptrend and upward pivot in downtrend should be taken as an entry signal in the opposite direction. These trades are very high probability trades and are worth waiting for. Oversold and overbought levels of the RSI and stochastics can be used to trade these ranges. The successfully retested bottom or top could be used as a stop. This setup can be applied in any time frame and you can capitalise on the big trends by using this technique. This is because all big uptrends or downtrends generally start with a successful retest. (*See* Figures 4.9, 4.10 and 4.11)

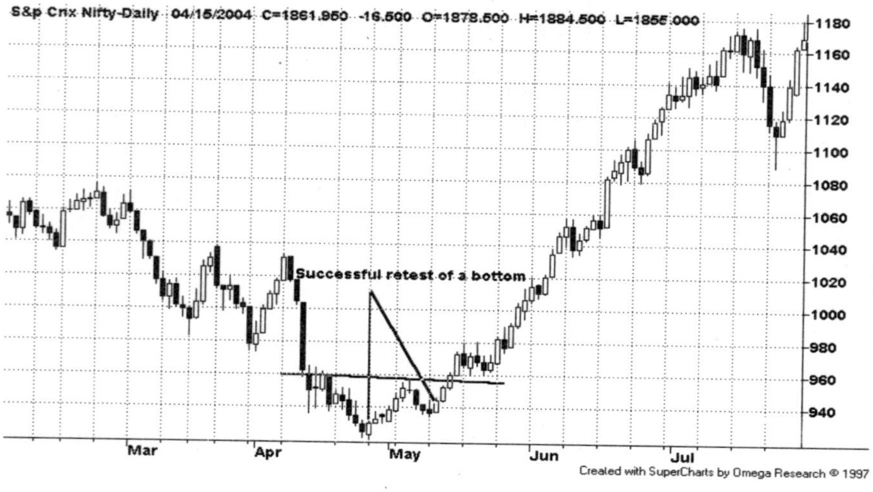

Figure 4.9

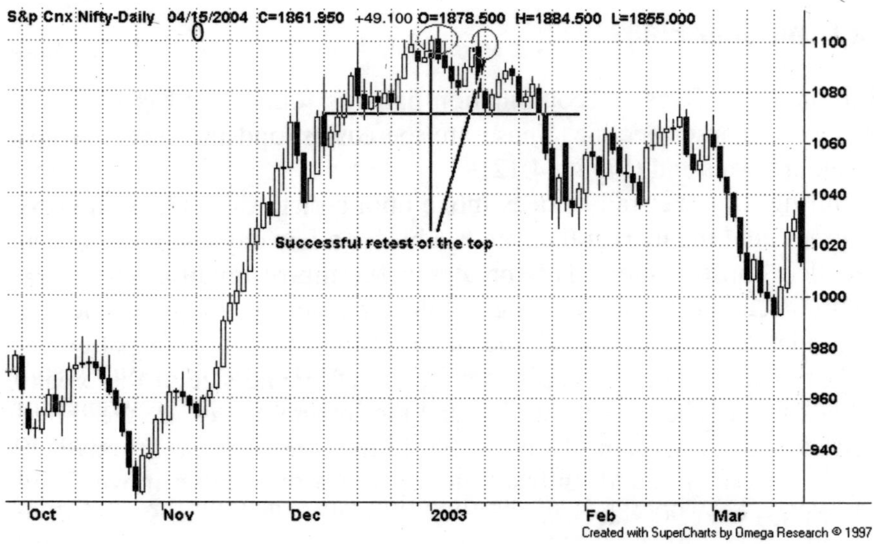

Figure 4.10

Figure 4.11

Bull and Bear Flags

Bull and bear flags are continuation patterns found midway during a rally or a market decline. These are the easiest and the surest setups for entering a trend (Figure 4.12).

During a market rally prices move up a certain distance with good volumes, and the market then stalls a bit for a few days, a phase which is called consolidation. This creates a flag-like formation shown in Figure 4.12 and is easily recognisable. This set up involves entering the trade in the direction of the main trend when the flag pattern is broken. The advantage here is that the direction and size of the break-out is known. The size of the first and the second moves are the same, so traders can have a profit objective of the size of the first move. A flag is generally found midway during an up or a down move. This pattern has over 90% accuracy.

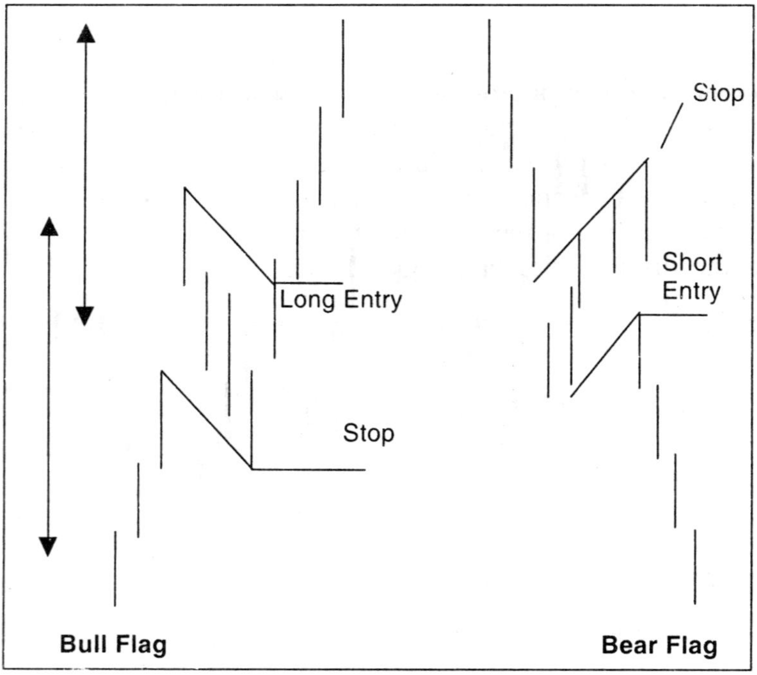

Figure 4.12

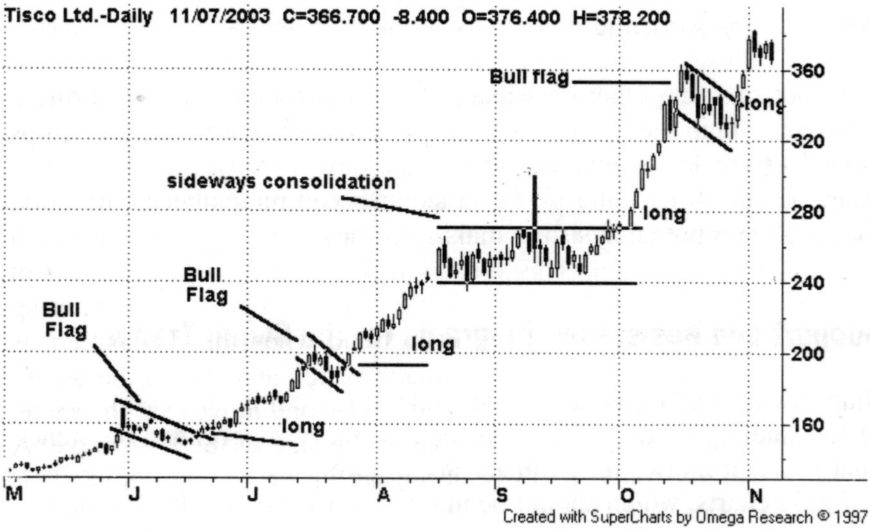

Figure 4.13

The way I use it in real life is that if I see a stock rising or declining, I keep following it closely till it stalls and forms some kind of a consolidatory sideways pattern. The important thing for traders to keep in mind is not to get too involved in the shape or the semantics of the sideways consolidation. Instead, the critical aspect is to look for a temporary stalling of the trend and to get in when the market breaks out in the original direction. Once I find a low volume sideways

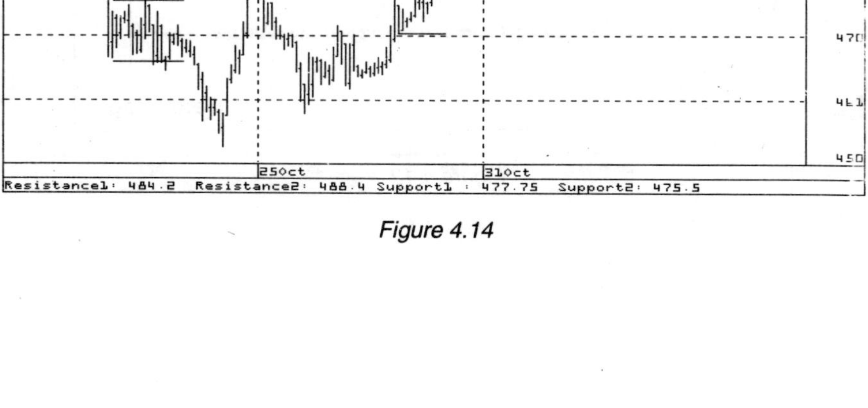

Figure 4.14

consolidation subsequent to a rally — or a decline — on a daily chart, I like to follow the stock on the intraday chart, looking for a trend line breakout or some other classical breakout pattern in the direction of the trend which then provides me with a low risk entry. Stops can be placed at the lower end of the flag as shown in the accompanying charts (Figures 4.13 and 4.14). Traders should remember at all times that our job is not analysis but making money.

Support and Resistance Diagrams for the Swing Trader

Since swing trading is largely dependent on trading successful retests of low and highs, all swing traders should carry support and resistance charts of at least two time frames (*see* Figure 4.15).

These charts, which should be updated daily, are helpful in entering high probability trades. Traders should be alert as significant resistances and supports are reached, particularly in a range-bound scenario, to take the retest trades.

Some practical advice: while these signals are quite reliable, markets do not move according to any given script. Try to go long at least

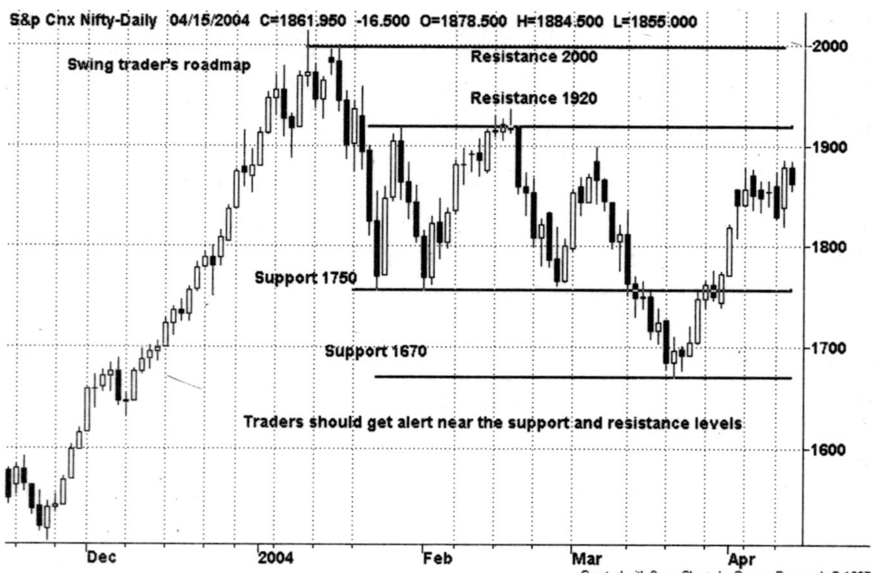

Figure 4.15

above an intraday pivot on the upside, or short at least under an intraday pivot on the downside. Sometimes markets gives whipsaws before taking a particular direction. At other times, the market starts moving in a narrow range before revealing its direction. Every trader has seen the market apparently in a downtrend in the morning, then suddenly turn course and end up with a healthy gain. This is one of the reasons traders should never have strong opinions; because the market as well as other traders do not care about your opinion. If the market goes contrary to your analysis, change your analysis and your trade. Look at a trading day as akin to finding your way through a thick forest. You need to make this journey daily, and every evening you need to prepare maps according to what you expect the route the next day may be. But if your map does not work, and you find you are heading the wrong way, you must quickly change your course. When the market does not behave as you expect it to, do as the market tells you to do. Keep losses small till you figure out what the market is doing, but do not overtrade.

I start out with the map. If I believe the market is in a downtrend, I wait for the market to make some sort of an intraday high. This can be achieved by:

1. Having all the supports and resistance marked on the intraday chart, and
2. Using the slow stochastic, the fast stochastic and the 20-period moving average to try to sell an intraday high.

You sell when both the stochastics reach overbought and then you sell the first black candle from the top. Sometimes that is not the top, so I use at least a one per cent stop to make sure that I differentiate any noise from an upmove. Also, you need to be watching the intraday chart all the time if the daily time frame is your canvas, like it is for most traders. For a while the index or stock might behave as you anticipated, but you need to change stance as soon as you see things changing.

One way of keeping a tab is to keep watching the intraday advance decline ratio: this is available on the Yahoo India Finance section. Generally, it is safe to trade in the direction of the advance decline ratio. If the number of decliners are more on a certain day, then you are fine being short; if the number of advancers are more, you are safe being long. When this ratio starts changing from 5:1 and heads towards 1:1, the market is changing direction. Also, learn to differentiate between intraday bounces and genuine upmoves. One rule of doing so is that after an intraday bounce, the market should come down with velocity. If, on the other hand, the market starts consolidating at higher levels, you need to move out of shorts. If breadth also stalls at that point, then something is certainly changing. So you need to keep looking for evidence to make sure that you are in sync with the market. Will you always be successful? No. If you are not successful, keep a stop in place and re-evaluate if you are wrong. You need to be on your toes in any market. Expect the punch coming from the left hook or right hook. Do not be surprised or shocked by any market move. Act quickly to fall in line with the market. Do not expect or hope the market will move in sync with you.

The same thing holds when buying the intraday low. Do I always catch it? Of course not; some days I have to reverse my position midway and take the opposite position as I see the market moving contrary to my expectation. There are some days when I have to do this twice, or even thrice. Those are the bad days when the market is whipsawing me all over the place. At such times I quit for the day and let the market first decide on where it wants to go. You cannot be stubborn with the market. You need to dance in step with its movements.

Once your trade moves at least one per cent into profit by the day's close, you should decide to carry it to the next day. The reason for this is that overnight gains can be substantial if the market opens with a gap in favour of your trade. If, on the other hand, the gains have been less than one per cent and the market dilly-dallies towards the close, it's a good idea to close the trade and come back fresh for the next trading session. If you are long at close of trade, you must watch for excellent market breadth (at least 2:1 in favour of advances) and a closing rate near the high. If you are short, the market should close weak, preferably near the low of the day and with poor market breadth (at least 2:1 in favour of declines). The trade should be carried so long as the market keeps acting right.

For a long trade, keep watching the breadth of the market after the market has moved in your direction; if it starts to deteriorate rapidly, book partial profit, then wait to see the breadth of the market as it bounces. If it seems just an intraday correction, rebuild position above intraday high. If the market fails to take out the intraday high, book the rest of the profit. If there is a sudden sell off, wait for a bounce and look at the strength of the bounce; if the bounce looks weak and so does the breadth, book all your profits. As a rule of thumb, if you are unsure about what is happening, book your profits entirely and stay out. Profits earned once should not be allowed to erode. Wait for the market to show its hand. More opportunities to buy or sell will always come again. Remember the two Dalal Street adages:

- In bull markets, buy all corrections. Same is the case with short positions.
- Do not short a dull market.

Remember these two. In later chapters, we will discuss the concept of trailing stop.

Chapter 5

Day Trading Rules and Setups

I often think of day trading as being similar to a military operation, where pulling the trigger is probably the easiest part. Day trading is about discipline and training of the mind. It is about waiting in the trenches till the right opportunity (setup) appears. It is about quantifying the risk in every trade. It is knowing when to hit and when to run. Yes, it's about guerrilla warfare. It's about recognising temporary demand-supply mismatches and capitalising on them. It's not about standing in the way of large trends and letting the institutions maul you. It's like the Vietcong fighting the US army, where the Viets got the better of the Americans by using guerrilla tactics. Collectively, the Americans could maul them but in guerrilla warfare the Americans got a bloody nose. A guerrilla is just that, and he should never think of himself as a general. Similarly, the day trader should always remember that he is in the trade for a day, maximum two. He should not try to be a position trader. If a trader tries to wear too many hats at the same time, he will end up failing at everything. Just as all wars are first won on the planning table, it is critical that a day trader have a plan before starting to trade. A trading plan is essential for success. It is utterly impossible to succeed at trading without a concrete plan. The following are suggestions, some general, others specific, that I believe will help day traders achieve their goals.

Do Your Homework

The study of specific stocks or derivatives and their relationship to the overall market is an absolute essential. It is suggested that the trader work at least one hour outside of market hours on familiarising himself with stocks that could be traded the next day. As this book is focused on derivatives, the number of futures and options to be scanned becomes limited. For Indian derivatives, this can be done on the Internet on the following sites:

www.moneycontrol.com
www.capitalmarket.com
www.sharekhan.com
www.equitymaster.com
http://in.biz.yahoo.com/commentary/
www.sify.com
www.walletwatch.com
www.nseindia.com

And, many more.

Day traders in particular and traders in general should remember that trading is a global profession and they should thus be receptive to ideas from traders of other countries. Also, traders should study global currency and commodity charts, not only because it will enhance their knowledge of charting but also because these derivatives are also likely to be launched in India in the future. Gold and silver futures are already available for trading with most Indian stock brokers.

With experience, a trader will have greater understanding of the widely traded stocks and will be able to better judge information for potential opportunities. In addition, a trader should spend some time every day in honing his craft; studying trading techniques, refining trading ideas, etc. Weekends require at least two to three hours of study looking for setups for the following week. A trader should be prepared to spend a minimum of twelve hours a week outside market hours on such planning and study. A serious day trader should acquire a good charting software and try to get hold of as many trading books as are available. You need to understand that successful trading is a passion and the rewards are enormous. Also, it is critical to take your mind off trading with some other activity as well. I, for one, play tennis every morning to keep myself fresh for the day ahead.

Stick to a Schedule

A standard schedule is essential. A trader should arrive at his trading centre half-an-hour or more before the market opens and plan on being there all day. Before the market opens, the trader should have a list of potential trading stocks or derivatives based on his homework of the previous evening.

He should review how these stocks and derivatives behaved the day before, and draw conclusions as to whether or not he will follow them when the market opens. The trader should have his attention on the market, and on nothing else; he should also be rested and ready to attack the market. If there is some distraction that threatens to take his attention off the market, he should cease trading until the situation is addressed and until he can trade again with full concentration. If you get up in the morning, fight with your wife, and then your neighbour over parking space, your chances of winning at trading are greatly reduced.

Learn How to Manage Your Losses

Not being able to manage your losses, or letting them run, is the number one reason why traders lose money. Losses are inevitable. Nobody makes money everyday. The key to winning overall is to limit one's losses and to be able to offset them with profitable trades. All big losses start by being a small loss. If the market is not acting according to your expectation, just get out. Also make sure you don't overtrade, and be extremely careful on entries. It's much easier getting into a trade than getting out of one. The trader should never take more than a set limit of points. It is my personal experience that it's extremely difficult to set a number limit on points, such as one-half a point, etc. An easier way to tackle the problem is in terms of limiting the rupee value loss on a trade, for example, Rs.10,000. The per trade figure you set should be no more than 2% of your total trading capital, you can then figure out how many shares that means. Thus, if you are trading 1,000 shares of any stock or futures, then your stop loss cannot be more than Rs.10. You should also be aware of the range a market is trading in during the day in order to make an assessment of the stop loss in terms of points. In a day trading scenario, and unless there is some unexpected news, eight times out of ten the market forms a range in the first couple of hours by establishing a high and low, and then towards the end of the day breaks out or down from that range and establishes a direction.

Another strategy is to look for a move in one direction and then look for some intraday consolidation or continuation patterns to be able to trade breakouts or breakdowns. As a good day trader, you should have a view on the trend and try to trade in the direction of that trend. Traders can make exceptions in special circumstances where there is no daily trend, namely when the market is choppy or you are able to short at the top or bottom of the range and an intraday counter-trend move; these are low percentage trades.

Money Management

Another thing most Indian traders tend to overlook is the proper use of leverage. Most unsuccessful traders feel that if they have enough money to pay the margin, they are ready to play. Or, that whatever capital they have should be used in taking the maximum possible position. Both these are very dangerous methods of trading.

Based on his trading capital, a trader needs to carefully work out the amount of leverage he will employ so that even a string of losses do not put him out of business. Drawdowns are a part of every trader's life. A streak of losses can easily reduce your equity by 15-20%. A trader should trade only a given number of contracts against his entire capital based on whether he employs a conservative or an aggressive approach to trading.

For example, at the time of writing one Nifty futures contract at 1500 Nifty level was worth Rs. 3 lakh. Accordingly, a conservative investor should have a minimum of 66% of the total contract value as his account equity, i.e. Rs. 2 lakh. So if such a trader has an account equity of Rs. 30 lakh, he should be trading no more than 15 Nifty contracts at any time. By taking this approach a trader would be able to absorb a 15-20% drawdown and still recover. He will never be thrown out of the game. A more aggressive trader might have 33% of the total contract value as his account equity. Thus, for a similar Nifty contract worth Rs. 3 lakh, he should have at least Rs.1 lakh as his account equity. This trader would be in greater trouble if he has a 15-20% drawdown.

One's position size should be increased only when one's trading capital doubles. Money management will be discussed in greater detail later in Chapter 12 which is exclusively dedicated to the subject. Leverage produces some very exciting returns but can easily wipe out a trader if used excessively.

Maximum Shares per Trade

Traders with little experience get wiped out in short order by trading large numbers of shares. Until the trader is consistently making money, i.e. ten trading days in a row with no losing days, the number of shares should be limited. In choppy sideways markets, you should also reduce your volume. Remember, bull markets should not be confused with brilliance. Conversely, choppy markets will not allow you to be brilliant. When the markets are slow, reduce your exposure size.

Number of Trades per Day

Trading too much in a day is the third reason why traders consistently lose money. There is absolutely no reason to trade more than five trades per day. The maximum number of trades should be limited to five per day. And even five trades are justified only if a trader is trading more than one stock at a time. I like to look at a successful day when I make one entry and one exit or position. Successful trading is about making entries extremely careful and then a period of inactivity while the market does what you want it to, followed by an exit when you have made profits several times the risk. Overtrading is the single biggest pitfall a trader has to combat everyday. And overtrading happens because traders have no plans. The intraday gyrations of a market need to be viewed in the context of a larger time frame, only then can a trader develop a direction bias and take a high probability trade. So, have your plan ready every day before the market opens.

Avoid Trading During the Slow Period of the Day

Trades are consistently more successful before 11.00 a.m. and after 2.00 p.m. This is because before 11.00 a.m. you tend to catch the highs or the lows of the day and after 2.00 p.m. you catch the breakout or breakdowns. Trades are consistently less successful between 11.00 a.m. and 2.00 p.m. There is only one exception; if a particular stock is in play (being traded heavily due to some factor such as a big news announcement), this rule can be broken with relative safety.

But trying to find a trade between 11.00 a.m. and 2.00 p.m. is almost always a bad move and should be avoided. It is safer to miss a few opportunities than to consistently lose money when the market is slow. Personally speaking, I like to observe the market action in the first couple of hours before taking any positions. Technical analysis is a hypothesis, the market tells you where it actually going.

Wait For the Best Entry Setups

It is worth waiting for the best entry setups to initiate trades, particularly in futures. A lot of heartburn and losses can be avoided if day traders wait for the right setups before entering trades. A lot of setups are discussed in this chapter. It is also important to keep a view of the overall market and take a trade in the direction of the larger trend. The market often gyrates up and down before it breaks out in the desired direction. So better the entry, the higher the probability of a winning trade. A day trader should desist from what I call compulsive gambling. Compulsive gambling is when a day trader comes to trade without preparation, and enters trades without any regard to setups. All traders need to find the bias of the market in order to increase their probability of winning trades. Day traders should remember that each trade contributes to, or takes away, from their overall bottom line. This is a business that they are running and it should not be mistaken as an adventure or a thrill.

When you trade without knowledge or preparation, the stock market turns into a casino. I cannot stress enough that the day trader needs to develop enormous amounts of self control before he can win in the market. A very simple technique of reducing risk in day trading, and even in a swing trading situation, is to buy oversold and sell overbought. Sounds simple, doesn't it? Well, here is how you can accomplish it. I use the Yahoo India's intraday charts to identify a low risk buy or sell by putting on the slow as well as the fast stochastic indicators.

Consider the intraday chart in Figure 5.1 which was taken from Yahoo India Finance site (link: http://in.finance.yahoo.com/). On this chart put the slow stochastics and fast stochastics indicators and also a 20-period moving average. These two indicators show the relative overbought position of the market over the 80 level and oversold positions of the market under that level. The chart further has a 20-period moving average on it. Now, let's consider two scenarios:

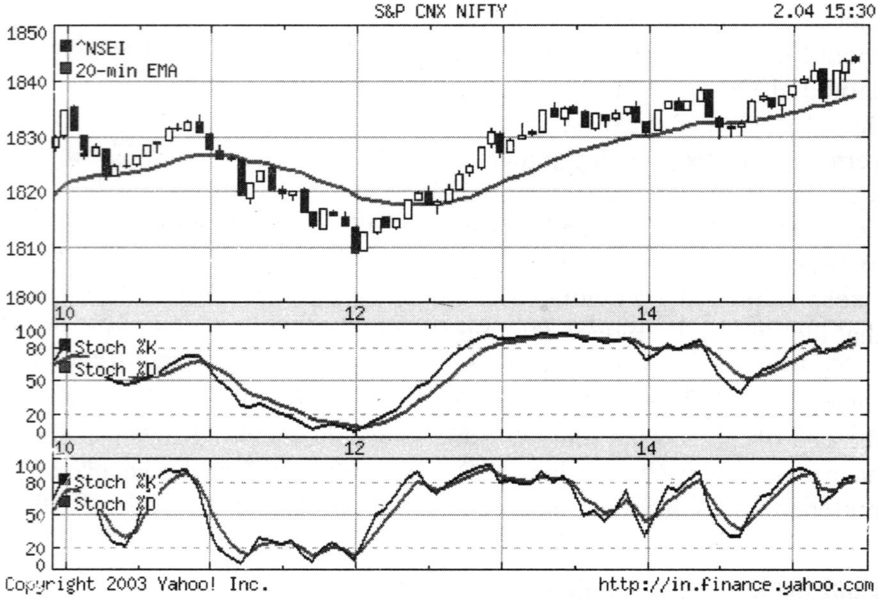

Figure 5.1

1. The market is in a strong daily up (down) trend. In such a case, day traders should try to buy when both slow and fast stochastics on the daily chart reach the oversold (overbought) levels below (above) 20 (80), and the price chart rises (falls) above (below) the 20 minute moving average.
2. When there is no apparent daily trend. In this case, day traders should make sure that they make trades when only both the indicators are in extreme territories.

This increase the chances of a successful trade since a trendless market usually tends to swing from overbought to oversold levels during the day. Overall, as the margin of error is very small in day trading, day traders should trade only when the markets are overstretched in either direction, which can be ascertained by indicators such as stochastics.

Use Stops and Targets

It is critical for day traders to use stops and targets as, indeed, it is for all traders. But it is all the more important for day traders since most times they square up their positions by the end of the day. Day traders should have a clear plan before they come to the trading centre. They should also book profits on a regular basis so as not to lose profits on the table; they need these profits to cover the inevitable losses. It is very critical that the day trader should have a risk/reward ratio of at least 1:2. Also, day traders should be alert and open to reversing position if the patterns are not working out because failed patterns lead to extremely strong moves in the opposite direction. As a rule of thumb, I keep stops at the previous pivot in the direction opposite to the trend that I am trying to trade in all time frames.

Time stops is another effective technique which works well for day traders; for example, they can keep a stop loss of three hours, and at the end of three hours into the trade they can square up, whether they have made a profit or a loss. There are other traders, however, who prefer stop losses based on rupee value or percentages.

Limit the Number of Positions at One Time

A trader should try and limit himself to one open position at a time. Two positions are acceptable, but three are not. A trader should understand the benefits of a narrow focus. Each trader needs to find his own niche. If a trader is good at trading technology stocks, he should keep doing that. If someone is good at Nifty futures and index options, as I believe I am, there is no reason to move to stock futures or options. A day trader should remember that at the end of the day the colour of the money is the same, no matter which stocks, or how many stocks, you are trading. I agree with the school of thought that after a point diversification is a hedge for ignorance.

While the above is generally true, obviously it won't apply if you are doing basket trades — but most people don't trade a basket of stocks. Holding a position overnight is done only if the market closes strong and the trader expects some follow through action the following day. The maximum number of positions needs to be seen in the light of the worst possible situation because the worst can, and does, occur. The worst, of course, is that all positions start losing. At that point a trader should not lose more than a certain percentage of his trading equity. You always need to live to be able to fight another day.

All rules can be safely broken under certain circumstances. But in my experience breaking more than one rule is a grave mistake, and reduces the possibility of success to less than 25%. It should not be done.

Each Trader Should Have His own Trading Regimen

Every batsman in cricket has his own style — Sachin Tendulkar cannot bat like Rahul Dravid, and Dravid should not try to be a Tendulkar. Similarly, every trader has a regimen, a style or set of rules that he follows in choosing trades. For example, most day traders use technical analysis as a part of their personal regimen to form conclusions.

A trader must have a personal regimen, a specific set of rules or guidelines that he follows. A trader's personal regimen would include the specifics of what indicators he uses and why. The regimen should be constantly refined and polished owing to the fact that the market changes all the time, and what worked six months ago may not work now. Traders in Indian markets should avoid stocks with questionable fundamentals which show high volume as these can attract manipulation and are sooner or later confined by the exchange to the trade-to-trade category where each transaction must result in delivery. Often these stocks then lose all their liquidity and drop sharply in price as well. The chances of this happening in the derivatives market is lower as derivates are allowed only in large cap and widely held stocks.

Your trading guidelines must be in writing. These guidelines must be your own. You must not rely on another trader's recommendation as a buy signal, some "hot tip", or a computer program, or anything else to make your final decisions. Personally, I think the best way to lose money in the market is to sit at a broker's terminal. In India, often day traders are bunched up in a broker's office, sometimes as many as five to six traders to every terminal. There are lots of recommendations flying around. There may well be successful traders among them — but how do you tell?

Also, the software available at a broker's office may not always be good enough for decent intraday technical analysis. And, of course, your opinions are likely to get coloured by all kinds of rumours.

I consider trading to be a loner's job and a trader should trust only his own analysis. Trading is not about reaching a consensus. A trader must make his final decisions himself, and he can't do so without a personal regimen. Lack of a personal regimen means a trader is open to the vagaries of whoever or whatever is making the decisions around him. The trader himself must make the call, not something or someone else. A personal trading regimen helps the trader refine his skills and learn what works for him and what does not. He can change his regimen at any time, of course, but he must have something to change.

Importance of Intraday Charts for a Position Trader

A lot of position traders, people who keep their positions from a few days to a couple months, may be tempted to ignore this chapter. But I have found that intraday charts are critical to a position trader for making low risk entries close to one's stop loss pivot. If a market is in an uptrend and the position trader is waiting for a retracement in order to enter a position, it is often difficult to decide whether the market has reversed or is in a relief rally. At that point intraday charts, and reversal patterns they exhibit, can be extremely useful to the position trader. When trading a higher time frame, it's useful to keep tabs on all the lower time frames possible. An example of this is given later in this chapter in the 1-2-3 continuation setup.

The Day Trader's Guide to Price and Volume

There is a close connection between price and volume and it is important for every day trader to understand at least the basics of this relationship. Generally speaking, increasing volume indicates the continuation of a trend and decreasing volume indicates the end of a trend, or a reversal. You need to be familiar with this when you are day trading.

Let's have a look at some scenarios from day trading perspective:

1. A Price Advance with Steadily Increasing Volume

A good way of implementing this strategy is to look for market's volume leaders around 11 a.m. These volume leaders can be seen on both the NSE and BSE terminals and on the Yahoo India Finance site, which I have found contains highly useful information in terms of price, volume and charting. Once you have identified the heavy volume stocks, whether those moving higher or lower, it's often profitable to take trades in the direction of the market in such stocks. This should however be done only with that particular day's perspective.

Often a basket of three or four shares can be bought which have the heaviest volumes and are moving in the direction of the market. While this is not my preferred style of trading, but there are people making a living out of it.

In general, higher prices need to be supported by higher volumes. Higher volume is the fuel which sustains an upmove and which indicates continuing upward momentum. As the price rises, more and more buyers get attracted until the price reaches a stage of euphoria that usually indicates the end of the price advance.

2. A Slowing Pace of Buying with Decreasing Volume

Remembering an Old Dalal Streets adage might be in order here: Don't buy a quiet market at the top, and don't sell a quiet market at the bottom.

A quiet market at the top indicates that the top is near, and that buying is drying up. It has two possible outcomes:

- Sellers realise that the top might be near and start selling, causing the price to reverse lower.
- The stock starts consolidating and gets supported by strong bids, which indicates that an up-move is likely later.

In such a case, traders who are long should book profits and wait for new patterns and re-enter later in case the trend continues.

3. Higher Volume During Price Advances with Lower Volumes on Pullback

This indicates a continuing uptrend. A lower volume during the pullback indicates that there are not enough sellers in the market to drive the stock down, although low volume is seen as evidence of a counter trend move. Day traders can use a 5-period RSI under 40 to identify oversold areas in an uptrend, and overbought areas over 60 in a downtrend, and accordingly enter a low risk trade.

4. Big Buying Volume Without the Price Going Higher

This indicates distribution which, in turn, means resistance. A big seller may well be in the market. There is no way to tell at this point whether the buyers would win this battle and drive the price higher, or whether they would give up and the stock will eventually reverse. In such cases, traders should wait for new patterns before initiating further trades.

5. A Slow and Steady Movement Upward with Consistent Volume

This indicates a continuing upward momentum. There might be a buyer in the market who is steadily buying shares and trying to not attract too much attention while doing so.

6. An Extreme Acceleration in the Advancing Price Which is Not Sustained

This indicates the end of the euphoric stage of the upward move. This is a very common scenario. When everyone is getting into something, I like to avoid it altogether and prefer waiting for the market to change direction. Instead of stampeding on the way in, it's often more beneficial to wait for the market to reverse and enter on the short side, or *vice versa*, when the panic or euphoria dies down. For me, those stages of euphoria and panic are very important exit signals. They can also present very interesting entry points, especially after a stock has had a panic sell off.

Day Trading Setups

1-2-3 Continuation Pattern

Criteria

1. Wide range bar breaking out of support.
2. Narrow range bar near or at the highs of the previous wide range bar. Often this narrow range bar is also an inside range bar.

Entry

Switch to a smaller time frame and take a breakout from the base or use above the highs of the narrow range bar of bar 2.

Stop

Under the lows of the base or last major pivot low on the smaller time frame, under the lows of the narrow range bar, or under the lows of the third bar at the time of the setup.

Target

Bar 1 = Bar 3

Now that you see the setup on the daily chart (Figure 5.2), get ready to capitalise on the lower time frame. Let's now consider the 30-minute chart, as the setup appears (Figure 5.3).

When I was about to enter the above trade, my broker told me that there was a lot of uncertainty; there was a futures and options expiry the next day, state election results were due in the same week, and the FIIs were expected to book profits because of their year-end considerations. In other words, he tried his best to give me all the reasons for not taking the trade. But the beauty of technical analysis is that when you see a setup, and see supporting evidence on other time frames and indicators, you need to pull the trigger. The above trade gave me 50 points in three trading sessions, which on my volumes of 3,000 shares of the Nifty is Rs.1,50,000 — and that is not bad for three days of work. The key here was waiting for the breakout since the market was choppy. Things can never be totally certain in the market, so there is no point waiting once the charts suggest a buy.

Figure 5.2

Figure 5.3

The 2B Setup

Criteria

A high followed by a slightly higher high.

Entry

When the high of the first high (Point 1 in Figure 5.4) breaks on a pullback from the second high (Point 2 in Figure 5.4).

Alternate Entry

Under the prior bar's lows after the second high is made. For instance, if the lows of the bar making the second high is Rs. 510, entry is under Rs. 510. The only time it is not under the bar that made the second high is if that high is followed by an inside range bar, in which case you would use a break in the lows of the inside range bar.

Stop

Over the second high.

Target

Target should be the width of the trading range from the point of breakout or breakdown.

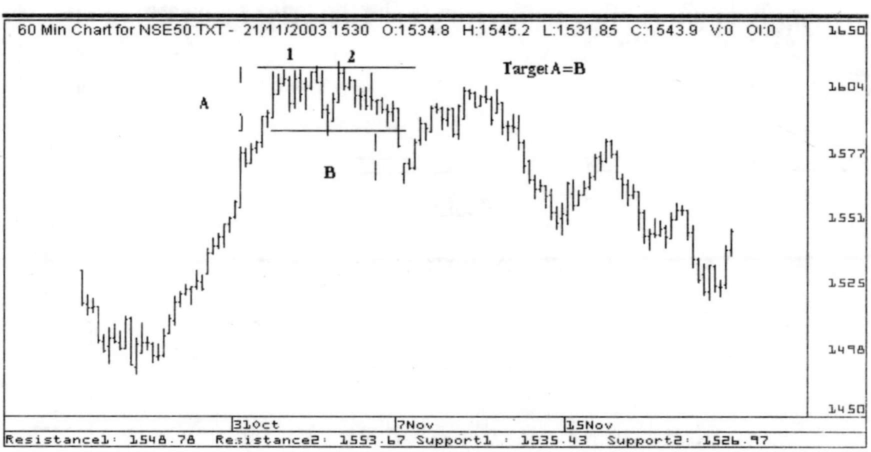

Figure 5.4

Ascending Triangle

Criteria

Equal or nearly equal highs and higher lows on reducing volume.

Entry

Breakout from the trend lines on higher than average volume as the trend lines converge.

Stop

Under the lows of the base, or last major pivot low on the smaller time frame, or under the lows of the setup bar.

Target

Equal distance on a breakout comparable to the distance between the first high and first low in the triangle. Ascending triangles tend to breakout higher (Figures 5.5 and 5.6).

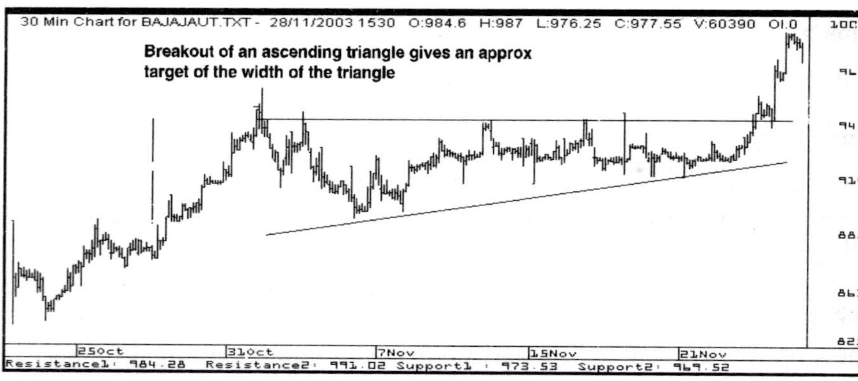

Figure 5.5

Figure 5.6

Trading Range/Congestion

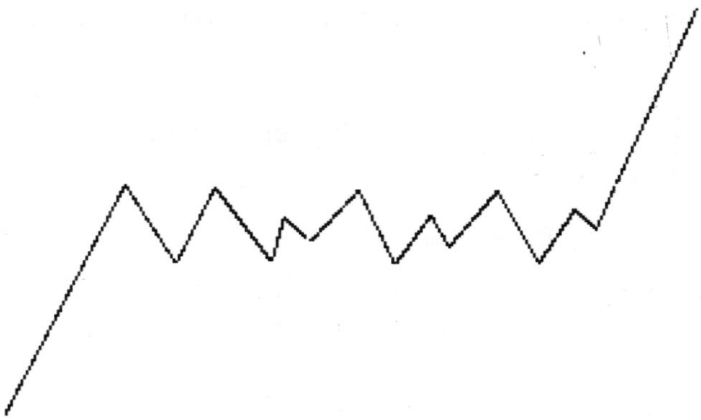

Trading Range / Congestion / Basing / Consolidation

Breakout

Criteria

A base/trading range at highs or lows.

Entry

A breakout in the most recent section of the trading range or trend line in the direction of the trend prior to the trading range (Figures 5.7 and 5.8).

Stop

The stop would be under the last pivot low within the trading range.

Target

An equal move to that before the trading range on the move out of the trading range.

Head and Shoulders

Criteria

High (left shoulder) followed by a higher high (head) and then a lower high (right shoulder) which is comparable to the left shoulder.

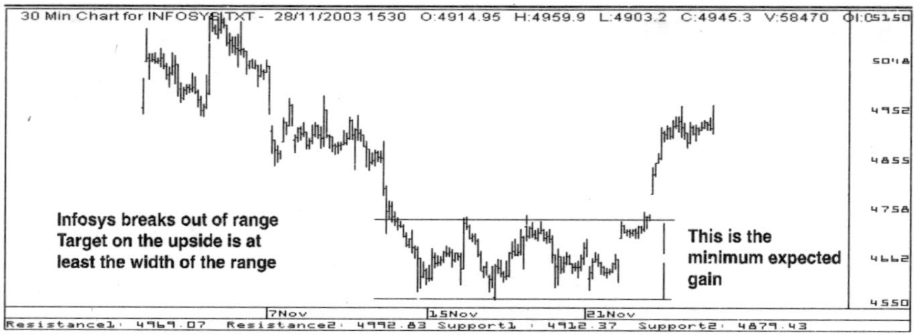

Figure 5.7

Figure 5.8

Entry

Breakdown from the neckline. The neckline connects the lows on either side of the head. Alternative and preferred entry is using a bear flag breakdown to enter after the right shoulder has formed (Figures 5.9 and 5.10).

Stop

Over the past pivot high.

Target

The height of the head from the neckline is the target from the neckline after the breakdown.

Figure 5.9

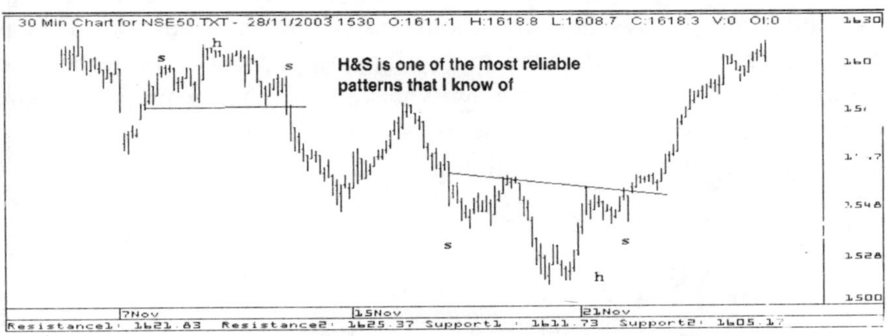

Figure 5.10

Pennants/Wedges

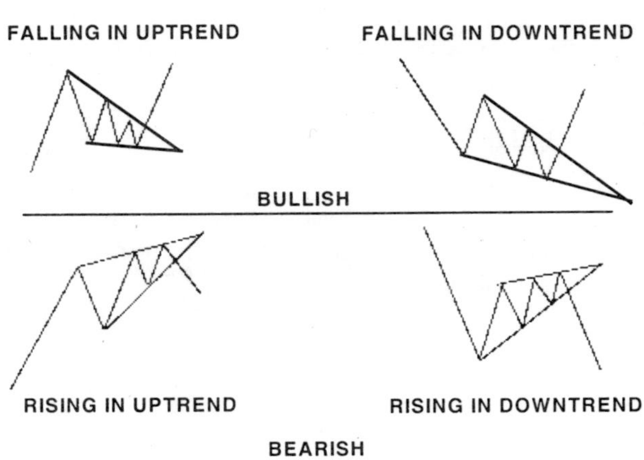

Flags, Pennants and Wedges

Flags, pennants and wedges are extremely important for a day trader. These are little stalling patterns in an ongoing trend which provide the day trader both with a low risk entry and a stop loss. These patterns often occur in the middle of an up or a down move in all time frames (Figures 5.11 and 5.12). So a target on the upside or downside of a move preceding these patterns is good bet. I know traders who make a living trading just these patterns. As I would like to stress again, we are here to make money and not be right in predicting tops and bottoms. In fact, I am often asked if we are at the top or bottom of a market and I am always hesitant about answering the question. This is because knowing whether the market has topped out or bottomed out is not the key to making money. The key to making money in any time frame is entering trends with a low risk entry and then using proper money management techniques.

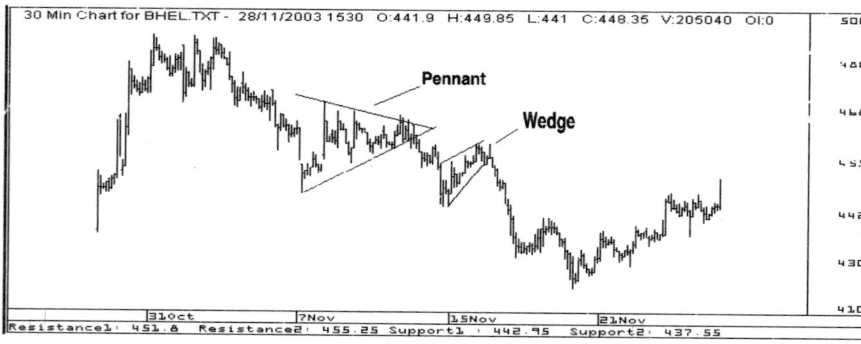

Figure 5.11

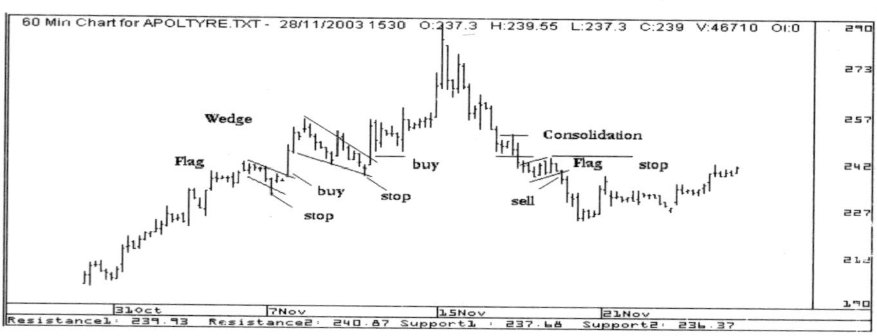

Figure 5.12

Reverse Head and Shoulders

Criteria

Low (left shoulder) followed by a lower low (head) and then a higher low (right shoulder) which is comparable to the left shoulder (Figures 5.13 and 5.14).

Entry

Break higher from the neckline. The neckline connects the highs on either side of the head.

Stop

Under the past pivot low.

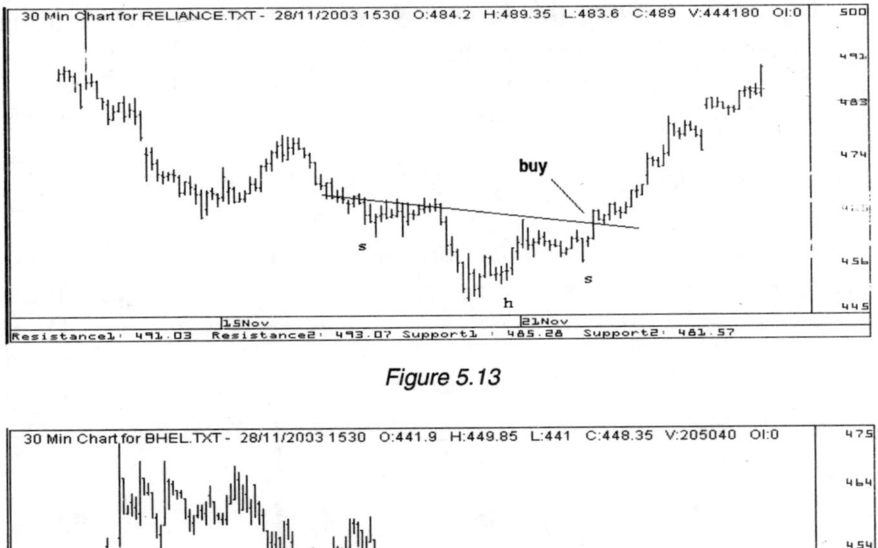

Figure 5.13

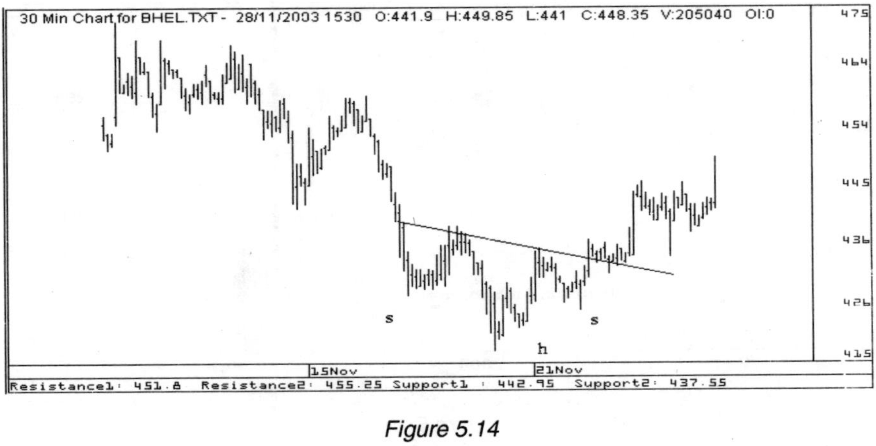

Figure 5.14

Trading News-Based Gaps

Trading gaps is probably at par with trading flags, pennants and wedges in terms of ease but far superior in terms of the returns offered in the shortest possible time. In India, bad news often occurs overnight, such as a terrorist strike, political parties withdrawing support to bring down governments, companies announcing results either after the market closes or before it opens. And not only bad news; sometimes there is good news as well that comes after the markets close. The good news could be companies announcing spectacular results, government announcing divestment, companies announcing acquisitions, etc. The reaction to such news is often in the shape of a gap up or a gap down opening — a logical reaction to such news. The trouble is, the discounting mechanism of the market often quickly over-reacts. The technical reason for this is that the market becomes oversold until strong hands then pick it up from the lower level. In my experience, 95% of the time the reaction does not see follow through in the direction of the gap and can be successfully traded in the opposite direction.

Let us consider an actual event to understand the market's discounting mechanism.

When the late Mr. Dhirubhai Ambani was critically ill in hospital, the Reliance share moved lower every time there was news of further

Figure 5.15

deterioration in his health. Now tragic as it was, there was no doubt that his sons were then ably running the company and, in a business sense, his death was not going to make a dramatic change to the company's operations. Yet the Reliance share lost ground day after day for about two weeks and went down from Rs. 285 to about Rs. 260. Traders would watch television the whole day for updates from Ambani brothers. The news that Mr. Ambani had finally passed away came after the markets closed. Investors and traders were jittery about the market reaction considering Reliance's heavyweight status. The next day the Reliance share gapped down Rs. 5 but recovered almost immediately and finally closed higher by about Rs. 10. This incident shows that the market was discounting the event well in advance of when it happened, and actually moved to look ahead once it did. It is such events that a trader needs to look for to get into great setups and potentially very rewarding trades (Figure 5.15).

Another situation that easily comes to mind were the quarterly results of Indian IT companies announced in July 2003. Market veterans would remember that in the earlier quarter of that year, Infosys reduced its guidance to about 10-15% growth in net profit for the year and the share immediately tanked 30% in a day. Subsequently, there was a July bloodbath in all the IT stocks. So when the next quarter results were

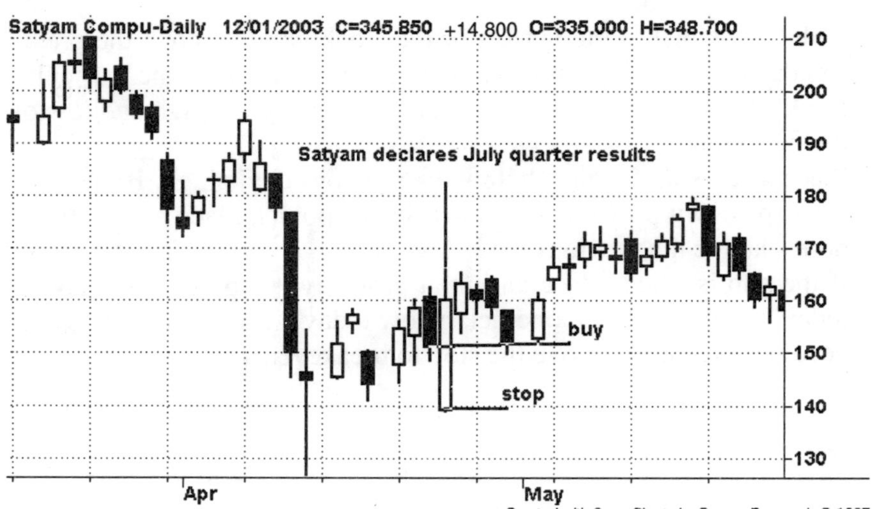

Figure 5.16

about to be declared IT stocks started declining in value and the sentiment was such that as each IT result approached, the particular stock would start declining. I particularly remember Satyam as it fell from Rs. 175 to about Rs. 150 in a matter of a week, with wild rumours of extremely poor results floating all over the place. Satyam results were declared before the markets opened and were lukewarm. Satyam gapped down Rs. 5 but then immediately went up Rs. 15 and closed strong for the day. This incident again shows how the market anticipates news and often the reaction is contrary to the news declared (Figure 5.16).

There are other types of news, such as the Gujarat earthquake or an overnight terrorist strike, which the market cannot foresee. Tragic as such events are, they provide some very useful opportunities to the day trader. At the time of the Gujarat earthquake, for instance, the Sensex gapped down 80 points at the opening and went down by a total of 160 points. But as news came in that the industries located in Gujarat were safe, the markets recovered and closed the day only 35 points down. The cement stocks even closed positive because of people betting on the ensuing reconstruction.

Strategy for Trading on News

1. Identify the previous day's high and low for the market index, or the particular stock;
2. If the news makes the market or the stock gap up above the previous day's high by at least 10 Nifty points — or 2% on the particular stock — wait for the first half-hour and identify the high and low of the half-hour;
3. Place a sell stop 5 points below the previous day's high. If the market gaps down previous day's low by 10 points, place a buy stop 5 points above the previous day's low.
4. If the gap is filled, place an initial protective stop one point above today's high (for buys, one tick below today's low). As the position becomes profitable, move the stop to breakeven.

Chapter 6

Cash and Futures Arbitrage

As I began writing this chapter in January 2004, Indian batsmen were thrashing the Australian bowlers all over the park Down Under. I mention this as I see an important analogy between cricket and trading in the stock markets. In batting, they say, the job of the openers is to see off the new ball so that a foundation is laid for the middle order batsmen to get to a big total. Similarly, in trading it's important to see off some of the choppy sessions, overbought periods, or periods of uncertainty so that when the market again resumes trending, traders can get back into the market.

Knowing when not to trade is perhaps as important as knowing when to trade.

All experienced traders would recall the expensive mistakes they made at times when it would have been better to have kept out instead of taking unacceptable risks. It is perhaps the pressure of "idle cash" that makes traders take risks that they should not. This pressure can be eliminated by taking advantage of the arbitrage returns offered between the cash and the derivatives market. The returns can be of the order of 15-22% annualized risk free, hardly something to be sneezed at when your cash is idling any way.

The cash and futures arbitrage is a strategy which often offers risk free returns at rates better than savings accounts deposits and most other risk free liquid asset classes.

The futures price of any security, or the index, is a combination of two factors; the cash price of the asset, and the cost of carry for the period remaining to expiry of the futures instrument. For example:

The one month futures price of Reliance Industries =
Cash price of the Reliance stock + the cost of carry for a period of one month.

In the Indian markets the cost of carry currently varies between a negative 35% per annum to a positive 35% per annum. It can even be higher or lower than the 35% figure but that would be an extraordinary event. The method of capturing this risk free return is simple.

Futures Price Higher than the Cash Price

We all know that at expiry the futures price closes at the cash price of the security or index. So in the above Reliance example, if the futures price of Reliance is higher than its cash price, you can buy the Reliance stock and sell a similar quantity of Reliance futures. This will allow you to earn the cost of carry of the Reliance futures.

For example, if the price of Reliance is Rs. 400 on the day of execution and the Reliance futures is trading at Rs. 406, it is possible to buy the Reliance stock for Rs. 400 and sell the Reliance futures at Rs. 406. On expiry, assuming Reliance closes at Rs. 450, you make Rs. 50 by selling the Reliance stock and lose Rs. 44 by buying back the futures, which is Rs. 6 in a month, or 18% annualized, risk free. This is, of course, before commissions. The stock itself is accepted as margin for the futures position.

Futures prices are generally higher than the cash prices in an overbought market.

Cash Price Higher than the Futures Price

Intuitively, the cost of carry should always be a positive figure. In the Indian markets, however, we often see futures prices being lower than the cash prices, generally in an oversold market. This may be due to the fact that the Indian market is cash settled and not delivery settled, so the futures price is more a reflection of sentiment, rather than that of the financing cost.

Let us assume that the cash price of the Reliance share is greater than its futures price. Suppose the cash price is Rs. 406 and the futures price is Rs. 400. The obvious thing to do would be to sell the stock in the cash market and buy the futures. So at expiry if Reliance closes at Rs. 450, you will buy back the stock at a loss of Rs. 44 and make Rs. 50 on the settlement of the futures position. But since there is an interest to be paid for borrowing the stock, it has to be deducted from the cost of carry earned from this strategy. Assuming an interest of 12% is paid on the stock borrowed, and there was a 20% margin on the futures position and a 50% margin on the borrowed stock, it will lead to a return of 8.5%, which might not amount to much after commissions. So, this strategy should be applied only when the cost of carry is abnormally high.

Also, since the Indian markets follow the T+1 settlement, the stock has to be delivered the next morning. And while most large brokers like Kotak Securities, etc. do some stock lending which would make it possible to capture this return, the mechanism is not yet well developed and the smaller brokers usually do not have this facility. With the large brokers we could have borrowed the stock from the depository and sold it in the market, paying an interest which would be lower than the cost of carry of the futures. When using borrowed stock, you need to make sure that you are making money after paying the interest on borrowed stock and commissions.

Sebi has put in place margin trading and stock lending system from 1 February 2004. This system is provided to investors only by corporate brokers. This facility will take time to develop and it will be interesting to see if it can be employed for selling the stock short in the above case.

Returns Possible with Cash and Futures Arbitrage

Table 6.1 shows the kind of returns that are possible through cash and futures arbitrage. Traders should remember that these are risk free returns. These are returns through cash and futures arbitrage from January 2004 which was a wildly bullish market; such costs of carry may not be available at other times. So this strategy cannot and should not be applied at all times, typically much better returns are possible in bull markets.

Personally, I like to lock in extraordinary mispricings in the futures price and anything near 3.5% per annum would excite me.

Why the Cost of Carry Varies According to the Market Sentiment

I think Indian traders can understand this better than traders from anywhere else.

Table 6.1

Security	*Cash Price Jan 2004 (Rs.)*	*Futures Price Jan 2004 (Rs.)*	*Difference (Rs.)*	*Cost of Carry (Annualized)*
ACC	265.55	268.00	–2.45	13.47%
Bajaj Auto	1120.00	1137.90	–17.90	23.33%
BHEL	538.80	545.00	–6.20	16.80%
BPCL	479.15	485.00	–5.85	17.83%
Canara Bank	141.10	143.20	–2.10	21.73%
Digital	749.00	758.00	–9.00	17.54%
Dr Reddy	1450.00	1468.75	–18.75	18.88%
HPCL	460.00	466.30	–6.30	20.00%
Infosys	5691.30	5755.00	–63.70	16.34%
Larson	538.00	543.50	–5.50	14.93%
Maruti	381.00	385.50	–4.50	17.24%
National Alum	203.00	206.35	–3.35	24.09%
Nifty Futures (near)	1950.25	1960.00	–9.75	7.30%
ONGC	916.00	926.60	–10.90	17.37%
PNB	239.50	242.50	–3.00	18.29%
Ranbaxy	1109.25	1123.40	–14.15	18.62%
Reliance	587.10	592.80	–5.70	14.17%
Satyam	375.75	381.50	–5.75	22.34%
State Bank	570.00	576.60	–6.40	16.34%
Tata Power	328.70	332.75	–4.05	17.99%
Telco	457.05	463.00	–5.95	19.01%
Tisco	451.70	458.00	–6.30	20.36%

Remember the good old days of the *badla*? Now *badla* too was a financing cost and it varied wildly, from 12-13% to as high as 48% at times. The *badla* rates depended on the market conditions. Higher *badla* rates meant a high demand for money which, in turn, meant that the markets were bullish. Lower *badla* rates prevailed when the demand for money was low because the markets were either flat or bearish.

By keeping this financing cost principle in mind, traders can make money by cash and futures arbitrage, and also get a sense of the market's direction when the cost of carry is at its extremes. Typically, when the costs of carry of most Nifty stocks is upwards of 35% per annum, it's a good time to take profits on your long positions and use the arbitrage strategy to earn a further 35% on those profits. Costs of carry above 35-40% are unsustainable over the long term and would sooner or later lead to a correction in the market, or at least a sideways movement. Conversely, when the cost of carry is negative, something which should not theoretically happen but does in the Indian market — a similar extreme value would signify an oversold market and one which should be bought into.

Advantages of Using Cash and Futures Arbitrage

Reasonable Returns When No Other Trade is Visible

This strategy can offer 18-22% returns annually for traders when there are no trades visible on the horizon. This is a much better option than keeping your funds at no interest with the broker, or even keeping them in your savings account. Good trades are like music; they flow very simply and naturally. Often the stresses of running a household, peer pressure, etc, can lead a trader into a false trade. In my years of trading, I have found that the best trading is done when these is no pressure. Which is why I spend a lot of time looking for opportunities which can help me make money from activities other than pure swing trading. Cash futures arbitrage is one such; writing covered calls is another. Returns of 18-22% annually may not excite stock market punters, but stock market trading is as much about stability and consistency of returns as it is about the quantum of returns on every trade. These are all issues professional traders need to think about. These extra returns take some pressure off the need to trade all the time, thus enabling the trader to wait for the best setups, confident that he is making money somewhere else.

Waiting for good trades in my case could mean the following two scenarios.

Waiting For a Market Correction to Take a Swing Trade

We have discussed earlier the low risk entry technique of buying in an oversold condition in a lower time frame in the direction of the trend established in the higher time frame. Now during strong bull trends, sometimes the market does not correct for a long time and just keeps going up. This happened, for instance, between December 2003 and January 2004. I was having my complete exposure through most of the trend; I then booked profits when the market turned sideways and my targets were achieved. But the market rallied some more without first correcting substantially. Now at the risk of not participating in the subsequent move and, again, not getting the best entry into the trend, I decided I would go in for my complete exposure.

Generally, based on my money management methods I am long or short 3,000 shares, or 15 contracts of Nifty,. So I decided to let the market run and took a one-third position of 1,000 Nifty, which kept me comfortably in the trend while waiting for the perfect set up, which in my case would have meant an oversold level in the daily chart plus a reversal. Some could argue that I let go of profits that might have been mine. But a mature trader realizes that no market goes up forever and corrections are inevitable. A trader can hold a position confidently if he thinks that he entered the best setup possible. Chasing momentum can be a dangerous game and one that can leave you with drawdowns of 15-20% if your run into a correction as soon as you enter. The cash futures arbitrage strategy makes money even when you are waiting for good a setup.

Waiting For Covered Call Setups

One of the big dangers in covered call writing, as we shall see later in the book, is looking at downsides bigger than the call premiums you earn. This can happen if calls are written in a market that has been moving upward for a while and is susceptible to a correction. I have often been in such a situation. And every time the wait has been worthwhile since each time the market corrects, it's easier to make money on the covered call. Again, nobody knows when the correction might take place. So there is need for a strategy which gives liquidity and reasonable returns on idle cash. Cash futures arbitrage fulfils that space.

Perfect for Cash Which You Cannot Risk

All traders have cash which they don't want to directly risk in the stock market. Cash futures arbitrages can be a technique to earn a decent risk free return on cash that cannot be risked. All traders keep some reserve cash or an account where they keep their profits for times when the market stop being helpful. These funds can be deployed in risk free strategies such as cash futures arbitrage.

Perfect for Choppy Sideways Markets

Markets go through periods of consolidation and up and down action when trading becomes very difficult. The costs of carry of futures are reasonable till about the 15th of every month. So it's always possible to wait a few days if one has to till some extraordinary mispricings appear. These mispricings are very quickly taken care of by smart arbitrageurs, so waiting once you spot such an opportunity is not the smartest thing to do.

Reduces the Market Risk of a Portfolio

A lot of high net worth investors and mutual funds have very high weightage in index stocks. There are times when the market might look overheated and these investors may want to reduce the risk of possible market declines for the next few weeks. At such times they can sell index futures worth the entire, or a part of, the market value of their portfolio to hedge against market declines and also earn the cost of carry in the bargain. Index futures arbitrage may not be profitable for individual trader because of the inefficiencies in buying the cash Nifty or the Sensex portfolio.

Although it is possible to buy the Nifty cash portfolio through the Nifty basket, which is a portfolio of Nifty stocks bought by shooting bids at all the stocks in the weightages that they represent in the Nifty. But the overall acquisition price of the Nifty bees may turn out to be higher than the Nifty cash at the same point since some of the Nifty constituents are not liquid at all times. In such a case, if the trader wants to invest Rs. 10 lakh in index arbitrage, he can buy Rs. 10 lakh worth of Nifty bees and sell an equivalent amount of Nifty index futures. But traders purely in the arbitrage game for the cost of carry returns will not find the Nifty premiums too exciting.

The other option is buying the Nifty bees, which is a product by a company which closely tracks the Nifty. The bees trades at one-tenth the value of the cash Nifty. For example, if the Nifty is at 1,900, the Nifty bees would be around 189-190. But the liquidity is so poor that serious traders cannot trade a large quantity. As of writing this book, the liquidity was something like 3,000 shares traded in a day. So this also does not seem to be a very viable option though things might change as the markets develop some more.

Possible Outcomes of the Cash Futures Arbitrage

Like most things in life, if executed properly the returns from the cash futures arbitrage strategy can be juiced up. The highest costs of carry are found when the market is greatly overbought which makes the shifting of profits from swing trading or covered call writing to this strategy very convenient.

There are two possible outcomes once such a strategy is implemented.

- If the futures maintain a premium till expiry, let the futures expire and sell the stock. For example, I had bought 6,900 shares of Nalco for Rs. 201.50 and sold 6,900 Nalco futures for Rs. 204.50 with 25 days left for expiry. It turned out to be 24% annualized return, and I pocketed approximately Rs. 21,000 in profit.
- Sometimes if the market corrects in the interim, the cost of carry can become negative during the month because of temporary demand supply mismatch. This opportunity should be used to unwind both legs of the strategy and thus enhance your profits even further. For example, if in the above Nalco case a correction had occurred before expiry and the Nalco stock fallen to Rs. 195 and the futures to Rs. 193, I would have unwound both legs and made approximately Rs. 35,000 in the process.

It is not possible to trade full-tilt in the stock market every minute or target maximum possible returns all the time. There are times when you need to operate in a lower gear, also times when you need to press on the gas pedal, so that overall your returns are above average. The goal has to be protection of capital, along with generation of returns while taking the lowest risk possible. Cash futures arbitrage is a great way to manage volatility in returns over a period of time and also deploy idle cash at a decent rate of return while waiting for better trading opportunities. As good as the cash futures arbitrage strategy sounds, traders should remember that capturing extraordinary mispricings is not possible all the time. You need to assess whether the cost of carry is high enough to deliver worthwhile returns.

Chapter 7

Getting to Grips with Options

Before the introduction of derivatives in India, you could either buy or sell stocks. The smarter investors and traders would either earn *badla* on the shares they held or earned *badla* by margin lending activity to the exchange. I like to think of options as the bass, treble and volume controls of a music system that is the stock market. If there were no bass, treble and volume controls, you could either switch the radio on or off, and be forced to listen to the songs and news at the same volume and tone. With the advent of derivatives, a lot more flexibility has come available to traders. They can adjust and massage their stock market exposure with the various derivative instruments, particularly options and a combination of options, futures and stocks.

An options contract involves the payment, or receipt, of a premium for the right to buy or sell the underlying asset at a particular price, within a specified period. Each transaction in the options market involves either opening a new position or closing an existing one.

Let us now discuss options from a trader's point of view and without getting lost in too much mathematics.

Stocks and futures are linear products where the downside could be as much as the upside. The huge benefit of options, on the other hand, is that they are non-linear products with only limited downside but unlimited upside for the buyer.

The option seller, conversely has limited upside but unlimited downside risk.

But this asymmetry comes with certain risks and rewards for both options buyers and sellers. The naked options buyer does not lose more than the option premium he pays. An option position is called naked if it is not hedged by another options or futures position, or a spread strategy. Accordingly, simply buying a call or a put is called buying naked options. In order to enjoy the benefit of limiting the loss only to the premium, a trader needs to take many other kinds of risks, namely:

- The risk of sideways movement of the market;
- The risk of adverse movement of the market; and
- The risk of time to expiry.

A little later we will compare whether it is the buyer or the seller who is actually able to reduce risk in the options market.

Generally speaking, options are spoken of in terms of *hedging* and *speculation*.

Speculation (Trading) with Options

By speculation, I mean buying naked puts or calls and the various strategies that make use of a combination of futures, options and/or stocks, with the intention of making a profit instead of hedging another position. Profitable trading with any instrument in any market requires strong trending moves because of the risks listed above, though the options market does have some strategies for a range-bound market on the option selling side. Also, it is critical to remember that because of fixed contract sizes, the minimum position a trader can take is defined by the stock exchange.

Personally, I use options for speculation only in a strongly trending market. One of the reasons for this is that Indian options are liquid only for the near month expiration.

Also, I never buy options for hedging purposes because I do not think it is worth paying extra to hedge, except in the case of covered calls (which is selling calls against stock positions). The covered call actually puts money into your account. The covered call is dealt with, in exclusive detail, in Chapter 9.

Hedging with Options

Hedging is defined as taking a position in conjunction with a stock or a futures position to reduce the risk of adverse movement. Hedging in the above sense requires payment of a premium, much as an insurance policy does and, in turn, puts the return bar higher for achieving profit targets. Both are worthy causes in themselves but I would like to focus in this book on the enhancement of returns and management of risk through options. Still, we will discuss some hedging strategies as well in later chapters.

Buying options for purpose of hedging reduces returns and actually increases risk except, maybe, in the case of very long term investing. I would rather sell than buy an option any day, since at-the-money puts can be priced up to 4% of the underlying contract. In extraordinary circumstances where a portfolio needs to be protected, out-of-money puts can be bought. Or sometimes when the next month's futures contracts become active in the middle of the current month, traders can hedge for at most one-and-a-half month by selling individual stock or Nifty futures. Another good way of hedging is to keep selling calls against a portfolio (covered calls) and over a period of time earn enough premia to cushion any fall in the market. In general, for traders the best way to protect profits is to bring them home. Positions can always be re-entered later on after a correction.

But if options are used according to one's view of the market and volatility, etc., they can be effective in most situations. Generally speaking, options can and should be used in conjunction with other products like futures and stocks. Options can thus reduce the downside during adverse market movement and also offer steady returns in a sideways or trending market. All these strategies will be discussed in this and later chapters of this book.

Options: Some Important Concepts

Market Lots

The stock exchanges in their wisdom decided to limit the Indian derivatives market to the relatively larger players and thus introduced market lots with a minimum contract size of Rs. 2 lakh. As the derivatives market was first implemented at a Nifty level of about 1,000 (or Sensex 3,300), the average contract sizes in some cases rose to over Rs. 10 lakh when the market rallied. As of writing this book, the lots have been re-sized in order to bring the exposure back down to Rs. 2 lakh per contract. But since stocks keep rising and falling, this problem will exist till a stable policy is put in place*. The option trader needs to understand the overall risk he is taking, both in terms of his total exposure to the derivatives market, as also for each individual derivative contract. This is discussed in detail in the chapter on money management later in the book (Chapter 12). If the exposure of a particular options contract is more than a trader's pre-determined exposure to the derivatives market because of the lot size, he should desist from taking positions in such options.

Strike Price

The price at which the underlying stock of an option can be purchased or sold by the contract buyer is called the strike price. The strikes in options of most Indian shares are in multiples of Rs. 5 and Rs. 10. Generally speaking, five to six option prices are available on both sides of the current price of the underlying. Of course, this depends on whether the prices have been moving up or down at a given point of time. For example, the ACC stock trading at Rs. 200 might have options listed with strikes of Rs. 150, Rs. 160, Rs. 170, Rs. 180, Rs. 190, Rs. 200, Rs. 210, Rs. 220, Rs. 230, Rs. 240 and Rs. 250.

But sometimes there may not be so many strikes available in real life. For example, if Nifty moves up from, say, 900 to 1500, it may have options of all strikes between 1,300 and 1,500 but only two strikes of 1,510 and 1,520 on the upper side on any given day. It is important for traders to factor in the time it takes exchanges to list new strikes. In fast moving markets, sometimes the exchanges can be a little slow and there is nothing we can do about it.

Another problem is that strikes which are closer to the price of the underlying are more liquid than are the others. As explained later under "The Greeks" section, I like to buy the higher delta option. A higher delta option, in general, is an option which is deep in-the-money; in other words one which is on the profitable side of the strike price by quite a margin. Sometimes that is difficult with the liquidity being low for deep in-the-money options. So you need to strike a balance by buying sufficient in-the-money strike and one that has reasonable liquidity in proportion to the volumes that you are expecting to

* (Please see Appendix I for the latest lot sizes for derivatives contracts on all stocks and indices)

trade. Check with your broker if you can easily buy and sell the quantity you want to trade and what quantities are other buyers and sellers putting their bids for.

In-the-money

- A call option whose strike price is below the current price of the underlying; or
- A put with a strike above the current price.

For example, if the ACC stock is trading at Rs. 200, the ACC call options with strikes 190, 180, 170 and below are all in-the-money.

Out-of-the-money

- A call option whose strike price is above the current price of the underlying stock or
- A put with a strike below the current price.

When ACC is trading at Rs. 200, the ACC call options with strikes 210, 220, 230 and upwards are out-of-the-money.

At-the-money [ATM]

This is an option that has a strike price equal to the current price of the underlying stock.

The ACC option with a strike of Rs. 200 is at-the-money when the stock is trading at or near the strike price.

Expiration Date

The date when the term of an options contract terminates is called its expiration date. The expiry of Indian options mandated by the stock exchanges is the last Thursday of every month. Technically speaking, options contracts are available for the near month (current), mid-month (next) and far month (the month after next). Currently, however, only the near month options usually have tradable liquidity and only towards the last week of the near month do options of the mid-month gather enough liquidity to be traded comfortably.

Presently in India, therefore, the number of days to expiration has more relevance than is apparent. Options for the subsequent month (mid-month) become active in the last week of the current month. As a rule, traders should try to buy as much time value as possible so that their positions have enough time to work out. Unless the market is in a strong trending mode, long options should not be held after the 15th or 20th of the expiration month. This is because the time component of the option expires very fast, and usually during the last few days of the month the loss due to time value is equal to or even more than the gain on the underlying stock. The decay of the time value is known as time decay and the rate of time decay is available as theta (*see* the section on "The Greeks" later in this chapter) on most option calculators.

Underlying Stock or Index

The stock or index that an option gives its buyer or seller the right to buy or sell is known as the underlying. For example, in the case of ACC call option, the underlying stock is ACC and the behaviour of the option depends on the movement of the ACC stock.

Option Holders (Option Buyers)

The buyers of options are often designated as option holders. This is also the same as creating a long position in the options market. The option buyer needs to pay just the option premium and his risk is limited to the premium he pays since that is the maximum he can lose.

Option Writers (Option Sellers)

Writers receive money (premium) for writing, i.e. selling, options. They are considered to have short positions on the particular option of the stock or index. The option writer has to pay an upfront margin to the broker which can vary from 20% to 70%. The short position in options has unlimited risk and limited return, and a short position in the options market is treated as a short position in the futures market. This means that a naked short options position attracts margins and mark to market rules of a short futures contract because, in theory, the loss on an options contract could be unlimited, much like in the case of a short futures contract.

Types of Options

There are two types of options contracts — the call and the put. Then, too, options can be either European or American. European options can be exercised only on the exercise date, whereas American options can be exercised at any time.

In India, as in most parts of the world, only the index options are traded as European options while the stock options are traded as American options.

There are also two kinds of instruments available under options:

- Call is the right to buy the underlying asset at a particular price within a specified period.
- Put is the right to sell the underlying asset at a particular price, within a specified period.

Option Value

The option value is composed of two parts:

- Intrinsic value, and
- Time value.

Intrinsic value is the amount by which an option is in-the-money. For example, let us suppose the ACC stock is trading at Rs. 220 and the 200 ACC call option is trading at a premium of Rs. 32. Of the premium of Rs. 32, the intrinsic value is Rs. 20.

Time value is the part of an option premium that exceeds its intrinsic value. In the above example, therefore, the time value is Rs. 12.

Just to clarify in terms of which options to buy; if I am bullish on ACC and the share is trading at Rs. 200, I would take the quotes of 200, 210, 220 ACC call options and compare the intrinsic values with the time values and buy the one with the maximum intrinsic value.

Out-of-the-money (OTM) options cost less than in-the-money (ITM) options because the chances of appreciation are higher in ITM options. Personally, I buy only in-the-money options with the least amount of time value in them. Thus, in the above ACC example, if the 200 call is selling for Rs. 30 and 210 call is selling for Rs. 25, I would buy the 200 call even if this means paying Rs. 5 more. This is because the less time value there is in an option, the lower is the value that is lost because of time. Currently, in India only the near month (or current month) options are actually liquid enough to trade. Accordingly, unless there are strong trending moves, the option's time value can evaporate in a hurry.

Options with more time till expiration cost more than those with less time.

Factors That Determine the Price of an Option

There are four major and two minor factors that determine the price of an option:

The major factors are:

- Price of the underlying.
- Volatility of the underlying.
- Strike price of the option.
- Time remaining until the option expires.

The minor factors are:

- Prevalent risk free interest rate.
- Dividend rate of the underlying stock.

Volatility

Volatility is a measure of the fluctuation in a stock's (or index's) price and often plays the most important role in options trading.

Knowing volatility can help you:

- Choose and implement an appropriate options strategy.
- Improve your timing in entering or exiting positions.
- Identify overpriced and underpriced options.

Understanding Volatility

Volatility is a measure of the amount by which an asset's price fluctuates in a given time. Mathematically, volatility is the annualized standard deviation of an asset's daily price changes.

There are two types of volatility:

- Historical volatility, and
- Implied volatility.

Historical volatility is a measure of the actual changes in an asset's price over a specific period of time. Historical volatility is available in most trading software, such as Trade-station, Super-charts, EI 2000, etc. It's also provided by many technical analysts and data providers.

Implied volatility is a measure of how much the "market" expects an option's price to move. Thus, it is the volatility that the market itself is implying, rather than that indicated by the past movements of the stock's price. Implied volatility can be calculated on the options calculator or obtained from several financial websites (*see* Appendix II). The moment you decide to buy or sell options or implement any strategy using options, it is critical to remember that implied volatility (IV) is an important part of the puzzle.

Let's go through an example as a step-by-step guide to buying or selling options.

Table 7.1

Implied Volatility Calculator

Risk Free Interest Rate:	6.00%
Underlying Asset:	
Market price (Rs.):	322.00
Dividends:	
Ex date	
Amount	
Or	
Continuous rate	20%
Option:	
Option type:	
Option market price (Rs.):	25
Strike price (Rs.):	320.00
Value date:	11/18/03
Expiration date:	11/27/03
Days to expiration:	9
Pricing:	
Pricing model:	Black Scholes
Number of steps for binomial model:	100
Implied Volatility:	118.33%

Suppose you want to take a long position in the Satyam 320 call option at Rs. 25, and the current price of Satyam stock is Rs. 322. Let us assume the current date to be 18 November 2003 and the expiry is on the 27 November 2003. You have to include either the 18th or the 27th in your calculation of implied volatility, not both. Now let us calculate the implied volatility (Table 7.1).

As you can observe, the inputs you needed to calculate implied volatility are very simple. You need the current date and the date of expiry, the options strike price, the current price of the underlying, risk free interest rate (which we will take as 6%), and historical volatility. Given these, you will automatically get the implied volatility in the option. At the time of writing this book, the Satyam share had a historical volatility of 50% and the implied volatility in the particular option example we have chosen is 118.33%, which means this option has a lot of volatility premium — or time value — in it. Traders should avoid strategies which consist of buying such an option. Instead, one's strategy should be to sell a high volatility option.

Table 7.2

Implied Volatility Calculator

Risk Free Interest Rate:	6.00%
Underlying Asset:	
Market price (Rs.):	322.00
Dividends:	
Ex date	
Amount	
Or	
Continuous rate	20%
Option:	
Option type:	
Option market price (Rs.):	10
Strike price (Rs.):	320.00
Value date:	11/18/03
Expiration date:	11/27/03
Days to expiration:	9
Pricing:	
Pricing model:	Black Scholes
Number of steps for binomial model:	100
Implied Volatility:	43.29%

Now, let's consider the same Satyam 320 option with the other parameters remaining the same except for the option premium, which is assumed to be Rs. 10, and again calculate the implied volatility (Table 7.2)

The same 320 Satyam call, having the same number of days to expiry, and with obviously the same price of the underlying and other inputs but with a premium of Rs. 10 has an implied volatility of 43.29% which is lower than Satyam's historical volatility of 50%. With all other things, such as one's view on the market and the stock being equal, the lower implied volatility immediately makes this Satyam call option appropriate for buying.

It is important to understand why it's not a good idea to buy options which have high implied volatility.

The stock market goes through alternate phases of high and low volatility. Periods of high are followed by periods of low volatility, and *vice versa*. Let us suppose a trader buys a high volatility option, and the volatility of the stock or the market — and hence the implied volatility of the option — goes down. Even if the underlying subsequently moves in a favourable direction, the option premium may not appreciate beyond the option's purchase price, and may even depreciate as the days to expiry reduce. This kind of option buying will be considered a high risk buy. On the other hand, if a trader buys a low implied volatility option, and both the volatility of the underlying and the implied volatility of the option go up, even if the movement of the underlying is marginally unfavourable, the option will at least hold its value.

The implied volatility can be high or low compared to the historical volatility. The important point is that one should buy a low implied volatility option which will be cheaper than a high volatility one of the same strike, expiry and underlying instrument. You should choose strategies which involve selling of options when the implied volatilities are high, and buy options when the implied volatility is low.

We will discuss the buying and selling of volatility further in the chapter on options strategies (Chapter 8).

The Greeks

The Greeks help the trader to understand the rate of change of the option premium with changes in the price of the underlying, time to expiry, volatility, etc.

Our discussion of the Greeks will include delta, gamma, vega, theta and rho. These greek letters denote the sensitivity of the option premium to changes in the above criteria. It is useful to understand the Greeks because they are an aspect of the buying or selling decision in the options market. While it is helpful to understand that call values rise and put values fall when the underlying index or stock rises and other factors remain constant, it is much more helpful to have a specific estimate of such changes in value. Such an estimate makes it possible to choose from among a number of strategies that are appropriate for a specific market forecast.

Delta

Delta deals with the most important determinant of an option price, namely the price of the underlying. Personally, I consider delta to be the most important Greek of all. As we would all remember from Class XII Maths (yes, the dreaded calculus), delta of an option is the first derivative of option value with respect to change in the price of the underlying.

We will not delve into the mathematics of delta but instead focus on its concept and utility. Delta is an estimate of the likely change in an option's value given a one-unit change in price of the underlying instrument, assuming other factors remain constant. Deltas can vary between +1 and –1.

In simple language, in the case of a higher delta option, the change in the option premium would be more for each rupee of change in the underlying stock or index, whether upward or downward.

In the case of a lower delta option, on the other hand, for each rupee of change in the underlying, the change in option premium would be lesser. In other words, the correlation of an option's premium to its delta is positive. As a trading strategy I always trade the higher delta option because for each unit of move in the underlying, the higher delta option premium moves more relative to a lower delta option.

Table 7.3

Price of the Underlying (Rs.)	Calculated Option Premium (Rs.)	Delta (Rs.)
280	5.75	+.29
285	7.32	+.343
290	9.15	+.397
295	11.26	+.452
300	13.64	+.508
305	16.30	+.562
310	19.22	+.614
315	22.39	+.664
320	25.81	+.71

Now, what is a high delta option? The more in-the-money an option is, the higher is its delta. The less in-the-money an option is, the lower is its delta, everything else being constant.

Let's now look at an example to put to test what we have said above. Let's consider the Satyam 300 November Call, where the date of valuation was 14 November 2003, the expiry date of the option was 27 November 2003, the historical volatility 64%, risk free interest rate of 6% and divided rate of 20%.

We now examine how the option premium of this Satyam 300 November Call changes, as the option moves from deep out-of-the-money to deep in-the-money (Table 7.3).

The above table brings out the procedure for buying options. As you can see, there are benefits of buying higher delta and more in-the-money options. The delta is moving towards +1 as the option becomes more in-the-money, which means that for each rupee of upward movement in the underlying stock, the option premium increasingly moves closer to +1. All else being equal, I would always buy the higher delta option. The higher delta option behaves more like a future as its delta approaches +1. Hence by buying a deep in-the-money option, a trader gets the upside of a future while limiting the downside.

The other way I look at it is that the more in-the-money option you buy, the higher is the intrinsic value in its premium. As we know by now, the time value part of the option can evaporate very fast. So the option which has greater intrinsic value is the one that I like to buy, since I want to pay as low a time premium as possible. Such an option behaves more like a future and my downside remains limited.

Calls Have Positive Deltas

The plus sign (+) associated with the delta of the Satyam 300 Call in Table 7.3 indicates a positive, or direct, relationship between changes in the price of the underlying instrument and change in the theoretical value of the call. As the table illustrates, when the underlying stock level rises, so does the theoretical value of the 300 Call.

It should be noted that a plus or minus sign associated with an option value may be different from the sign of an option position. The subject of position deltas will be discussed later.

Puts Have Negative Deltas

Let's now examine the Satyam 300 Put option, keeping all other parameters exactly the same (Table 7.4).

It's quite apparent that even in the case of puts buying a higher delta, in-the-money put is much better than a lower delta put, at-the-money put, or an out-of-money put.

The minus sign (–) associated with the delta of the 300 Put indicates a negative, or inverse, relationship between the change in the underlying instrument price and change in put's value. As indicated in Table 7.4, a rise in the index level caused the put value to decline.

The other Greeks are more important from a theoretical and a conceptual point of view and we will discuss these only briefly.

Table 7.4

Price of the Underlying (Rs.)	*Calculated Option Premium (Rs.)*	*Delta*
320	7.44	–.29
315	8.99	–.336
310	10.78	–.386
305	12.82	–.438
300	15.13	–.492
295	17.71	–.548
290	20.57	–.603
285	23.70	–.657
280	27.10	–.71

Gamma

Refer back to the delta tables (Tables 7.3 and 7.4) and note that the delta of +0.29 does not exactly predict the 300 Satyam Call value after a one-point increase in the underlying index. This is because the difference between the estimated changes in value and the actual change in value occurs because the delta changes when the price of the underlying changes. Gamma is an estimate of the change in delta for a one unit change in price of the underlying instrument, assuming other factors remain constant. Mathematically, gamma is the second derivative of the option pricing formula with respect to change in price of the underlying. The importance of this factor is captured by delta.

Vega

Vega is the change in option value that results from a one per cent change in volatility, assuming other factors remain constant. Vega answers the question: if the volatility changes by one per cent, how much does the option value change.

Mathematically, vega is the first derivative of option price with respect to change in volatility. Since first derivatives are theoretically "instantaneous rates of change," and since vega estimates the impact of a one per cent change, there will be frequent rounding errors.

Let's look at our Satyam example again (Table 7.5).

Strike: Rs. 300
Price of underlying: Rs. 295
Days to expiry: 13
Volatility: 64%

Table 7.5

Change of Volatility	*Vega*	*Option Premium (Rs.)*
54%	0.16	4.00
59%	0.17	4.86
64%	0.18	5.75
69%	0.185	6.66
74%	0.189	7.596

As Table 7.5 show, option premiums rise as the volatility increases and so does vega. This is the reason we have been stressing that you buy only low volatility options.

Theta

Theta is an estimate of the change in option value given a one unit change in time to expiration, assuming other factors remain constant. Now, this is the all-important time factor that we have been discussing. Time factor is currently critical in India because we are really talking only about the near month options as the others do not have sufficient liquidity to be relevant.

Going back to our example of the Satyam 300 Call, let's look at the time decay of this option. (Table 7.6)

Strike: Rs. 300
Price of underlying: Rs. 295
Volatility: 64%

Table 7.6

Time to expiry	*Theta (7 day theta)*	*Option Premium (Rs.)*
25	–2.3	9.96
20	–2.6	8.36
15	–3.026	6.55
10	–3.53	4.46
5	–.536 (1 day theta)	1.99

Without getting too deeply involved in the mathematical details, I would like to point out that a trader should note the increasing negative values of theta as the option nears expiry. The theta values are negative because the longer an option is held, the greater is the time decay effect on it.

We should clearly understand that in India, where there are about twenty trading sessions in a given month, the odds are stacked heavily against an option buyer. Personally I would be very hesitant to buy any options after the 15th of any month for the same month's expiry. Please remember that unless the market is trending, the loss in time value could exceed even the gains from a favourable movement in the underlying.

Rho

Rho is an estimate of the change in option value given a one percent change in interest rates, assuming other factors remain constant. Rho is not important from a short term trading perspective as interest rates do not change very often.

Factors to Keep in Mind When Buying Options

Do Not Use Options Solely as a Timing Tool

It is important to understand that options have a limited time horizon and personally I do not know of any time cycle analysis which works consistently. This is because even obvious-looking trends take time to develop but the time clock is always winding down in the options market. It's therefore important to buy options with low volatility so that there is no possibility of loss because of volatility.

Buy Deep In-the-Money Options

As we have seen in this chapter, it is always better to buy deep in-the-money options because each unit gain in the underlying stock or index leads to a higher gain in the option premium. Also, deep in-the-money options suffer less from time decay as the intrinsic value in such options is high.

Always Be Ready to Adjust Positions

If the market is not acting as you anticipated it would, get out of your options position. The last thing you should do in the options market is hope and pray. Quickly readjust your position with regard to the new market reality but do not over hedge as that raises your investment — remember, there is no risk-free trade.

Try to Reduce Your Net Investment by Selling Calls Wherever Possible

We will be discussing the use of spreads in later chapters. This is critical in India because the option has very little time to work. I would go to the extent of saying that it is always preferable to buy a stock or a future and sell calls against them because they do not have any attached time value. Covered call strategies are discussed in Chapter 9.

Keep a Reasonable Profit Target

I generally believe anything over 50% is a reasonable return in the options market. Unless the market is really trending in one direction, it is worth booking profits as and when more than 50% profits are achieved and move on to the next trade. This 50% is the absolute return in a month because that is the time to expiry of Indian options.

Do Not Buy More Naked Options Than Is Justified by Your Trading Account

It is very important to understand that the options market provides the kicker to your portfolio, and this cannot be 100% of your account. Personally speaking, I never keep my account exposed more than 10% to naked option buying.

In India, the culture of service in the brokerage industry is just about starting. Before the mid-nineties, there were few brokers and these people did not bother a lot about customer service. At that point, just getting an honest broker was considered being lucky. Now though things are improving, most of the small brokers still like to put the onus of responsibility on the client. As readers, must be aware, in the derivatives market, in each monthly settlement each buy should correspond to a sell, which the broker has to mark as the closure of the position. But this has to be reminded to him that a long or a short position already exists and the second transaction is the closing transaction.

Chapter 8

Strategies for Trading Options

Introduction

Different option strategies are used for taking advantage of the expected movement in a particular stock or index. An options strategy may involve buying and selling puts or calls, or both at the same, or different strikes of stocks or the index. This is done in order to take advantage of all kinds of views on the underlying stock or index, such as:

Bullish	Trending up move expected
Mildly bullish	Mild up move expected
Neutral	Range bound movement expected
Bearish	Trending down move expected
Mildly bearish	Mild down move expected

How to Develop a View on the Market or a Particular Stock

Views on a stock or index are developed on the basis of technical analysis, fundamental analysis, or expected news.

In my experience a view on the basis of technical analysis works best in the case of trading options. Am I biased? Maybe. Making money in the equity market is challenging enough most of the time, it gets even more challenging if there is a time element attached to it.

Charts and current prices often have all the fundamentals and news built in, more so in India because here some people are more informed than others and insider trading is rampant. This is proven by the fact that stocks move spectacularly days before announcement of any important relevant news. So the only way to beat these insiders is to know what they are doing, and that can be discovered on the charts. There is no question that over the long term stocks move because of fundamentals, but whether they do so for the same reasons over the short term is open to question. Option trading has nothing to do with long-term fundamentals because such trades last only one month. This leads us to important time-related issues which we shall now discuss.

Why Time to Expiry is so Important in Choosing Options Strategies in India

In India, the most important point to remember is that presently the most liquid options are those of the current month. So no matter how sure one is about a stock's movement, if the expected movement does not take place by the time to expiry, the options expire worthless.

Strategies that work in India are thus a little different from those that work worldwide mainly because the Indian options buyer needs to deal with time to expiry issues. Worldwide far month options which expire several months from now, or even years later, are quite liquid. Accordingly, we will discuss only those strategies in this chapter which are particularly useful for Indian traders. Traders interested in other strategies will find a lot of excellent literature available on the topic on the Net. Also, we will discuss the practical trading issues and concepts without going into detailed theories, as this book seeks to help you become a better trader and not PhDs in derivatives. If you wish you can consult standard textbooks on options which really get into pay-off diagrams for a theoretical explanation of strategies.

The time factor discussed above thus calls for codifying some certain unwritten rules (being written for the first time in this book) that Indian traders should follow. Following these rules would greatly improve your chances of making in the Indian options market. These are rules which experience in the Indian equity options market has taught the savvy among the Indian traders.

Use Option Strategies Which Involve Selling of Options as Well

Most successful strategies in the Indian context involve the selling of options. Traders do so in order to reduce their net investment. Traders and investors need to remember that even if the news they have is correct, it can take time before the price moves in the expected direction. But if they run out of time on an option, they are in any case going to make a loss. Option buyers should remember that option sellers are very smart people and the chances of their having priced in fundamentals and expected news is very high. In some cases sold options can even be twice the number of bought options. We will discuss this further under the strategies section.

Net Investment Should be Kept to the Minimum Possible and Returns Should be Calculated on Net Investment Basis

Investors and traders need to remember, particularly when using strategies that involve buying options, that they can lose even if the stock moves in their expected direction. This can happen if a very expensive strategy is used and the favourable movement is not dramatic enough to offset the high cost. This can also happen if very expensive options have been bought and the seller has priced in the expected movement of the stock.

Traders need to always remember that the options game is loaded in favour of the option seller who likes to price in every conceivable event and movement in the market or a given stock. All strategies discussed in this chapter seek to minimize the net investment.

High Implied Volatility Should be Consistently Sold either as a Straddle or a Covered Call

The implied volatility concept was discussed in detail in Chapter 7. As discussed there, and also in the later chapter on special situations (Chapter 10), selling options offers the best odds for making money. Again, it's important to remember not to sell unhedged (naked) options and to take protective action in case of unhedged options once they near breakdown.

Selling high volatility options makes the task of the option buyer even more difficult as it raises the bar above which he can make money. Also, high volatility periods are followed by periods of low volatility. Thus, not only does the option buyer lose volatility premium, he also loses valuable time value.

Traders Must Always Remember that Markets Trend only 30% of the Time, so Strategies to Capture Range Bound Movement are a Must

With options it is not possible to capture range bound movement either in stocks or the market. The important point to bear in mind here is that trending moves are followed by consolidations, which are again followed by trending moves. 70% of the time the market moves in a trading range, making no significant moves either up or down. It is only 30% of the time that markets actually trend. So the options market now gives a trader the opportunity to take a view on the range bound market.

As we discussed in an earlier example, traders must remember that it's not important for your view to be completely right; what is important is that you keep changing your strategy as the view changes. Often when you position yourself for a range bound market, the market may well start trending, or *vice versa*. This can happen to the best of traders in the world. What is important is for a trader to realize this quickly and make the appropriate changes to his strategy. Of course, at such times it is helpful to have bought cheaper options and sold the more expensive ones.

Be Careful of Well-advertised Strategies, They are More Expensive to Execute; It is Sometimes Worthwhile to Pursue the Opposite Strategy

Financial media often try to "help" retail traders by suggesting option strategies. I wish it were that simple. For example, often during the budget period they recommend a strategy called buying the straddle which involves buying a call and a put of the same strike price. Since everyone tries to get on to this supposedly money making bandwagon, the straddle ends up being very expensive and it becomes impossible to make any money by going in for it. There are other times when buying calls or puts is highly recommended for reducing risk. At these times it is worthwhile to do the opposite since the market would have already discounted the entire expected price move; of course, this must be done with appropriate hedging.

Don't Get into Options Trading without a Thorough Knowledge of Technical Analysis and Access to Charting Information

As discussed earlier, it is my opinion that consistent money in options can only be made by using technical charts. This is particularly true in India because of the lack of liquidity involved in the longer-term options. I believe only charts can give a reasonable view of the price movement expected in a one-month time frame.

Market Timing is Not the Key to Making Money in Options

I would like stress that options trading is not about timing the market. While it is important to have a view on the market, buying or selling options or strategies just because you believe the market is going up or down is a little simplistic. Once you have a view on the market, it is critical to determine the amount of time in which the expected movement might take place. Thereafter it is important to determine the implied volatilities of the options involved. A trader should then consider the implications of his trade not working out, and have a contingency strategy to keep one's loss to the minimum. In other words, you need to clearly work out the risk reward ratio. Options trading is rather like a game of chess where the winner may not have the best analysis but he would bet when most parameters are in his favour.

Gathering Preliminary Information

The following drill can be followed in making a good options trading decision:

- Develop a view on the market, or the particular stock.
- Try to assess the number of days it will take for the view to materialize.
- As far a possible, use a credit strategy (one that puts money into your account) instead of a debit strategy (one that takes money from your account). A credit strategy works even if the stock or the market does not move as much as you expect it to.
- Calculate the implied volatilities of the options involved.
- Think about the adverse scenario in case the strategy were not to work out.
- Work out the breakeven point of your trade and, if possible, try to make the trade risk-free once the trade moves in your favour by booking profits on certain options and buying or writing new options with different strikes.

Armed with the above techniques and a view of the market, we are now prepared to enter the exciting world of option strategies. In each case, we will first describe a strategy and then show how it is implemented in the Indian context The use of Peter Hoadley software for evaluating option strategies is explained in Appendix III.

Vertical Spreads

A vertical spread always consists of one long option and one short option, where both options are of the same type (both calls or both puts), and have the same expiration, but differ in their exercise or strike prices. Traders who already have a view as to the direction of the market use these spreads. Consequently, we see that vertical spreads are of two varieties, the bull spread and the bear spread. What determines whether a spread is bullish or bearish is not whether it is composed of puts or calls. Rather, if the trader/investor buys the option with the lower exercise price and sells the option with the higher exercise price, the spread is bullish. Conversely, if he buys the higher exercise price and sells the lower one the spread is bearish.

Credit Spreads

A credit spread is, simply put, one in which the receipt of cash from the short option exceeds the amount of cash paid out for the long option, inclusive of transaction costs. Thus, the following would be considered as credit spreads:

- Bear call spreads;
- Bull put spreads.

Debit Spreads

Conversely, a debit spread is one in which the amount of cash paid out for the long option exceeds the amount received for the short option, inclusive of transaction costs. Thus, the following are debit spreads:

- Bull call spreads;
- Bear put spreads.

There is no better way to introduce the benefits of spreading than by directly comparing a spread's risk reward profile with that of purchasing of the underlying or a "naked" option. This will highlight why spreading can be so valuable.

Naked Options

Assume we were dealing with the purchase of 1 Satyam Computers April 200 call @ Rs. 15 and the underlying was trading at Rs. 205. The risk reward profile would look as follows:

1. Breakeven: Since I paid Rs. 15 for it, I would breakeven on the April 200 call if the Satyam stock was trading at Rs. 215. Why? Because I have to recoup the Rs. 15 I paid as premium

Rs. 200 + Rs. 15 = Rs. 215.

2. Profit: I would make money on this April 200 call when the underlying Satyam share moves above the breakeven point. Since theoretically the stock price could go up infinitely, my potential profit is unlimited.

3. Loss: If the Satyam share were to close below Rs. 215 upon the option's expiry. I stand to lose money. Now, here is the great thing about options; I don't have to worry about how far below Rs. 215 the stock closes. Unlike in the case of my owning the stock, the most I can lose is the total premium I paid for the call option, Rs. 15 in this case. Not a bad deal. (Figure 8.1)

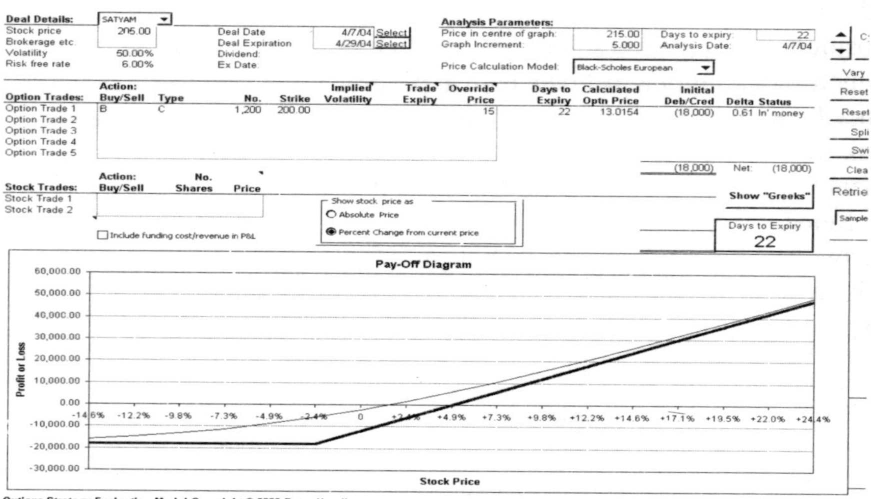

Figure 8.1 (a)

P/L at Expiry:		4/29/04															
Stock Price:	175.00	180.00	185.00	190.00	195.00	200.00	205.00	210.00	215.00	220.00	225.00	230.00	235.00	240.00	245.00	250.00	255.00
Brokerage etc.																	
Options:																	
Option Trade 1	-18,000	-18,000	-18,000	-18,000	-18,000	-18,000	-12,000	-6,000		6,000	12,000	18,000	24,000	30,000	36,000	42,000	48,000
Option Trade 2																	
Option Trade 3																	
Option Trade 4																	
Option Trade 5																	
Stock:																	
Dividends																	
Stock Trade 1																	
Stock Trade 2																	
Net Funding:																	
Total P/L:	-18,000	-18,000	-18,000	-18,000	-18,000	-18,000	-12,000	-6,000		6,000	12,000	18,000	24,000	30,000	36,000	42,000	48,000
	-14.6%	-12.2%	-9.8%	-7.3%	-4.9%	-2.4%	0	+2.4%	+4.9%	+7.3%	+9.8%	+12.2%	+14.6%	+17.1%	+19.5%	+22.0%	+24.4%
P/L at Analysis Date:		4/7/04															
Stock Price:	175.00	180.00	185.00	190.00	195.00	200.00	205.00	210.00	215.00	220.00	225.00	230.00	235.00	240.00	245.00	250.00	255.00
Brokerage etc.																	
Options:																	
Option Trade 1	-15,954	-14,817	-13,278	-11,286	-8,809	-5,837	-2,382	1,529	5,850	10,531	15,517	20,752	26,188	31,778	37,486	43,282	49,141
Option Trade 2																	
Option Trade 3																	
Option Trade 4																	
Option Trade 5																	
Stock:																	
Dividends																	
Stock Trade 1																	
Stock Trade 2																	
Net Funding:																	
Total P/L:	-15,954	-14,817	-13,278	-11,286	-8,809	-5,837	-2,382	1,529	5,850	10,531	15,517	20,752	26,188	31,778	37,486	43,282	49,141
Position "Greeks:"																	
Delta (ESP)																	
Gamma (ESP)																	
Theta																	
Vega																	
Rho																	

(Press button at top of screen to calculate) For help: www.hoadley.net/options

Figure 8.1 (b)

The Bull Call Spread

The bull call spread comes into play when a trader is bullish in his view of the underlying share, but perhaps not so bullish as to simply buy the share itself, or buy naked calls. He wants to gain from the anticipated increase in the underlying's price, but believes that a breakeven of Rs. 15 might be difficult to achieve in the mildly bullish scenario. A hedged position, then, is the best bet for him. So he settles on a bull call spread which enables him to bet on a bullish position but with a bit of an insurance built in, if you will, for a lower cost than a naked call and a lot less risk than owning the stock itself. We shall see why this is so in a moment.

Remember we said that a bull call spread is simply a combination of two options, a long one with a lower strike price and a short one with a higher strike price, where both options are of the same type and expiration but have different strike prices.

Let's look at an example:

Buy 1 Satyam April 200 call @ Rs. 15
Sell 1 Satyam April 220 call @ Rs. 7
Net Cost of April Satyam Bull Spread = Rs. 8

Let us now see what the possible risk, reward and breakeven point of this bull call spread would be and how it compares with the risk and reward profile of an outright call.

1. Loss: The most this bull call spread can lose is Rs. 8 (or Rs. 9,600 per lot), because we incurred a debit of Rs. 15 for one April 200 call, but one April 220 call sold generated Rs. 7 credit. Considering the worst case scenario — because options are the right but not the obligation to engage in a transaction — traders can just let them both expire worthless if they so wish.

Thus, the loss = Rs. 15 – Rs. 7 = Rs. 8.

That's a lot better than losing Rs. 15 on the straight call purchase.

2. Profit: The big compromise in spreading is that a trader loses the potential for unlimited gain that he has with the naked long call, or in owning the underlying stock outright.

This is because profit in a bull call spread is limited to the difference between the strike prices (higher *minus* lower), *minus* the difference between the premiums (premium 1 *minus* premium 2), if and only if the underlying is above the second strike at expiration.

Accordingly in the above example the profit would be:

Rs. (220-200) – (15.7) = Rs. (20) – (8) = Rs. 12.

3. Breakeven: The breakeven point is equal to the lower strike price *plus* the difference in premiums.

In our example:

Rs. (200) + (15–7) = Rs. (200) + (8) Rs. = Rs. 208

So, the breakeven on our vertical spread is a price of Rs. 208 for the Satyam share.

As described in the introductory section of this chapter, spreads can help a trader calibrate the risks he takes in line with his degree of bullishness or bearishness. For example, if a trader is feeling more bullish, he can enter into a spread that offers a greater possibility of reward on the upside; the accompanying trade-off being a higher cost on the downside. [Figures 8.2(a) & (b)].

The Bull Put Spread

Now let's take a look at the bull put spread. In the put market, the bull put spread is the functional equivalent of the bull call spread in the call market in that the trader opting for this spread has a bullish view of the market, and he sells the higher strike put while purchasing the lower strike put. This scenario creates a net credit on the position as a whole because the premium of the short put is greater than the premium of the long put.

Let's look at the maximum profit we can make, the maximum loss, and breakeven point:

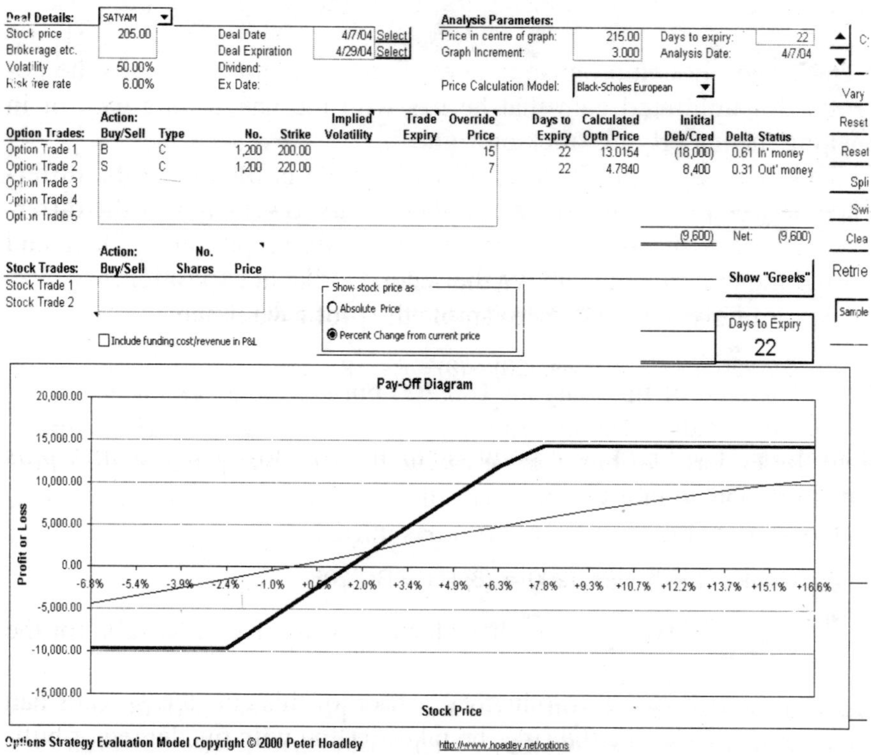

Figure 8.2(a)

P/L at Expiry:		4/29/04															
Stock Price:	**191.00**	**194.00**	**197.00**	**200.00**	**203.00**	**206.00**	**209.00**	**212.00**	**215.00**	**218.00**	**221.00**	**224.00**	**227.00**	**230.00**	**233.00**	**236.00**	**239.00**
Brokerage etc.																	
Options:																	
Option Trade 1	-18,000	-18,000	-18,000	-18,000	-14,400	-10,800	-7,200	-3,600		3,600	7,200	10,800	14,400	18,000	21,600	25,200	28,800
Option Trade 2	8,400	8,400	8,400	8,400	8,400	8,400	8,400	8,400	8,400	8,400	7,200	3,600		-3,600	-7,200	-10,800	-14,400
Option Trade 3																	
Option Trade 4																	
Option Trade 5																	
Stock:																	
Dividends																	
Stock Trade 1																	
Stock Trade 2																	
Net Funding:																	
Total P/L:	-9,600	-9,600	-9,600	-9,600	-6,000	-2,400	1,200	4,800	8,400	12,000	14,400	14,400	14,400	14,400	14,400	14,400	14,400
	-6.8%	-5.4%	-3.9%	-2.4%	-1.0%	+0.5%	+2.0%	+3.4%	+4.9%	+6.3%	+7.8%	+9.3%	+10.7%	+12.2%	+13.7%	+15.1%	+16.6%

P/L at Analysis Date:		4/7/04															
Stock Price:	**191.00**	**194.00**	**197.00**	**200.00**	**203.00**	**206.00**	**209.00**	**212.00**	**215.00**	**218.00**	**221.00**	**224.00**	**227.00**	**230.00**	**233.00**	**236.00**	**239.00**
Brokerage etc.																	
Options:																	
Option Trade 1	-10,830	-9,344	-7,679	-5,837	-3,820	-1,635	712	3,211	5,850	8,619	11,506	14,498	17,584	20,752	23,993	27,295	30,649
Option Trade 2	6,423	5,849	5,157	4,338	3,379	2,274	1,014	-405	-1,985	-3,728	-5,631	-7,692	-9,906	-12,264	-14,761	-17,386	-20,131
Option Trade 3																	
Option Trade 4																	
Option Trade 5																	
Stock:																	
Dividends																	
Stock Trade 1																	
Stock Trade 2																	
Net Funding:																	
Total P/L:	-4,407	-3,495	-2,522	-1,499	-441	639	1,726	2,806	3,865	4,892	5,875	6,806	7,679	8,488	9,232	9,909	10,519

Figure 8.2 (b)

Figure 8.2 (a & b): **Payoff diagram for the bull call spread**

Profit: The sale of this Satyam 180/200 put spread gives an inflow of Rs. 8. This credit is the maximum profit one can achieve. If at expiration, the underlying has a price *above* the exercise price of the short put, then both options expire worthless, because these are both puts, and a put is in-the-money only if it has intrinsic value.

Sell 1 Satyam April 200 put @ Rs. 15
Buy 1 Satyam April 180 put @ Rs. 7
Credit Rs. 8

Loss: The worst-case scenario for the bull put spread would be if the underlying expires below the higher strike price, less the premium collected at expiration. Accordingly, the seller of this spread can lose the difference in the strike prices, minus the initial credit. Thus:

Maximum Loss = (Rs. 200-180) — 8 = Rs. 12

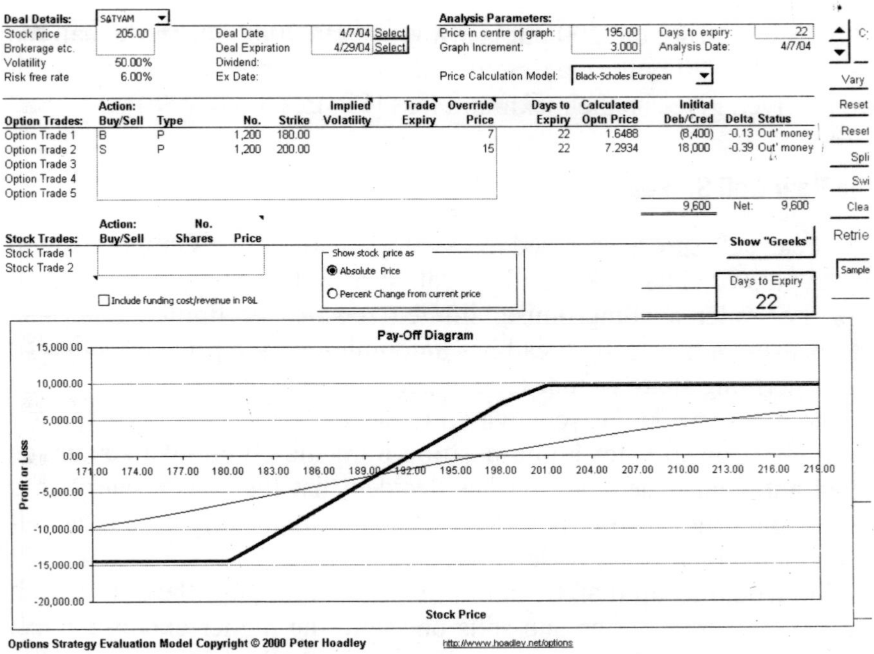

Figure 8.3 (a)

P/L at Expiry:	4/29/04																
Stock Price:	**171.00**	**174.00**	**177.00**	**180.00**	**183.00**	**186.00**	**189.00**	**192.00**	**195.00**	**198.00**	**201.00**	**204.00**	**207.00**	**210.00**	**213.00**	**216.00**	**219.00**
Brokerage etc.																	
Options:																	
Option Trade 1	2,400	-1,200	-4,800	-8,400	-8,400	-8,400	-8,400	-8,400	-8,400	-8,400	-8,400	-8,400	-8,400	-8,400	-8,400	-5,400	-6,400
Option Trade 2	-16,800	-13,200	-9,600	-6,000	-2,400	1,200	4,800	8,400	12,000	15,600	18,000	18,000	18,000	18,000	18,000	18,000	18,000
Option Trade 3																	
Option Trade 4																	
Option Trade 5																	
Stock:																	
Dividends																	
Stock Trade 1																	
Stock Trade 2																	
Net Funding:																	
Total P/L:	-14,400	-14,400	-14,400	-14,400	-10,800	-7,200	-3,600		3,600	7,200	9,600	9,600	9,600	9,600	9,600	9,600	9,600
	-16.6%	-15.1%	-13.7%	-12.2%	-10.7%	-9.3%	-7.8%	-6.3%	-4.9%	-3.4%	-2.0%	-0.5%	+1.0%	+2.4%	+3.9%	+5.4%	+6.8%
P/L at Analysis Date:	4/7/04																
Stock Price:	**171.00**	**174.00**	**177.00**	**180.00**	**183.00**	**186.00**	**189.00**	**192.00**	**195.00**	**198.00**	**201.00**	**204.00**	**207.00**	**210.00**	**213.00**	**216.00**	**219.00**
Brokerage etc.																	
Options:																	
Option Trade 1	7,663	5,500	3,534	1,767	193	-1,194	-2,404	-3,449	-4,344	-5,101	-5,737	-6,266	-6,702	-7,059	-7,348	-7,580	-7,765
Option Trade 2	-17,317	-14,195	-11,190	-8,316	-5,588	-3,017	-612	1,620	3,675	5,551	7,250	8,777	10,136	11,338	12,391	13,307	14,097
Option Trade 3																	
Option Trade 4																	
Option Trade 5																	
Stock:																	
Dividends																	
Stock Trade 1																	
Stock Trade 2																	
Net Funding:																	
Total P/L:	-9,654	-8,695	-7,655	-6,550	-5,395	-4,211	-3,015	-1,829	-668	450	1,513	2,510	3,434	4,279	5,043	5,727	6,333

Figure 8.3 (b)

Figure 8.3 (a & b): **Pay off diagram for bull put spread**

Below Rs. 180, the 200 put is always worth 20 points more than the 180 put. The 20-point maximum value of the spread *minus* the credit we received gives us the maximum loss [Figures 8.3 (a & b)].

The Bear Call Spread

The bear call spread is a hedged strategy that can be composed with either puts or calls. Like the bull call spread, the bear call spread offers the trader a compromise: limited reward for limited risk. The trader using a bear call spread has an opinion on the price direction of the underlying share or index; he expects it to decline.

There are various reasons why a trader may use a bear call spread: he might want to enter into a position immediately to take advantage of an anticipated decline, but has decided that the cost of entry of a naked long put position is too high; or, the trader might have a specific price target on the underlying.

You would recall that, by definition, if a trader buys the option with the lower exercise price and sells one with the higher exercise price, the spread is bullish; conversely, if he buys the higher exercise price and sells the lower one the spread is bearish.

It follows, then, that if we are going in for a bearish spread, and one with calls, it would look something like this:

Buy 1 Satyam April 220 Call	@ Rs. 7 debit
Sell 1 Satyam April 200 Call	@ Rs. 15 credit
Net	Rs. 8 credit

Note that if Satyam were below Rs. 200 at expiration, both options would expire worthless because calls have intrinsic value only when the underlying is trading above the option's strike price. The two strike prices being Rs. 200 and Rs. 220, anything under Rs. 200 means no intrinsic values for the calls.

This is a bear spread we have opted for, so clearly we expect the market to go down. Remember, we have already collected Rs. 8 when we put on the spread. So if both options expire worthless, then we simply pocket the credit of Rs. 8.

If Satyam were to expire above Rs. 220, then the spread would be worth its maximum of Rs. 20. Above Rs. 220, both options have intrinsic value. The maximum a spread can be worth is the difference between the strike prices of its legs.

Now in this case, we don't actually collect Rs. 20. Remember, we have already received a Rs. 8 credit. Since we are short the spread, we received a credit of Rs. 8 for a spread that ended up being worth Rs. 20. We just lost Rs. 7 on the deal. Not so great, but possibly better than being short the stock or naked calls.

To summarize:

- Maximum profit for a bear call spread is the credit received; in this case, Rs. 8.
- Maximum loss for a bear call spread, is equal to the maximum possible value of the spread, minus the credit received. In the above case,

Rs. (220 – 200) – (8) = Rs. 20 – Rs. 8 = Rs. 12

The breakeven is the short strike plus the amount received for the spread. In this case:

Rs. 200 + Rs. 8 = Rs. 208

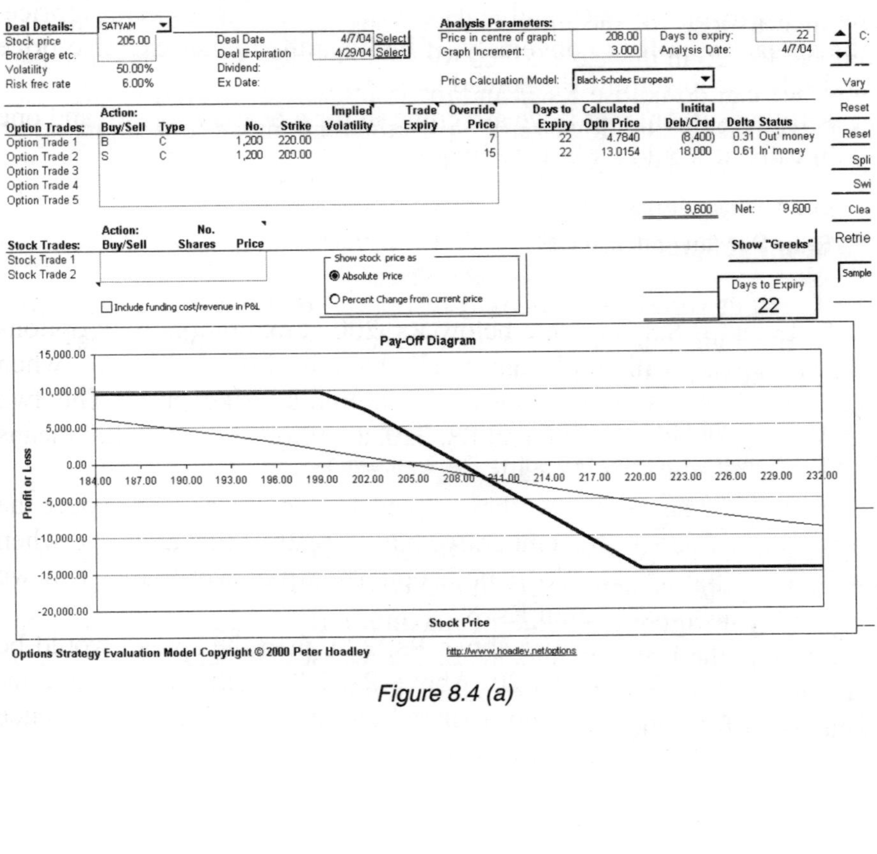

Figure 8.4 (a)

P/L at Expiry:		4/29/04															
Stock Price:	**184.00**	**187.00**	**190.00**	**193.00**	**196.00**	**199.00**	**202.00**	**205.00**	**208.00**	**211.00**	**214.00**	**217.00**	**220.00**	**223.00**	**226.00**	**229.00**	**232.00**
Brokerage etc.																	
Options:																	
Option Trade 1	-8,400	-8,400	-8,400	-8,400	-8,400	-8,400	-8,400	-8,400	-8,400	-8,400	-8,400	-8,400	-8,400	-4,800	-1,200	2,400	6,000
Option Trade 2	18,000	19,000	18,000	18,000	18,000	18,000	15,600	12,000	8,400	4,800	1,200	-2,400	-6,000	-9,600	-13,200	-16,800	-20,400
Option Trade 3																	
Option Trade 4		/															
Option Trade 5																	
Stock:																	
Dividends																	
Stock Trade 1																	
Stock Trade 2																	
Net Funding:																	
Total P/L:	9,600	9,600	9,600	9,500	9,600	9,600	7,200	3,600		-3,600	-7,200	-10,800	-14,400	-14,400	-14,400	-14,400	-14,400
	-10.2%	-8.8%	-7.3%	-5.9%	-4.4%	-2.9%	-1.5%	0	+1.5%	+2.9%	+4.4%	+5.9%	+7.3%	+8.8%	+10.2%	+11.7%	+13.2%
P/L at Analysis Date:		4/7/04															
Stock Price:	**184.00**	**187.00**	**190.00**	**193.00**	**196.00**	**199.00**	**202.00**	**205.00**	**208.00**	**211.00**	**214.00**	**217.00**	**220.00**	**223.00**	**226.00**	**229.00**	**232.00**
Brokerage etc.																	
Options:																	
Option Trade 1	-7,378	-7,028	-6,590	-6,052	-5,401	-4,626	-3,715	-2,659	-1,452	-86	1,440	3,129	4,979	6,988	9,151	11,462	13,914
Option Trade 2	13,621	12,537	11,286	9,859	8,254	6,471	4,512	2,382	87	-2,362	-4,955	-7,683	-10,531	-13,490	-16,546	-19,688	-22,905
Option Trade 3																	
Option Trade 4																	
Option Trade 5																	
Stock:																	
Dividends																	
Stock Trade 1																	
Stock Trade 2																	
Net Funding																	
Total P/L:	6,243	5,510	4,695	3,806	2,853	1,845	797	-278	-1,364	-2,448	-3,515	-4,554	-5,552	-6,502	-7,394	-8,226	-8,991

Figure 8.4 (b)

The call we are short will lose money when the stock rises. It will continue to lose till the upper strike stops the losses, thus the maximum of Rs. 20 in this case. Since we collected Rs. 8 to begin with, the worst we can do is lose Rs. 7 and the point where we start losing (the breakeven) is that the lower strike plus the amount we took in, namely Rs. 208 [Figure 8.4 (a & b)].

The Bear Put Spread

The bear put spread is composed of both a long put and a short put where the long put has the higher strike and the short put has the lower strike price. For example:

Buy 1 Satyam April Rs. 200 put @ Rs. 15 paid
Sell 1 Satyam April Rs. 180 put @ Rs. 7 received
Cost = Rs. 8 debit

The cost of the spread is the difference between the premium paid for the long option, and the credit received from the short option.

Let's try to figure out what the maximum risk and reward would be for our hypothetical Satyam spread. The worst-case scenario is if Satyam closes above Rs. 200 at expiration in which case both legs would expire out-of-the-money.

Since both options expire worthless, the trader would lose the Rs. 8 he paid for the spread. Thus:

Maximum Loss: The bear put spread is a debit spread. The maximum amount of loss in a debit spread (one that has been purchased) is the amount paid for it. In this case, Rs. 8.

Rs. 15 debit *less*
Rs. 7 credit

Maximum Profit: Figuring out the profit (reward) is a bit more complicated, but should still present us with only a little difficulty. Note that in our hypothetical Satyam spread, the short Satyam Rs. 180 put has value if Satyam were below Rs. 180. In which case, the value of the short put would match, rupee for rupee, the value received for the in-the-money Rs. 200 put.

When the underlying is below strike 1 at expiration, the maximum profit in a bear put spread is limited to the difference in strike prices (strike 2 – strike 1), *minus* the difference in the premiums (option 2 – option 1).

(Assuming underlying below Rs. 180)
Long 1 Satyam April Rs. 200 put @ Rs. 15
Short 1 Satyam April Rs. 180 put @ (–) Rs. 7

The maximum profit equals the difference between the two strikes (Rs. 200 – Rs. 180) less the money spent/received (Rs. 15 – Rs. 7)

(Rs. 20) – (Rs. 8) = Rs. 12

Thus, the most we can make on this spread is Rs. 12

Breakeven: Finally, the breakeven in this spread is the higher strike price *minus* the net premium paid:

Rs. 200 – Rs. 8 = Rs. 192

It is important to note that the degree of bearishness of the bear put spread is determined by the strike price of the short put.

Again, this makes intuitive sense. The farther away, or out-of-the-money the short put is, further the underlying has to drop for the spread to reach its maximum value [Figure 8.5 (a & b)].

Deal Details: SATYAM

Stock price	205.00	Deal Date	4/7/04 Select		
Brokerage etc.		Deal Expiration	4/29/04 Select		
Volatility	50.00%	Dividend:			
Risk free rate	6.00%	Ex Date:			

Analysis Parameters:

Price in centre of graph:	192.00	Days to expiry:	22
Graph Increment:	3.000	Analysis Date:	4/7/04
Price Calculation Model:	Black-Scholes European		

Option Trades:	Action: Buy/Sell	Type	No.	Strike	Implied Volatility	Trade Expiry	Override Price	Days to Expiry	Calculated Optn Price	Initital Deb/Cred	Delta Status
Option Trade 1	S	P	1,200	180.00			7	22	1.6488	8,400	-0.13 Out' money
Option Trade 2	B	P	1,200	200.00			15	22	7.2934	(18,000)	-0.39 Out' money
Option Trade 3											
Option Trade 4											
Option Trade 5											
										(9,600)	Net: (9,600)

Stock Trades:	Action: Buy/Sell	No. Shares	Price
Stock Trade 1			
Stock Trade 2			

☐ Include funding cost/revenue in P&L

Show stock price as
◉ Absolute Price
○ Percent Change from current price

Show "Greeks"

Days to Expiry 22

Vary
Reset
Reset
Spli
Swi
Clea
Retrie
Sample

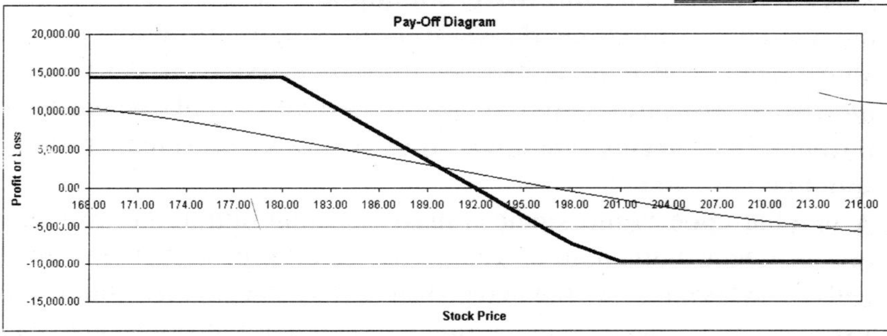

Options Strategy Evaluation Model Copyright © 2000 Peter Hoadley http://www.hoadley.net/options

Figure 8.5 (a)

P/L at Expiry: 4/29/04

Stock Price:	168.00	171.00	174.00	177.00	180.00	183.00	186.00	189.00	192.00	195.00	198.00	201.00	204.00	207.00	210.00	213.00	216.00
Brokerage etc.																	
Options:																	
Option Trade 1	-6,000	-2,400	1,200	4,800	8,400	8,400	8,400	8,400	8,400	8,400	8,400	8,400	8,400	8,400	8,400	8,400	8,400
Option Trade 2	20,400	16,800	13,200	9,600	6,000	2,400	-1,200	-4,800	-8,400	-12,000	-15,600	-18,000	-18,000	-18,000	-18,000	-18,000	-18,000
Option Trade 3																	
Option Trade 4																	
Option Trade 5																	
Stock:																	
Dividends																	
Stock Trade 1																	
Stock Trade 2																	
Net Funding																	
Total P/L:	14,400	14,400	14,400	14,400	14,400	10,800	7,200	3,600		-3,600	-7,200	-9,600	-9,600	-9,600	-9,600	-9,600	-9,600
	-18.0%	-16.6%	-15.1%	-13.7%	-12.2%	-10.7%	-9.3%	-7.8%	-6.3%	-4.9%	-3.4%	-2.0%	-0.5%	+1.0%	+2.4%	+3.9%	+5.4%

P/L at Analysis Date: 4/7/04

Stock Price:	168.00	171.00	174.00	177.00	180.00	183.00	186.00	189.00	192.00	195.00	198.00	201.00	204.00	207.00	210.00	213.00	216.00
Brokerage etc.																	
Options:																	
Option Trade 1	-10,021	-7,663	-5,500	-3,534	-1,767	-193	1,194	2,404	3,449	4,344	5,101	5,737	6,266	6,702	7,059	7,348	7,580
Option Trade 2	20,541	17,317	14,195	11,190	8,316	5,588	3,017	612	-1,620	-3,675	-5,551	-7,250	-8,777	-10,136	-11,338	-12,391	-13,307
Option Trade 3																	
Option Trade 4																	
Option Trade 5																	
Stock:																	
Dividends																	
Stock Trade 1																	
Stock Trade 2																	
Net Funding																	
Total P/L:	10,520	9,654	8,695	7,655	6,550	5,395	4,211	3,015	1,829	668	-450	-1,513	-2,510	-3,434	-4,279	-5,043	-5,727
Position "Greeks:"																	
Delta (ESP)																	
Gamma (ESP)																	
Theta																	
Vega																	
Rho																	

(Press button at top of screen to calculate) For help: www.hoadley.net/options

Figure 8.5 (b)

This section concludes our overview of the various types of vertical spreads.

Vertical Spreads: A Summary of Key Points

In this section, we will summarize some essential points that must be kept in mind in order to become a more proficient directional spreader:

1. Staying spread is staying alive: Putting on a spread means trading the possibility of unlimited reward for the benefit of limited risk.
2. Vertical spreads are combinations that are used by a trader who has an opinion on the direction of the underlying. A bear spreader believes the underlying would go down, while a bull spreader feels it should go up.
3. A vertical spread consists of at least one long option and one short option where both options are of the same type (whether puts or calls) and expiration, but have different strike prices. One-to-one verticals are typical, have limited risk reward profiles and have been discussed above. But ratio vertical spreads are also strategies that are popular amongst advanced options traders and carry very different risk characteristics.
4. A spread's maximum value is defined as the difference between the strike prices of the two legs that comprise it.
5. The maximum profit possible in a debit spread (one that has been purchased) is the maximum value of spread, *minus* the net amount paid.
6. The maximum loss in a debit spread is the amount paid for it.
7. The maximum profit potential of a credit spread (one that is sold) is the amount of cash received.
8. The maximum loss possible in a credit spread is the maximum value of the spread *minus* the amount received from selling it.
9. At expiration, the vertical spread will be worth zero if both options are out-of-the-money.
10. Be patient — and never overtrade.

Now, let us turn to some points that need to be kept in mind when trading options in India.

I would again remind traders and investors that options sellers can make money in more ways than can option buyers. So my personal preference is to take on credit spreads, where the trader makes money both when the underlying makes a move in the expected direction or simply hovers just above or below the sold put or call. Also, time is in favour of the credit spread. Buying naked options should be ruled out even in a hugely trending market because the breakeven is way too high.

Only in a clearly trending market do I take on debit spreads and then, too, I don't focus on the absolute amount of money I make but on the percentage return on my net investment. The other thing to keep in mind is that it's always possible for the underlying to first move in the expected direction and then retrace the entire move. So booking profits along the way is always advisable. Profits can be booked either by unwinding both legs of the spread or by rolling options up, down or out.

Rolling Options Up, Down and Out

Rolling of options is a strategy used to book profits on profitable options positions and strategies, and one which I highly recommend:

- Rolling of options consists of selling options of a strike which is deep in-the-money and buying a comparatively out-of-the-money option so that some amount of profits are booked.
- Rolling up is booking profits on the lower strike option and buying the higher strike option.
- Rolling down is booking profits on the higher strike option and buying the lower strike option.
- Rolling out means winding up the options position all together.

For example, if I am in profit in the 200/220 Satyam bull call spread, as soon as the stock reaches around Rs. 220, I would sell the 200 call and buy the 210 call, thus reducing the invested amount, sometimes even making the spread risk free. Or, I would roll out the entire spread, which means selling the 200 call and buying back the 220 call. This sometimes does not make sense if your short option is not depreciating because of time value, or in other words if there is lots of time left to expiry then the deeper in-the-money call appreciates more slowly than does the comparatively more out-of-money call, so rolling up to book profits is the only solution. Traders and investors need to remember that spreads should generally not be held till expiry. Whenever profits are available, traders should take them. If a spread is not working out, it should be wound up and something else considered instead.

Ratio Spreading

A ratio spread involves buying an at-the-money (ATM) or near-the-money option and selling multiple out-of-the-money (OTM) options with all of the options having the same expiration date. Ratio spreads can be constructed with either puts or calls. The ratio is usually two options sold for every one option bought. Though you can certainly have other ratios, just don't go overboard. Well, this is a strategy wherein you put up little or no money up front and profit if you are right but don't lose much — or even gain a small profit — if you are wrong.

Ratio Call Spread

Let's consider the example of an actual bullish trade on Reliance. The stock was then trading at Rs. 500. We believed that it could appreciate but was unlikely to go over Rs. 530 and that, therefore, we could do a ratio call spread. As noted above, a ratio call spread is constructed by buying an ATM call and selling two or more OTM calls. Consequently, we bought one Reliance April 500 call at Rs. 18 and sold two April 530 calls at Rs. 6 each. In essence, we would be paying Rs. 18 for the April 500 call and receiving Rs. 12 for selling the two April 530 calls. At most times Rs. 30 is enough in a big share such as Reliance but perhaps not in the kind of roaring bull market we were then in. On the other hand, I did not want to lose if there were a sharp correction. Sometimes if the premiums received are more than the premium paid, the spread might be done at a credit but I do not like to make the spread so risky that both the short calls get exercised against me. If ratio call spreads are done at a credit, you can eliminate all of your downside risk and get to keep the credit even if the underlying goes to zero. Two important things that option traders should always be aware of are their maximum profit potential and the breakeven point. They should know how much money they stand to make, and at what price would they breakeven.

I can use a complex formula to explain this but I would rather use this example. Equally, I'd advise traders to also work out the maximum profit potential and breakeven without getting into formulas.

Now since the net debit in this trade was Rs. 6, the breakeven point was Rs. 506. The maximum profit would be made at Rs. 530 where one would make Rs. 12 on the long call and get to keep Rs. 12 credit of the short calls. So the total maximum profit would be Rs. 12 + Rs. 12 = Rs. 24, which was four times the investment and a good percentage trade considering our view on the stock and the low breakeven.

On the other hand, one would start losing on this trade if the stock moved up much higher than Rs. 530 because the one long call is hedged by the one short call; and you have an extra short call which comes into play beyond Rs. 530. At Rs. 530 one would have made Rs. 12 on the long call (which provided a kind of protection over Rs. 530), plus Rs. 12 that was received as premium. So, on net basis on the upside, one would make a loss till the price went above Rs. 554. This is the way I look at ratio spreads.

We had initiated this trade on 4 April 2004. Reliance took its time getting to Rs. 530 during the month and the expiry was around the 27th. On the 23rd Reliance was quoting at Rs. 526, so since my long call was trading at Rs. 24 and the short calls trading at Rs. 4 each, I decided to roll out of my positions entirely and made Rs. 16 on an investment of Rs. 6.

A similar analysis is possible for ratio put spreads. An example would be buying 1 Reliance 500 Put and selling 2 Reliance 570 Puts. Traders should try to figure out the above values for the put ratio spreads as well.

There are however certain caveats that traders and investors need to remember:

- Earlier on we saw how important it was to establish the spread at a credit, since it eliminated the downside risk in the case of a ratio call spread — or upside risk on a ratio put spread. Many times it is not possible to obtain a credit when initiating a ratio spread. Only when there is a disparity in option premiums, and implied volatilities of OTM options are high compared to ATM options, are there good opportunities for ratio spreads.

- Traders should sell options that have a low probability of going in-the-money. Don't sell strikes that have a good chance of becoming in-the-money. Focus on selling strikes which are as far from the current price as possible.

The ratio spread is an excellent strategy from a risk-and-reward standpoint. It is a neutral to mildly directional strategy with little or no up front costs. You can profit when you're right and even profit when you're wrong. The only time you run into trouble is when you're proved too right. Good ratio spread opportunities are not available every day. But when conditions are right, you should start looking for them.

Straddles

Buying a Straddle

Strategy

Buy an ATM call and an ATM put with the same strike price and expiration date.

Time Decay Effect: Detrimental.

Situations: Look for a market with low volatility about to experience a sharp increase in volatility.

Profit: Unlimited. Profit requires sufficient market movement but does not depend on market direction.

Risk: Limited to the net debit paid. Margin is not required.

Upside Breakeven: Strike price *plus* net debit paid.

Downside Breakeven: Strike price *minus* net debit paid.

Buying a straddle consists of buying a call and a put of the same strike, whether of the index or a stock, when a sharp upward or downward movement is expected. It is a very expensive strategy as the net debit can be large and is justified only when a move commensurate with that kind of debit is expected. In India since there is only a month for this strategy to work out, it's important to wind it up once the particular news is announced, or equally if the expected move does not happen because the time value can eat away the premiums very fast. Also, since this strategy has become popular — because people tend to buy straddles around the budget or around result announcements — the implied volatilities of the concerned options rise to very high levels causing straddles to lose some of their sheen. It still remains viable at high market levels and in strong trending markets where the markets move more than the entire debit being paid. It can also be used if the volatility of the market diminishes, and the market is about to breakout in either direction. But because of the time factor, traders should be very careful of paying the high premiums involved.

As it is a risky proposition at most times, traders have found variations of straddles to trade sharp moves. For example, if a trader feels there is a 60% chance of a big sharp upmove and 40% chance of a sharp downmove, he can buy futures and at-the-money puts. This way he pays the premium of only one leg and gets exposure in both directions. As the market moves in one direction, one leg of this strategy can be covered while retaining the other.

Let's run through an example of a Nifty straddle [Figures 8.6 (a) & (b)].

Assume the Nifty is trading at 1,500, and a sharp move is expected in either direction.

The 1500 Call is bought for Rs. 52 and the 1500 Put is bought for Rs. 48, so the breakeven for this straddle is 100 points up or down, i.e. above 1,600 or below 1,400. In such a case, I would book profits if I am getting 150 points on either side. If the Nifty ends between 1,400 and 1,600 there will be loss, with the maximum loss occurring at 1,500.

If the Nifty ends between 1,400 to 1,600, the loss would be 100 (The absolute difference of the Nifty at expiry and strike price of the straddle, which was 1500. If the Nifty at expiry is at 1,464, the loss would be Rs. 64.

If the Nifty ends up at 1,640, the profit would be:

Rs. (1,640 – 1,500) – 100 = Rs. 40.

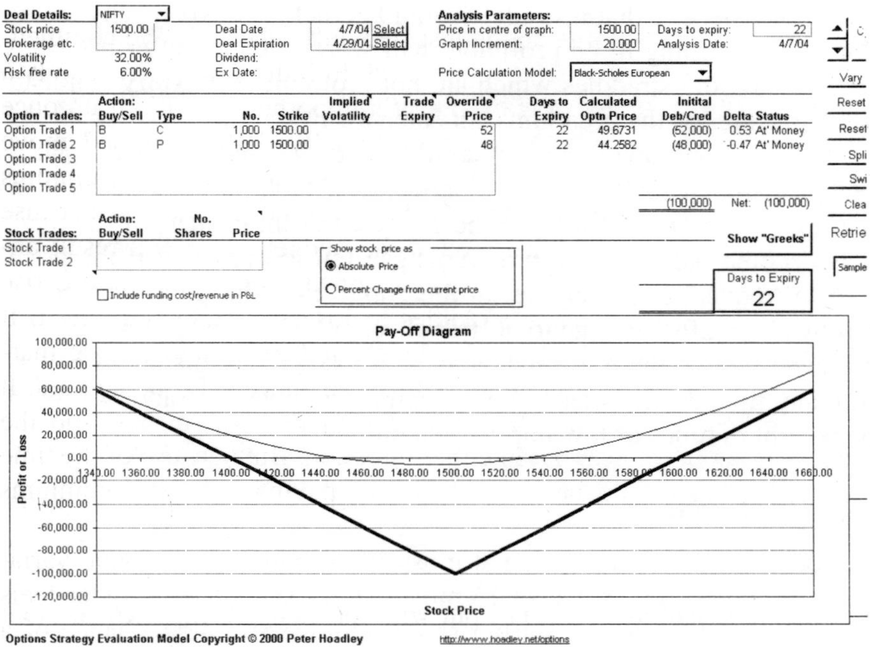

Figure 8.6 (a)

P/L at Expiry:	4/29/04																
Stock Price:	1340.00	1360.00	1380.00	1400.00	1420.00	1440.00	1460.00	1480.00	1500.00	1520.00	1540.00	1560.00	1580.00	1600.00	1620.00	1640.00	1660.00
Brokerage etc.																	
Options:																	
Option Trade 1	-52,000	-52,000	-52,000	-52,000	-52,000	-52,000	-52,000	-52,000	-52,000	-32,000	-12,000	8,000	28,000	48,000	68,000	[illegible]	[illegible]
Option Trade 2	112,000	92,000	72,000	52,000	32,000	12,000	-8,000	-28,000	-48,000	-48,000	-48,000	-48,000	-48,000	-48,000	-48,000	-48,000	[illegible]
Option Trade 3																	
Option Trade 4																	
Option Trade 5																	
Stock:																	
Dividends																	
Stock Trade 1																	
Stock Trade 2																	
Net Funding:																	
Total P/L:	60,000	40,000	20,000		-20,000	-40,000	-60,000	-80,000	-100,000	-80,000	-60,000	-40,000	-20,000		20,000	40,000	60,000
	-10.7%	-9.3%	-8.0%	-6.7%	-5.3%	-4.0%	-2.7%	-1.3%	0	+1.3%	+2.7%	+4.0%	+5.3%	+6.7%	+8.0%	+9.3%	+10.7%
P/L at Analysis Date:	4/7/04																
Stock Price:	1340.00	1360.00	1380.00	1400.00	1420.00	1440.00	1460.00	1480.00	1500.00	1520.00	1540.00	1560.00	1580.00	1600.00	1620.00	1640.00	1660.00
Brokerage etc.																	
Options:																	
Option Trade 1	-47,832	-45,734	-42,875	-39,103	-34,272	-28,259	-20,964	-12,328	-2,327	9,020	21,658	35,501	50,441	66,353	83,107	100,573	118,627
Option Trade 2	110,753	92,851	75,710	59,482	44,313	30,327	17,621	6,257	-3,742	-12,395	-19,757	-25,913	-30,974	-35,061	-38,308	-40,842	-42,788
Option Trade 3																	
Option Trade 4																	
Option Trade 5																	
Stock:																	
Dividends																	
Stock Trade 1																	
Stock Trade 2																	
Net Funding:																	
Total P/L:	62,921	47,117	32,835	20,380	10,040	2,068	-3,343	-6,070	-6,069	-3,376	1,901	9,588	19,468	31,292	44,799	59,731	75,639

Figure 8.6 (b)

Figure 8.6 (A&b): **Pay-off Diagrams for Buying a Straddle**

I do not believe that a straddle should be held till expiry; any straddle which is going to be profitable will work out soon after it's been put on. Holding straddles which are not profitable till expiry can lead to huge losses as the premiums get eaten away.

Traders should avoid buying straddles at very high implied volatilities because in such cases the sharp move might already be built in the option premiums and after the expected event or news if the markets become range bound, premiums can fall to even half if the price has not moved. For example, in the above case the premiums could fall by about 50% and the total straddle could be available for only Rs. 50, even though the Nifty may stay at 1,500 — and this could be before any time decay is taken into account. In general, straddles should be bought in times of low implied volatilities.

Selling a Straddle

Strategy

Sell an ATM call and an ATM put with the same strike price and expiration date.

Time Decay Effect: Helpful.

Situation: Look for a highly volatile market that seems to be entering a period of low volatility.

Profit: Limited to the net credit received. The less the market moves, the better chance you have of keeping premiums.

Risk: Unlimited on both sides. Margin is required.

Upside Breakeven: Strike price *plus* net credit received.

Downside Breakeven: Strike price *minus* net credit received.

Selling a straddle consists of selling a put and call of the same strike price. This is one of my favourite strategies and I don't think I have to repeat why. This strategy is best employed when options are trading at high implied volatilities and the market is expected to become range bound. Such a straddle makes money if the volatilities decline, it makes money because of time decay, and of course if the market stays range bound [Figures 8.7 (a) & (b)]. Here, too, the objective should not be to hold till expiry.

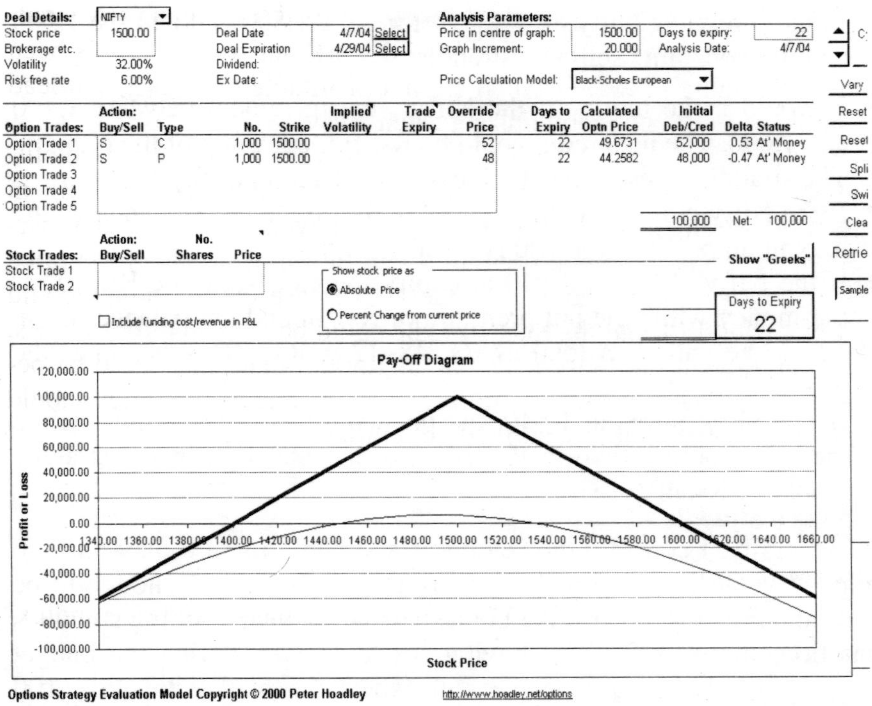

Figure 8.7 (a)

P/L at Expiry: 4/29/04

Stock Price:	1340.00	1360.00	1380.00	1400.00	1420.00	1440.00	1460.00	1480.00	1500.00	1520.00	1540.00	1560.00	1580.00	1600.00	1620.00	1640.00	1660.00
Brokerage etc.																	
Options:																	
Option Trade 1	52,000	52,000	52,000	52,000	52,000	52,000	52,000	52,000	52,000	32,000	12,000	-8,000	-28,000	-48,000	-68,000	-88,000	-108,000
Option Trade 2	-112,000	-92,000	-72,000	-52,000	-32,000	-12,000	8,000	28,000	48,000	48,000	48,000	48,000	48,000	48,000	48,000	48,000	48,000
Option Trade 3																	
Option Trade 4																	
Option Trade 5																	
Stock:																	
Dividends																	
Stock Trade 1																	
Stock Trade 2																	
Net Funding:																	
Total P/L:	-60,000	-40,000	-20,000		20,000	40,000	60,000	80,000	100,000	80,000	60,000	40,000	20,000		-20,000	-40,000	-60,000
	-10.7%	-9.3%	-8.0%	-6.7%	-5.3%	-4.0%	-2.7%	-1.3%	0	+1.3%	+2.7%	+4.0%	+5.3%	+6.7%	+8.0%	+9.3%	+10.7%

P/L at Analysis Date: 4/7/04

Stock Price:	1340.00	1360.00	1380.00	1400.00	1420.00	1440.00	1460.00	1480.00	1500.00	1520.00	1540.00	1560.00	1580.00	1600.00	1620.00	1640.00	1660.00
Brokerage etc.																	
Options:																	
Option Trade 1	47,832	45,734	42,875	39,103	34,272	28,259	20,964	12,328	2,327	-9,020	-21,658	-35,501	-50,441	-66,353	-83,107	-100,573	-118,627
Option Trade 2	-110,753	-92,851	-75,710	-59,482	-44,313	-30,327	-17,621	-6,257	3,742	12,395	19,757	25,913	30,974	35,061	38,308	40,842	42,788
Option Trade 3																	
Option Trade 4																	
Option Trade 5																	
Stock:																	
Dividends																	
Stock Trade 1																	
Stock Trade 2																	
Net Funding:																	
Total P/L:	-62,921	-47,117	-32,835	-20,380	-10,040	-2,068	3,343	6,070	6,069	3,376	-1,901	-9,588	-19,468	-31,292	-44,799	-59,731	-75,839

Figure 8.7 (b)

In the foregoing Nifty example, selling the 1,500 call and the 1,500 put would constitute selling a straddle.

- It would make money if the Nifty were to remain between 1,400 and 1,600. The net credit would be Rs. 100 per share of the Nifty.
- The straddle loses money both over 1,600 and under 1,400.
- If the Nifty closes at expiry at 1,500, the straddle could achieve the maximum profit of Rs. 100 per share.
- If the Nifty closes at 1,540 at expiry the call would be Rs. 40 in-the-money while the put premium of Rs. 48 and the balance of Rs. 12 on the call — a total of Rs. 48+12 = Rs. 60 — becomes the profit.
- If the Nifty closes at 1,640, the put would expire worthless while the call would be worth Rs. 140, so the total loss in the strategy would be Rs. 40.

Generally, I consider the selling of a straddle to be a play on high implied volatilities and if these drop, the profit is good enough to be carried home. In India during the last couple of years, selling straddles has been more useful than buying straddles even during the budget period. This is because people still expect the market to move 100 Nifty points post-budget, whereas smart professionals are now beginning to treat the budget as more or less a non-event. Most times the straddle is profitable if executed by properly capitalizing on the high implied volatilities. But during trending markets, action sometimes needs to be taken to change the position according to market conditions. Remember, in this strategy a margin of Rs. 40,000 may have to be paid for a one contract straddle, i.e. one call and one put sold. Also since selling naked options is always dangerous, it is important to keep open your hedging options as the prices move towards danger zones.

The example below would explain how a short straddle position may be managed.

This was a real trade I took on 21 October 2003. The Nifty had rallied non-stop to 1,570 from 920, and it then corrected about 30 points to 1,540. So I expected the Nifty to stay range bound between a 100-point range and consolidate. Also as only eleven days were left for expiry, with some holidays in between, so a straddle seemed safe. I, therefore, sold a Nifty 1,540 October straddle for about 60 points on

20 October. The lower boundary of the straddle was thus 1480 and higher boundary was 1600, which looked safe at that point.

What actually happened was that the very next day Nifty fell another 35 points to 1,505, and suddenly the straddle position seemed to look like the most dangerous position to have. The Nifty had a huge support at 1,500, and it bounced up from it a couple of times, but finally it went straight through, so I bought 1,480 puts for Rs. 16 in order to protect the downside. With the Nifty trading at 1495 and having decisively broken 1,500, I covered my short put, which was the losing position for Rs. 60 and took on a further bearish position buying in-the-money Nifty 1,500 puts for Rs. 30. As the market continued to weaken it became clear we were on the right side of the trade and so we held on. Nifty closed at 1,473 on 23 October. I checked the Nifty's daily 7-period RSI and it was close to 40. Now this was the signal that the market had dropped enough. So the next day as the market dropped to 1,460 we sold the 1,500 puts for Rs. 45 and the 1,480 puts for Rs. 32 which gave us a nice profit. The only position we then had was short 1,540 calls, which seemed like a safe distant position. As soon as we sold our puts intraday, the market started moving up and kept on moving up and finally closed at 1,506 after having touched 1,453 on the same day. This was on 24 October, the 25th and 26th were Saturday and Sunday. So now the short 1,540 calls came under threat, and we were close to the options expiry (31 October 2003) so we decided to buy 1480 and 1,500 November calls at the beginning of trade on 27 October, one set of calls as a calendar spread because the market was moving 40 points a day.

Well, thankfully, as we bought the calls on Monday the market started correcting and then rallied some on Thursday. The 1,540 calls expired worthless as the market closed at 1,520, which was what we had originally expected. If the 1,540 October calls had not expired worthless our plan was to sell one set of the November calls on the day of the expiry to cover any losses on the expiring call. As it turned out, in the beginning of November we were long two sets of calls — 1480 at Rs. 54 and 1500 at Rs. 47 — and the market rallied close to 90 points on the first two days and we liquidated these two sets of calls for Rs. 85 and Rs. 75, respectively. So the total transaction yielded us a profit of about 93 points, although the market had first gone down below our expectations and then rose beyond our expectations.

We were never right about the market, but we took the right actions as the market changed. We were nimble in recognizing that the market was not acting like we'd expected and took remedial action immediately, without hoping or praying. Also, we took quick profits as soon as we made 50% or more on our positions instead of expecting too much. The lesson is clear: the key to making money in the derivatives market is leaving your ego at home when you go trading. If the market is not behaving like you want it to, you need to fall in line with the market quickly. Of course, sometimes you are likely to get whipsawed but then that is an occupational hazard.

Chapter 9

The Covered Call

Who Says 4% Returns per Month are History

Times have changed since the early 1990s when even true-blue Indian corporates had to borrow funds at 16% per annum. As the Indian economy liberalised, interest rates started falling as otherwise the Indian industry would have been rendered uncompetitive in the world economy. Good as the fall in rates was for the Indian economy, it was bad news for those dependent on fixed income investments. Till 2001, Indian stock market traders had the *badla* system, which was a method of innovative stock market financing. In the *badla* system, the leveraged positions or margin trading was financed by borrowing funds from individuals and corporates at stock market determined rates. These rates could be as high as 4% per month in good markets, with the average being about 2.5%.

The problem was that some smart operatives like Ketan Parekh could take the system for a ride. They bought shares through *badla* by paying the 10% margin, and when the shares rose, they used their paper gains as further margin to buy even more shares. These highly leveraged shares were then pledged to co-operative and other banks from whom additional money was borrowed to invest in the market. Some banks merrily lent them money without any regard to banking norms. The stock market fell and we all know what happened. I consider these to have been more of banking scams rather than stock market scams. Once the technology stocks fell out of favour, what was an investment gone sour became a scam.

The regulators, however, concluded that the loophole in the system was that Indian cash and leveraged markets were inter-linked. Of course, that is the way it ought to be but in their zeal to be seen to be making the stock market a safe place to invest, the regulators held the *badla* system responsible for all ills in the country and banned it in

2001. Thus, a source of regular high returns from the stock market for traders and corporate also ended.

In 2001, the stock market regulator SEBI introduced the futures and options market in India. The derivatives market can actually be looked at as a leveraged market being financed by sellers (writers) of derivative products who take a fixed insurance premium for the risk they are assuming.

Why do these option sellers assume this risk? And how are they hedged against adverse movement of the underlying?

Well, the answer is that they do so by owning the underlying. Writing call options when you already own the underlying is called writing covered call options. Some people like to own particular stock futures or index futures instead of the actual stock or basket of stocks. If investors and traders find nothing else useful in this book, I think this one strategy will pay for the book's modest price more than a hundred times over. Readers should remember we are against writing naked options which can have unlimited risk.

Why Covered Call Writing Makes Sense in India

Let's understand how writing covered call options works. As discussed in Chapter 7, a call is the right to buy an underlying asset above a certain price, and before a certain date. Now the only liquid calls in India are the near-month expiry which means that there are, at most, 30 days for the calls to expire. If you eliminate Saturdays and Sundays, it leaves only 22 days. Throw in a couple of more holidays and the period reduces to an average of 20 trading sessions per month. Now let's understand the number of ways the covered call seller benefits:

1. If the options volatility reduces, he makes the difference of the volatility premium.
2. As the time to expiry reduces, he makes money on the time value.
3. If at expiry the price is below the strike price, he makes the entire premium, no questions asked.

Turn the above advantages on their head, and they turn into disadvantage for the call buyer. The poor fellow thinks he is minimising his risk because he has paid a fixed amount and that is all he is risking. Actually, though, he makes money only if the price of the stock rises, nay trends up, strongly. Experience shows that markets and stocks trend only 25-30% of the time. So who makes money most of the time? Clearly, the option writer does. World-wide data suggests that only 15% of the options are actually exercised. The reason for this is simple; markets don't trend most of the time. It is only during these relatively rare trending periods that option buyers make money, the rest of the time when markets consolidate or turn sideways, it is the option writer who makes a killing — or, as I call it, gets rent from his building. A month is simply too short a time for an option buyer to make money except in a raging bull market. The retail investors always forget that there is no free lunch in the market.

I like looking at stocks as assets and Indians identify very much with building and real estate and enjoy earning fancy rents every month. Well, now they can do so and all they need to do is to be a little careful.

If the stock starts trending upwards, how is option writer protected? Well, he is protected because he owns the underlying. In a delivery settled system he would deliver the stock but in India's cash settled system he needs to pay only the difference between the strike price and the stock price prevailing at the end of the month, which he can do by selling the stock he owns. So the upside risk is covered because of his ownership of the underlying. If the covered call writer writes a call all twelve months of the year in a good market and makes 4% per month, it's a return of 48% per annum, and that too without compounding. There are not all that many assets around which can give that kind of return with the level of risk being assumed. Generally, the call is not exercised till it is deep in-the-money. However when it is exercised, the trader can simply write a new, higher call option.

But, remember, the covered call writer may lose if the stock starts declining sharply. This is the only eventuality, in which the covered call writer can lose. But this possibility can also be reduced by a technical analyst who chooses his covered call stocks properly. The call writer can thus greatly reduce the risk of writing calls. In reality, therefore, the call buyer is not the one reducing his risk. Actually, he is the one that is taking all the risk and is giving the call seller a consistent, high return on his stock holding.

For the purposes of this chapter we will assume a one-to-one relationship between stock ownership and call writing, although ratio writing and mixed writing are also methods that are used. These are nothing but modification in the number of calls written or shares owned to change the risk/return equation. These methods can be developed by the call writer once he is comfortable with the concept. This is the gist of covered call writing; now let us delve into a detailed analysis of how to write covered calls.

Also, I would like to make it amply clear that this chapter assumes a sideways, mildly bullish, or an extremely bullish market. If the market environment is very bearish where every stock is getting slaughtered to half its value, writing covered calls may not do you any good. In such situations, it would be advisable to wait till the market completes its sharp falls and goes into a sideways mode in forming a basing formation. These bases often take six months to form, sometimes it could take as long as two years. Investors and traders can then again start writing covered calls once the market bottoms out.

What Kind of Returns Are We Talking About?

Let's have a look at all at-the-money call options which were available on 12 December 2003 to get an idea of the monthly and annual returns one can aim for. The expiry date for that month was 24 December while the contract started on 28 November. The way I like to calculate the nearest at-the-money call option is by using a rounding-off system. For example, if the stock price of ACC is between Rs. 210 and Rs. 215, the call option we consider is the Rs. 210 call option; if it is greater than Rs. 215 but less than Rs. 220, we consider the Rs. 220 call option, and so on. Such rounding-off fits well in my scheme of things. Aggressive investors can sell one strike further out-of-money, conservative investors can sell one strike further in-the-money; I just happen to like the middle ground. Readers should remember that since all of these options had only 12 days left for expiry, some amount of time value had already been realised. The option premiums at the beginning of a current month contract can be expected to be much higher. This exercise is just to give a flavour of the kind of returns available. Obviously, these returns are approximate and can vary from month to month since option premiums depend on various factors. (Table 9.1)

Table 9.1

Stock	*Prevailing Price of the Stock (Rs.)*	*Nearest At-the-Money Call Option (Rs.)*	*Premium till Expiry (12 days) (Rs.)*	*Premium Monthly (% return) (Rs.)*
ACC	226.55	230	5.85	6.40%
Andhra Bank	47.15	48	1.25	6.60%
Arvind Mills	61.10	60	3.40	13.90%
Bajaj Auto	1012.40	1000	32.00	7.90%
BEL	566.80	580	11.00	4.80%
BHEL	445.85	450	10.30	5.70%
Bank of Baroda	182.95	180	8.00	10.90%
Bank of India	59.30	60	1.95	8.20%
BPCL	393.70	390	10.50	6.60%
BSES	468.60	470	19.95	10.60%
Canara Bank	121.25	120	5.55	11.30%
Cipla	1188.75	1200	23.00	4.80%
CNXIT	21698.65	19700	900.00	10.30%
Digital	747.40	740	23.40	7.80%
Dr Reddy	1352.10	1350	36.30	6.70%
GAIL	194.20	190	10.30	13.25%
Grasim	916.75	920	15.00	4.09%
Gujarat Ambuja	303.80	200	11.75	9.60%
HCL Tech	282.10	280	9.30	8.24%
HDFC	362.65	360	11.00	7.50%
HDFC Bank	631.95	580	29.80	11.70%
Hero Honda	396.30	400	10.85	6.80%
Hindalco	1329.35	1320	40.60	7.60%
Hind Lever	186.95	190	3.35	4.40%
HPCL	410.35	410	9.80	5.97%
ICICI Bank	280.55	280	8.35	7.40%
I Flex	845.85	840	27.45	8.10%
Infosys	5032.10	5000	174.30	8.70%
IOC	407.70	410	11.25	6.80%
IPCL	214.45	210	11.20	13.00%
ITC	966.85	960	26.40	6.80%
Larson	437.20	440	8.05	4.60%
Mahindra	352.30	350	13.45	9.50%
Maruti	363.35	360	14.45	9.90%
Mastek	293.25	290	16.35	13.90%

Contd. . .

Table 9.1 (contd. . .)

Stock	*Prevailing Price of the Stock (Rs.)*	*Nearest At-the-Money Call Option (Rs.)*	*Premium till Expiry (12 days) (Rs.)*	*Premium Monthly (% return) (Rs.)*
MTNL	116.90	120	3.35	7.10%
Nat Alum	172.35	170	8.05	11.60%
Nifty	1698.60	1700	23.8	3.50%
NIIT	240.60	240	11.00	11.40%
ONGC	693.50	700	11.55	4.10%
Orient Bank	242.05	240	11.05	11.30%
PNB	182.92	180	7.50	10.25%
Polaris	201.15	201	11.00	13.60%
Ranbaxy	1073.90	1070	27.10	6.30%
Reliance	491.30	490	13.40	6.80%
Satyam	343.75	340	14.10	10.25%
SBI	475.05	480	10.35	5.40%
Shipping Corp.	159.90	160	6.80	10.62%
Syndicate Bank	32.65	33	1.25	9.50%
Tata Tea	314.45	310	13.10	10.33%
Telco	419.75	420	13.00	7.70%
Tisco	377.75	380	10.15	6.70%
Wipro	1609.40	1620	49.00	7.60%

Some of the above high returns may look very attractive, but there can be issues of liquidity and bid-ask spreads.

How Covered Call Writing Compares with Simply Going Long

Suppose one had bought ACC stock at Rs. 215, sold a 220 call for Rs. 15 on December of 2003 (Figure 9.1).

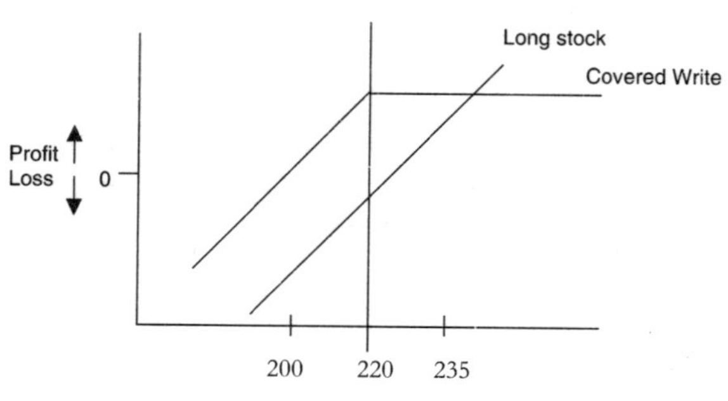

Figure. 9.1: **Stock Price at Expiration**

In the above case, the covered call performs better than just holding a long stock at all points other than above Rs. 235. We therefore make money if the ACC stock trades above the Rs. 200 mark. That is because if the prevailing stock price is Rs. 215, you get Rs. 15 up front and so your breakeven is Rs. 200. So theoretically we have a stop loss of Rs. 15 even before we get into the trade.

Now let's examine the three scenarios, which can occur.

ACC Closes Below Rs. 220

If the stock closes below Rs. 220 at the end of the month, say at Rs. 210, you pocket the entire Rs. 15 premium. In fact , we are fine so long as the stock does not close below Rs. 200, because we have a Rs. 15 hedge against a fall. As a rule of thumb it is reasonable to assume that the hedge is 50 paise to every rupee loss in the stock, i.e. if the stock goes down to Rs. 200, the option will go down to Rs. 7.5. The problem starts if the stock starts declining below Rs. 200. In my experience that can be avoided by:

1. Using technical analysis, and
2. Writing a deeper in-the-money call.

Typically, I would like to write an at-the-money call, or a call one strike above the prevailing stock price, if ACC and the market had just gone through a reaction and ACC was either at a support or at the lower end of a trading range. If the market and/or ACC had just rallied sharply, I would like to write one or two in-the-money strikes if possible in order to get more protection on the downside. This may get me lower time premium but the protection on the downside is welcome. For example, if the stock price was Rs. 215 after a rally, I would rather sell the 210 call which would sell for about Rs. 20. This would give me Rs. 5 as an extra hedge against a fall. I know traders who sell only one deep in-the-money strike, which is a conservative approach. Another choice would be to look for a different stock which has not recently rallied.

ACC Closes Above Rs. 220

If it closes above Rs. 220 you make Rs. 5 in stock appreciation and Rs. 15 in option premium, so your effective return for the month is about 10% If, however, the stock closes at Rs. 230 at the end of the month, you get Rs. 15 as stock appreciation but since the call you have written would be exercised against you, you end up keeping only Rs. 5 out of that and paying out Rs. 10. Above Rs. 220, your return remains constant at Rs. 20 (Rs. 5 + Rs. 15) and you get no further appreciation.

Assuming ACC closes at Rs. 235 for the current month, I would only write the call for the next month if the technical position of ACC indicated that the price would hold steady for another month. This could be a Rs. 230 or a 240 call depending on the technical position of the stock and the market. In case of a big vertical run, I would look for another stock that fulfils my criteria.

ACC Closes at Rs. 220

This is the ideal situation in terms of getting the best of both worlds and it does happen with a stock such as ACC. It allows you another month of writing at-the-money call options at Rs. 220. Since I look at a covered call in the Indian scenario as fresh investment every month, I would like to evaluate whether the conditions for writing the covered call are still the same as they were in the previous month, and the strikes available, or move on to some other stock.

There is one point investors and traders must remember if they continue to hold the stock for longer than a month and keep writing options on it. In the US, the stock is called when the call options is exercised and that is the end of the story. But in the Indian context of cash settlement, if the stock goes up every month and the calls against them are exercised, you will have a net cash outflow because you would need to pay the difference between the strike price and the prevailing price. No doubt the stock would have gained in intrinsic value as well during that period but those gains will remain notional unless, of course, one sells the stock. So if the stock drops sharply in value, which means way beyond the available option premiums, investors would stand to lose the gains they made from the covered calls. So it is important that an evaluation be done afresh every month as to whether the same stock should be used again for writing covered calls based on its technical position.

This was really the base case where an at-the-money call is written since the time premium you receive has the maximum time value. Later in this chapter we will discuss writing lower and higher cases and the conditions in which such changes might be necessary.

As we saw above, the covered call writer does better for all prices under Rs. 235. Which means we get a monthly return 6% if the stock sustains above Rs.215. If you are a long-term holder of the stock, and the stock does nothing for a year, you can make Rs. 180 in a year on a stock that hardly moved.

ACC is one of my favourite Indian shares to write covered calls on. There are several reasons why I like ACC. For one, I like to work in absolute numbers. At a stock price of Rs. 215, and with a market lot of 1,500 (you need to buy options in market lots of the underlying to hedge on the upside, so this is a factor) requires an investment of Rs. 322,500 at the time of writing, out of which you get Rs. 22,500 up front by writing a Rs. 15,220 call. This is a return of about 6.9%. This is unheard of return anywhere outside the stock market. The reason why many more stock market traders don't go in for this strategy is probably that it's not considered sexy to make money in this "passive" manner.

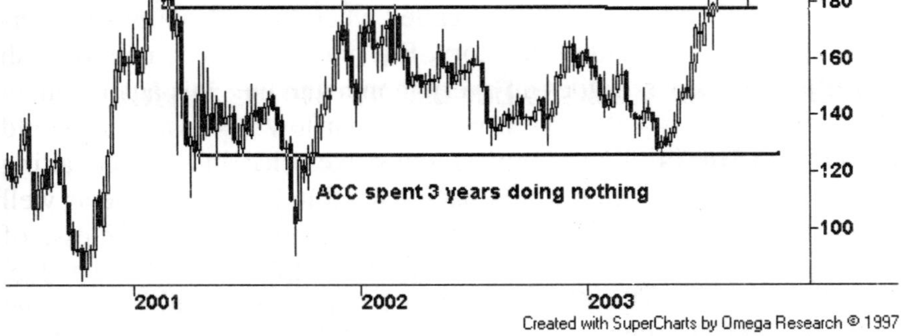

Figure 9.2

Let's now turn to the ACC chart for the 3-years period, 2001-2003 (Figure 9.2)

As you would note, the ACC chart really did nothing exciting for long periods of time. This is because the cement industry shows bursts of activity once in a while, but generally does nothing exciting. So ACC did nothing for about three years and moved in a range of Rs. 130-180, and when late in 2003 and early 2004 the entire market rallied 50%, it rallied only 20%, thus disappointing its long-term shareholders.

It is true that the 6% per month return is a bull market return for writing a covered call option, a good average for all times for an at-the-money ACC call could be 3 per cent monthly. If you had bought 1,500 ACC shares in 1999 at Rs. 180 and held on to them till 2003, you would not exactly be delighted. As an investor who was long only the stock you would have made Rs. 60,000 (at a price of Rs. 220). By writing covered calls at a return of 3% per month, which is about Rs. 8,100 per month taking an average price of Rs. 180, you would have made Rs. 97,200 annually. For the four years together you would have made Rs. 3,88,800. Yes, folks, and that is without compounding. So, in effect, you would have your entire investment back, plus your stock holding would have become free.

You can find the difference in the percentage return yourselves. And the important thing is that you don't have to watch the markets closely and continuously like you have to when trading futures. So what you have is a property which gives you rent every month, and where you have the option of deciding what you want to do every month. For the 70 to 75% of the time that the markets move sideways, I don't know of any strategy to beat this one.

Deciding on the Stocks to Buy and the Strikes to Write

Selection of Stocks

ACC is the perfect example of a stock for writing a covered call, a sideways moving stock of a large company which is not expected to go bankrupt any time soon. Such stocks are no longer growth stocks in the market and make perfect candidates for covered call writing. This is the first criterion for selecting stocks for writing covered calls.

You can select growth stocks as well but they are more volatile and the risk-adjusted returns may not be in your favour. We all saw what happened to the growth oriented technology stocks when the growth fell off in 2003. So with growth stocks you might lose the upside and get chopped on the downside. It is very important that the stock you choose should not have a speculative bubble, at least not of the kind that has taken the stock price ten times higher and made it clearly overvalued. That is the reason I select industries that are not currently fancied by the market. Also, I never select a stock that is not a market leader; under no circumstances do I want the stock's price to fall. Even if it does fall, it should not lose its bottom altogether.

I would not mind giving up a percentage on the premium for a lower risk stock. In fact, I would advise covered call writers to desist from choosing very risky or volatile stocks, no matter how high be the premium they might get, because if the stock drops 25-30%, investors will generally lose much more than the premium they receive.

My choices generally are stocks which trade heavy volumes even in the cash segment, such as Reliance (big market heavyweight), Satyam (yes, it's a technology stock, but I would take it when it's not in a sharply declining mood), Tisco, Gail (very stable stock, monopoly in its business), Hind Lever (which does nothing for years, has strong institutional holding and so will not see the bottom falling out; the premium you receive may be a little low, but well worth the capital protection it gives), and sometimes special situation stocks, but very carefully. These could be HPCL and BPCL when people are expecting a cabinet disinvestment committee meeting. (As of this writing the market has become used to political squabbling over disinvestments. So the divestment theme is not exactly as fancied as it was earlier). Other interesting candidates can sometimes be stocks of companies which are fundamentally strong but which decline for a couple of days before their quarterly results. The reason for capitalising on these situations is that unless the news is earth shattering, its implications are already built into the option premium as volatility. And even if the stock declines after the news is out, there is enough cushion. This is not an exhaustive list but certainly gives a flavour for what you might like to look at while choosing stocks for covered call writing.

In sum, the key here is that:

1. The stock should not be at a resistance or be overbought; and

2. The company should not be "operator driven" and should be well run and backed by institutions.

Although I am a technical analyst, I believe that technicals work much better with well-run and highly liquid companies which have widely-spread shareholding. I would avoid any stock which has had a vertical run and is up against overhead resistance, no matter which company it is.

Stocks for covered calls can be selected on the basis of an average knowledge of technical analysis. By average, I mean sufficient knowledge to enable you to select stocks which are either in uptrends or in sideways movement. I call this average knowledge of technical analysis because to ensure that a stock does not fall beyond a certain value is perhaps much easier than identifying a futures set-up which needs to work in three days. One should avoid stocks which have bearish patterns, or those which may have a tendency of declining very sharply. If you observe the chart of any stock over the last 4-5 years, you will be able to see its price "character".

Liquidity

The kind of stocks I like for writing covered calls are ones whose one strike in-the-money, out-of-the-money and at-the-money options are very liquid. Among the Indian stocks which have derivatives, this is presently not true for all. So the price discovery is not equally good in all cases. Also if you should decide to roll over your options position, you would need to find buyers and sellers.

Don't Let the Tail Wag the Dog

It is important for a trader to remember that it is the underlying stock which determines the value of the call, and not the other way around. It is sometimes easy to get carried away in trying to earn the maximum premium, but the objectives of this entire exercise are:

1. To ensure safety of capital, and
2. To make a consistent, steady return in the market and reducing the volatility of long-terms returns.

The objective is not to take undue risk by chasing the best premium, buying underlying stocks of questionable nature, or buying good stocks at overvalued conditions. I am stressing this point again because a wrong stock, or the right stock bought at the wrong time, can easily lead to a trader losing confidence in a good strategy.

Stop Loss

As the covered call only protects the covered call writer to the extent of the premium, it's extremely important that traders keep some kind of a stop loss in case the stock starts declining in a major way, such as breaking of crucial supports, breaking down from a range, some unexpected fundamental news, etc. Generally speaking, in most cases I would not keep the stock if it starts to give back the entire premium and/or starts breaking down supports. If you do not want to get rid of the stock then buying puts based on the chart patterns may not be a bad idea. But the key idea is never to get stuck on a sinking ship in the hope that a covered call will bail you out in the end.

Let's look at some charts of the Indian companies I consider worthy candidates for writing covered calls (Figures 9.3, 9.4 and 9.5).

Which Strikes to Write

Let's now take the ACC example further and see how one can decide which strike of covered call should be written (Figure 9.6).

The rules for this are very simple:

- Write one strike above the prevailing price when the stock has had a reaction, and

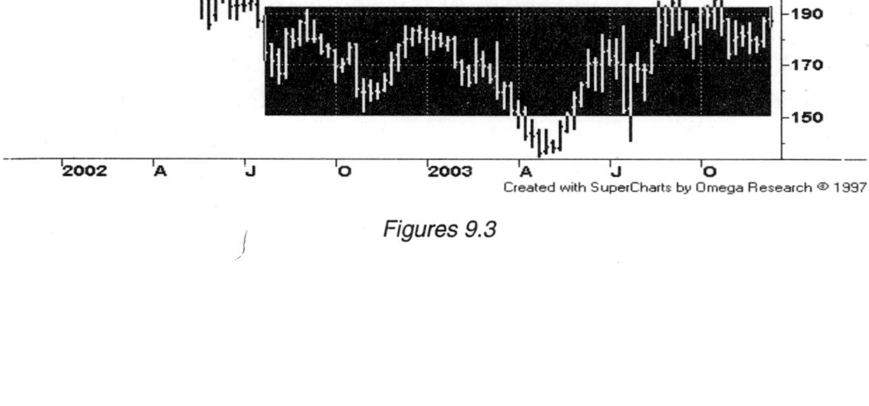

Figures 9.3

Figure 9.4

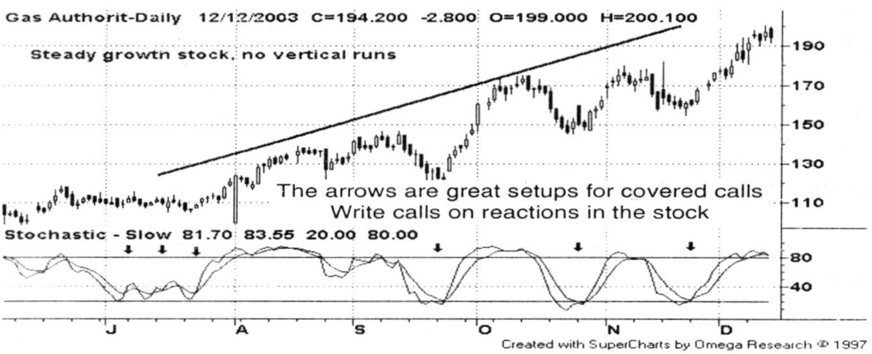

Figure 9.5

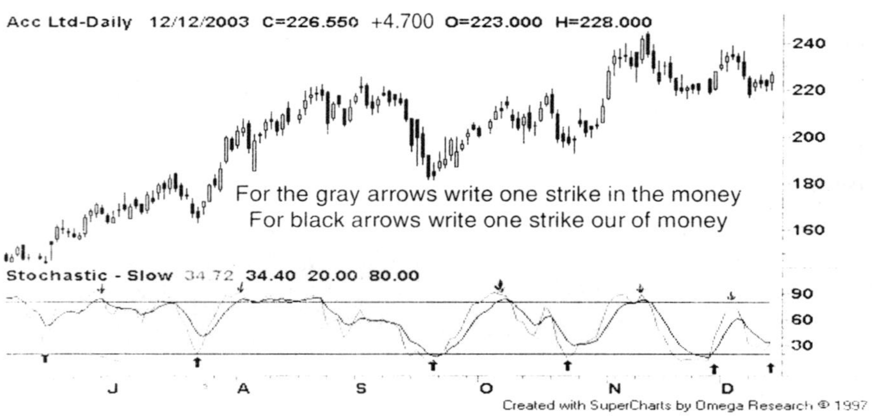

Figure. 9.6

- Write one strike below the prevailing price when the stock has had a rally.

Oscillators such as the stochastics can help us out in this.

Let us suppose, the prevailing price is Rs. 215. Check the stochastics; if it's in overbought territory, sell one strike in-the-money, i.e. the 210 call. In this case you are selling some extra protection to guard against a correction.

If the stock has had a reaction and is near its oversold territory, sell the Rs. 220 call so that if the stock rallies your returns improve because of stock appreciation as well.

The good thing about covered call is that it's not catastrophic if you don't choose the right strike. Choosing the right stock is much more important.

Investors who don't want to get rid of their stock and yet get some capital appreciation can choose two strikes out-of-money. In the case of our ACC example, they could write a 230 or a 240 call. They would then earn a lower premium, but it would reduce the chances of the option being exercised against them — and even if it is so exercised it would give them capital appreciation as well.

The Expiration Month

Life is easy in this regard since other than in the last five days before expiration, only the near-month options are really liquid in India. Now if I were writing a call option in the last five days for the first time, then I would like to do so for the next month and earn bigger time value. Thereafter in the last week of every month, I would like to re-evaluate my positions and judge which stocks are looking good for another round of writing, and which need to be dropped in favour of others. Always remember, a covered call in India is a position for a month. And since I am a swing trader, I do not believe in holding stocks long term.

Market Lot of the Option Being Written

Investors and traders should not have a lop-sided covered call portfolio. As discussed in the earlier chapters, changes in lot sizes often do not keep pace with the changes in stock prices. Yesterday's dog is today's hero. So if a trader wants to invest Rs. 20 lakh in a covered call portfolio, he should avoid all stocks which have huge lot sizes. For example, I would not include Telco at a price of Rs. 419 and a lot size of 3300 in such a portfolio. I would rather have four or five smaller stocks instead. The reason for this is that notwithstanding all the analysis in the world, the market will do its own thing. Having a lopsided portfolio means that the downside on a single stock could be very high. And that could wipe out all your gains on all other covered call writes. The chapter on money management (Chapter 12) provides detailed guidance on position sizing.

Follow up Strategies

Do Nothing

This is the strategy that works best in India since options of fundamentally strong stocks continue to have some time premium left till the last day. I prefer writing at-the-money calls since these give the maximum premium inflow. It is critical, however, that once covered call writing is accepted as a strategy, traders should write calls on an ongoing basis. On the last Thursday of every month, it should be a ritual to write fresh calls for the next month. Taking again the "rent from a building" example, traders and investors should look to invest their funds every month in order to get consistent benefits of call writing.

Generally speaking, options written in big stocks do not get exercised and it is possible to either square up the transaction on the last day, or let the option expire and sell the stock as well towards the close in order to initiate new positions. In case the same stock still looks good, traders can sell fresh calls while letting the old ones expire. This might entail some cash outflow if the stock had moved up very sharply in the previous month, the call sold deep in-the-money, and the fresh call is written for a lower premium inflow. The additional premium paid on the expensive call is captured as the intrinsic value in the stock, which remains notional if the stock is held. Again the approach is different for traders who are using covered call as a strategy and for those who have the stock as a position and just want some extra income.

What if the Call is Exercised Against You

In some cases the calls you write might be exercised by the buyer. Typically, this happens when the price of the stock rises very sharply. And this can happen since individual stocks have American options which can be exercised at any time during the month.

Should this happen, the trader needs to review the entire situation and decide whether the stock could be expected to rise much further, or if the rise was a one-off-move. This is never easy to determine. Nevertheless, some points such as volumes, breakout after a narrow range, or from a bullish pattern, would be the likely signals to look at.

In such cases traders should go on writing at-the-money calls as soon as a previous call is exercised against them. They can also write one or two strikes further from the at-the-money call if the stock looks bullish and is expected to rise further. You should not be worried about the exercise against you because you have captured the entire gain in the intrinsic value of the stock in any case. Fresh call writing needs to be looked at as a fresh situation. Sometimes writing a call on another stock which is range bound might be more useful.

Closing a Part or the Whole Position

There is only the situation when I would close my entire covered call position — if the stock breaks down below all its supports. As mentioned earlier, a covered call needs to have an ultimate stop loss should the stock start tanking. Despite the best technical analysis, sometimes a stock starts failing its supports and goes into a downtrend. At that point it is critical that the entire covered call position in the stock be closed at a stop loss determined by a strong support. You might toy with the idea of closing out a part of the position driven by the fact that your outlook on a given stock might have changed — you now have a more bullish view on the stock. This might tempt you to buy back a portion of your sold calls, maybe at a higher rate, and aim for some capital appreciation too. I do not subscribe to this because once you have decided to write a call, you should be clear that you are giving up the upsides. Changing one's objective midway only leads to higher transaction costs and sometimes the gain envisaged does not materialise.

Rolling Up

Rolling up is the condition of buying back the short call and writing a higher call. Again, in the Indian condition it is generally not useful to roll up even if the stock is trending in the given month. This is because it is generally difficult for a stock to beat the covered call return in a month. My experience is that over a period of twelve months, you generally end up making the same amount of money in covered calls, if not more, as in a trending stock. This is because all stocks take breaths, they pause for consolidation, which evens out things in the end. Thus other than increasing your transaction costs, I don't think rolling up serves any purpose. It would serve a purpose if mid-month calls could be written because there is a greater possibility of the stock slipping from sideways to bullish over a period of a couple of months.

Rolling Down

This is a strategy I often use when, in a given month, the stock that I have bought retraces a bit, or consolidates within a range, and the at-the-money call moves one strike lower. By doing this:

1. I buy back the short call cheaper, and
2. I get some extra premium by selling a lower call.

This is the only case where I would think of changing my strategy mid-month. Let's understand, I am talking of a mild retracement and not the stock getting butchered. If the stock starts falling sharply, your need to close the entire position.

In the game of covered call, you will generally not lose if you take in as much premium as you can.

Writing Index Covered Call Options

For a large mutual fund or very high net worth investors, it makes sense to write index options to enhance returns as well as hedge in times of uncertainty or consolidation. For smaller traders and investors, selling index options is a good way of playing in the index futures market. Trading naked index futures is generally pretty tough even for seasoned traders. For a retail trader, on the other hand, it is often easier to judge if the index will hold a particular level.

So by going long in the index futures and selling an at-the-money index call option, the retail trader gets a larger stop loss in terms of breakdown. By doing so, he gets into the advantageous situation of the option seller, rather than being the option buyer and getting the wrong end of the stick. Indian markets, and for that matter all markets, go sideways for long periods of time. So buying futures and selling at-the-money call options can be a profitable option. Still, as discussed earlier, it is critical to apply a stop loss in all futures and stock positions. Generally in bullish markets, at-the-money Nifty index call options sometimes sell for even Rs. 50, so the trader immediately gets Rs. 50 in his account as profit and as stop loss; in the case of Sensex this would be 150 points. I think that unless the trader really gets the trend wrong, a 50-point stop loss is generally enough. This is much better than the call and put spreads we discussed. However, since index options are still not so liquid in the Indian market, so squaring up two sets of illiquid options can sometimes be difficult. As with all futures related positions, the leverage — and hence the risk — of the entire strategy is greater.

Advance Implementation

Till now we have assumed that the number of calls written to stock owned is a one-to-one relationship, in terms of derivative lots. Also generally speaking, unless specified otherwise the calls are assumed to be written at-the-money. That is the way I do business and it works for my objectives. I have found that in the stock market the simpler you keep things, the greater are the returns. The less you need to change things, the better the returns. As a trader said very wisely, profitable trading should be boring. But now we will discuss strategies where the above rules are modified. It is not as if we recommend these strategies but these demonstrate the flexibility which can be achieved compared with options. One good reason why these strategies cannot easily be implemented by smaller players is because of the lot sizes involved. Most small traders and investors may be uncomfortable with multiple lots; by small I mean trading accounts of less than Rs. 50 lakh.

Partial Writing

This involves writing calls on a part of your stock holding thereby fine tuning your portfolio to achieve fixed as well as variable returns. Taking our ACC example, its derivatives lot is 1,500 shares. Assuming you have 3,000 shares, and though you think ACC is mildly bullish but you do not want to forego the entire upside if it does occur. Assume the prevailing price is Rs. 215, and you expect the quarterly results to be declared by the end of the month and would not like to take an unhedged bet on the results. Your target on ACC is Rs. 250 if the news from the company is good. So you sell a Rs. 230 call for Rs. 11 and leave the other 1,500 shares unhedged. If the results are indeed good, half of your shares will gain because of capital appreciation while the other half will provide you regular income and downside protection if the expectation is not met. As I have said before, writing covered calls on all of your stock holding is a good idea in the Indian scenario. In twenty trading sessions, it's difficult for most stocks to consistently beat the covered call premium.

Mixed Writing

Mixed writing is done by writing calls at different strike prices. Again there could be lot size problems here. This is another way of fine tuning returns but in the Indian scenario not very viable nor profitable, mainly because:

1. You end up having a large position in a single stock.
2. Stock movement might not be according to expectation unless the stock is trending.

In our ACC example, the stock was trading at Rs. 215 and if you have two lots, you can sell one 230 call, and another 240 call.

Ratio Writing

Ratio writing means writing higher calls in the ratio of 1:2, or more, to the stock held. I would not advise anyone to write more than 1:3, because I have seen stranger things happen in the market. This strategy is also used where you have a shortened month and the call premiums are high. It is critical to understand the breakeven in this transaction on both sides.

Let me take you through a trade I personally took and which I thought was a good percentage trade in a bullish market.

I was moderately bullish on the Reliance counter in a particular month but the month had only about ten trading sessions. So I went long on the Reliance futures at Rs. 500, and sold two Rs. 530 calls for Rs. 6.50 each which created an inflow of Rs. 13. This gave me a stop loss of Rs. 13 for breakeven. Another benefit was that I could even put an enhanced stop. Reliance had strong support at Rs. 480 but I did not want to risk more than Rs. 7 on this trade, so the extra Rs. 13 was financed by writing higher calls. On the upside, if Reliance did cross Rs. 530 before expiry, I would not have begun making a loss till Rs. 566 since I'd have gained Rs. 30 on the futures and Rs. 6.50 on the second written option. So my breakeven on the upside was Rs. 566.

Benefits of the Covered Call Strategy

It Improves the Odds of Successful Trading

The biggest benefit of the covered call strategy is that it can be implemented in two of the three possible stock movement scenarios. If the stock goes up, it's profitable. If the stock goes sideways, it's profitable. The only case when it's not profitable is when the stock goes down. Any strategy that works 66% of the time automatically has higher odds of success.

On the other hand, when buying either options or stocks, traders and investors make money only in one out of three possible eventualities, which is if the stock goes in the desired direction. Also, the covered call puts a premium on time; as time passes you gain the time value of the option. Being a very futures trader, the covered call both protects my capital and also makes my overall returns less volatile since my money is never idle but is always generating decent returns.

Your Best Chance for Making Money When Important News is Expected

When a company result or an election result is expected, or a divestment meet is being held by the government, often the smartest of minds are proved wrong in their anticipation of results. In such situations, the media analysts often advise people to take positions in options instead of futures or stocks. Every time I hear this, I lick my lips as I smell covered call opportunities. When news is expected, the normal response of people is to buy calls or puts. Now this increases the implied volatility of the options and makes them very expensive.

So generally the best course of action before an event is to take a covered call exposure because the expectation is built into the option premium. In my experience, unless the news breaks the company's or market's back, it is fairly well discounted in the call premium and you end up making money no matter which way the news announcement goes.

I particularly remember one instance when Tisco was expected to announce its quarterly results. Tisco had been rising steadily for the previous six months but had declined for the last couple of days on light volume and was then trading at Rs. 340, down from about Rs. 360 a day before the results. Since the steel cycle was up, the results were expected to be good. The problem to consider was whether the anticipated good results had been discounted and would there be sell-off after the results, or would Tisco's performance beat even the best of estimates and take the stock back up?

No amount of technical analysis will get you the answer to such a query. The results were to be announced on the next day at 12 noon. By 11 a.m. the stock had dropped to about Rs. 332. There was a strong support at Rs. 320, and it appeared oversold. So I checked the 330 call option and it was quoting at Rs. 26, which is a richly valued option because of expectation of the result built in. My analysis was that if the results were according to expectation, the sell-off would not take the stock to Rs. 304 which was my breakeven for this option. And since the stock had already sold off quite a bit before the result, it was likely it would, in fact, bounce back, or at least not fall a whole lot further. I had a decent stop loss for this trade and stood to make an 8% gain for the month — I would take such a call any day.

And, lo and behold, the results were slightly better than expected. Initially the stock sold off another Rs. 5, and then bounced back to close at Rs. 345. It then started going sideways and up and closed the month at about Rs. 358. As soon as the company declared the results, the call lost Rs. 6, since the uncertainty was over. So that was the immediate gain. In such circumstances where a naked position might appear risky, it's always better to take a covered call exposure. On the other side of this trade, some poor retail investor must have bought the

Tisco call for Rs. 26. Well, to be fair to him, he bought a good stock option; he forecast the results correctly, the stock moved up very nicely and, yet, what did he make? A gain of Rs. 2 compared to the Rs. 26 that were earned by the covered call strategy.

Had the results been below expectations, the stock would have taken a beating but we had a cushion of Rs. 26. And as the stock had fallen before the event, the technical position was looking much better for a rise or a sideways movement than a fall. It is, therefore, always worth remembering that the technical position of a stock is much more important than the premium being earned.

Beats Stock Market Returns Over the Long Term

In my experience, covered call writing has taken the stress out of stock market trading. The odds of making money in naked futures, options, and stocks are stacked against both the buyer and seller. This is because their probability for making money is one out of three. Covered call is the only strategy in which the trader makes money most of the time and even when he is wrong, the losses are lower than in the case of the other strategies. In long bear phases, markets as well as individual stocks take years to form bases and move up. Covered call is a good way to make money during such periods. In India, the call and put buyers would actually need a miracle to make money in the fifteen trading sessions that there effectively are in a month. This is because there are eight to ten holidays in a month and in the last five days before expiry, the decay in time value is often higher or equal to any favourable movement. In India, therefore, currently the covered call is as good as it can get.

Why Don't Many Other People Do It?

There can be a variety of reasons why many Indian traders don't currently write calls.

One of the reasons is the myth that futures and options are inherently risky. On the contrary, as we have seen futures and options are excellent tools for managing risk and returns. Like anything else they can certainly cause great harm if not used properly. If after reading this book, you still think futures and options are to be avoided, then I have truly failed.

Another reason is that most people like to follow the common practice and are suspicious of looking at anything new. Selling covered calls is not something that the earlier generations of traders ever had the opportunity to do. People were scared of computers when they first came, it was flying before that, etc.

There is another myth that the option buyer is the smartest and the most risk averse person around, and that options are sold by people who are either gamblers or very rich since selling options is, theoretically, very risky. Neither of the above is true, particularly in the case of writing covered calls. I have tried to prove time and again in this book that, in general, the option buyer always gets a raw deal, and this is particularly true in India.

Readers might also ask, "If this is so smart, why aren't the FIIs doing it?" Well, the FIIs probably are doing it, but they are not going to admit it on television! They are not supposed to get their fat salaries for writing covered calls. The FIIs do something even simpler; namely, borrow money at 1.5% in their country and arbitrage between the futures and the cash market in India and make about 6% per month.

Another possible reason why individual traders don't write covered calls is that they seem to believe it is only for professional traders and high net worth investors. Often they also mistakenly believe it's an investor's duty to stand by a stock through thick and thin even if it does nothing for them. Well, getting married to any stock is a cardinal sin, most investment books talk about. Be that as it may, the covered call strategy also caters to people who like retaining stocks forever by giving them a regular income. A stock is an investment position and nothing more than that.

My reason for writing covered calls is simple — it makes money and generally it does so better than most naked stock, futures or options buying. Actually, the concept is so simple that people get confused and think they are missing something. The best part about the covered call is that it outperforms the other methods 70 to 75% of the time when markets go sideways.

Sure, writing covered calls is not as exciting as swing trading, nor is it as glamorous as a futures trade but it gives you hard cash. You don't need to be a financial wizard to do this; you don't need the high levels of discipline or look for set-ups like we discussed in the earlier chapters on futures trading using technical analysis. And, at most times, it protects all of your capital. What else do you want?

Chapter 10

Derivative Strategies for Special Situations

There are some events typical to the Indian economic calendar when implied volatilities and the costs of carry are at abnormally high or low levels. As an active trader you should always be ready for such low risk, high return situations because derivatives give you the ability of adjusting risk and return. And this is done by selling options, not buying them. What happens in such situations is that retail investors often tend to buy calls or puts depending on the take of the media analysts, erroneously thinking that they can lose only a small amount and hence are reducing risk by buying options. The increased option price thus appears as increased implied volatility in the option price.

Also, the sellers are aware of the increased demand from option buyers at such times and tend to price the options higher than usual. Often the effect of the news is discounted in the option's price before the actual situation or event. So the seller of the option is still able to get out at almost breakeven if the news is adverse. What actually often happens after the news is public is that the demand of the call or put option goes down drastically and, regardless of the movement of the underlying, the implied volatility of the option drops. So the seller of the option immediately makes money on the lower implied volatility. This cushion helps the option seller both when the news is as per expectations, and even if the news turns out to be unexpected. It is important to understand that some of the events discussed here might lose importance over time, and new events may take their place.

Writing Covered Calls Just Before Important Announcements or News

The logic behind writing covered calls just before important announcements or results is that the option sellers like to price in the widest possible variation in the news. In doing so, they increase the implied volatility of the option to such a large extent that unless the news is catastrophic, the premium is more than sufficient to take care of everything. Of course, sometimes catastrophes do happen, but only rarely.

Let us recall what happened in April 2003 when Infosys reduced its annual guidance to 10-15% growth in profit. The stock lost 50% of its value in a single day. The way to guard against such events is to look at the results of the stock's peer group. If the stock in question is a bellwether and has a good management, it will do at least as well as its peers — or no worse. This due diligence exercise needs to be done before investing any money. Do not write covered calls on the results of the second and third rung companies, or ones with dubious management track record.

The other reason for writing covered calls is that volatility alternates between contraction and expansion. Thus by selling high volatility before an event or an announcement, it becomes likely that the volatility will reduce after the event and a profit can be made just by trading the volatility. This extra volatility premium also provides a cushion against an adverse movement in the underlying if the news is adverse, or if the underlying moves contrary to expectations.

Let's look at the accompanying Nifty chart and see how volatility varies over a period or time and how it can be traded. (Figure10.1)

As we can see in the chart, there are two lines which give a historical perspective of implied volatility, both high and low. The high-implied volatility is followed by low implied volatility, and *vice versa*. Therefore all other things being constant, it makes sense to buy implied volatility and sell high implied volatility.

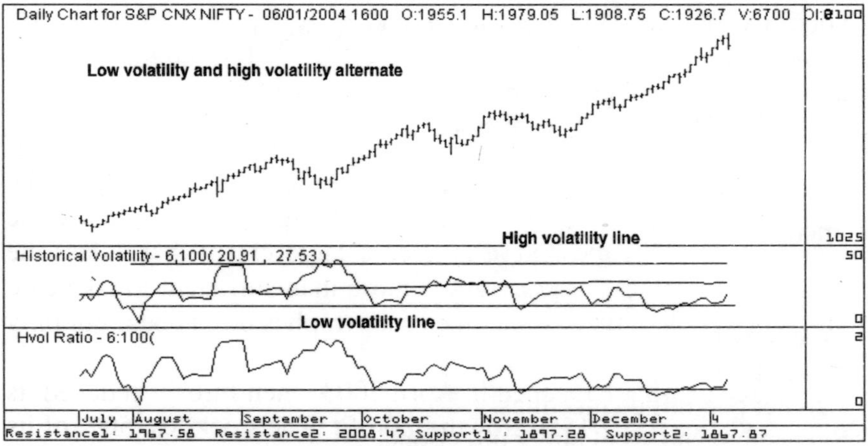

Figure 10.1

Favourable News

In most cases, it is wise to go in for a covered call, obviously hoping that the news would be positive. So, for example, if some news is expected in Reliance and the trader does not want to take the risk of a naked position, one can buy the Reliance stock, say at Rs. 455, and sell the Rs. 460 near-month call at Rs. 20. Once the news breaks, the call drops in value even if the price of the underlying moves favourably. So if a favourable news is announced and the stock moves up by Rs. 10 to Rs. 465, you might find the call appreciating only by Rs. 5 to Rs. 25. So, on expiry, the trader makes Rs. 5 till Rs. 460 and keeps the Rs. 20 premium from the call as well, in effect making Rs. 25 on Rs. 455, which is a trade equivalent to the stock moving 5.4% in twenty sessions. The trader can also unwind both positions and still make Rs. 5 if he is not interested in holding the position for the entire month.

Adverse News

In case the news is negative, and the stock goes down Rs. 10:

1. You are hedged to about Rs. 435 on the downside, since you have already made Rs. 20 from the call;

2. The call depreciates on the downside even faster as the implied volatility of the call goes down and it becomes further out of money. You might, therefore, find the call trading about Rs. 8 in the case of an adverse event. So you might still get out at break-even, even if the news is adverse.

Let us now consider some special events in the Indian economic calendar:

- Budget;
- Company results;
- Election results;
- Cabinet committee meetings;
- Events that can go in either direction.

Budget

The budget presented by the central government has traditionally been the most eagerly awaited event of the Indian economic calendar. All of the government's finances are discussed in it. New taxes are proposed, old ones waived or reduced, customs duties are levied or removed. There used to be a time when it was the only document which gave a complete, if not a correct, assessment of the economy's health. Also since most business was regulated by the government, an increase or reduction in taxes and duties used to make a big difference to the bottom lines of companies. So the budget always kept the capital markets interested in several ways. Of course, every year the capital market also had its own budget wish list. In the last few years, prior to derivatives being introduced in 2002, most capital market participants had grown used to seeing a 60-70 Nifty points rise or a fall on the budget day. As the capital markets were generally in the doldrums between 1999 and 2003, so these budgets either belied expectations or suddenly raised them very high.

Let's look at charts of some of the past budget sessions. (Figures 10.2, 10.3, 10.4 and 10.5).

Budgets from 1991-2002

In the year before 2002, the budgets used to trigger large movements in the market. Even on the budget day in 2002, the index saw a large intraday movement, but overall over a one-month period on either side, the market traded range bound. In most years before 2002, budget days saw huge movements in the index and established decisive trends.

I believe the budget is an index play and try to keep away from individual companies. Also, the budget does not now affect individual companies as much because of the rationalisation of taxes and duties into bands and the tendency of finance ministers not to change these abruptly. As time goes by, the budget will further lose its importance of being the annual ritual as the Indian economy becomes more developed and as governments make economic decisions throughout the year.

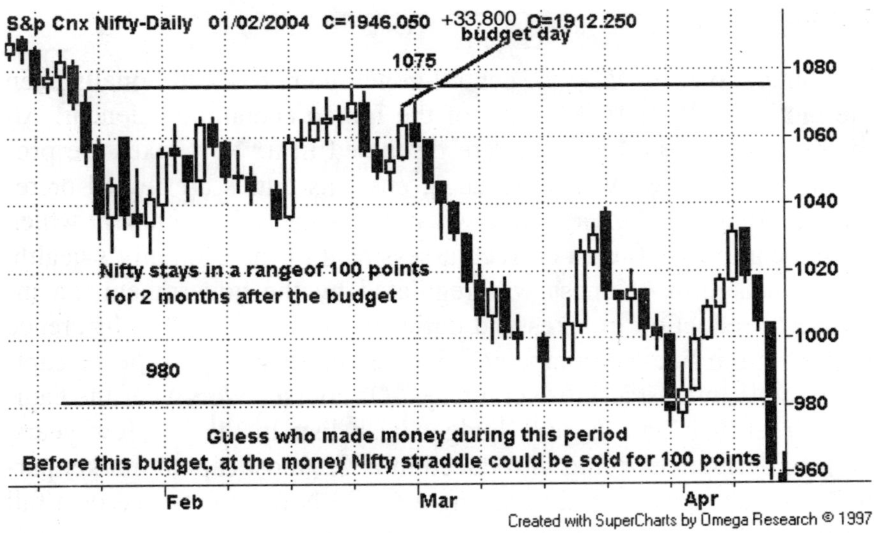

Figure 10.2: **Budget 2003**

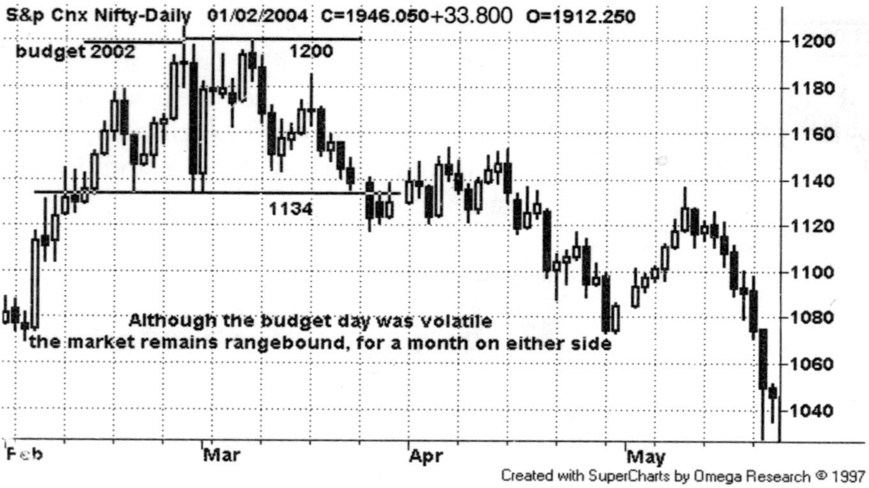

Figure 10.3: **Budget 2002**

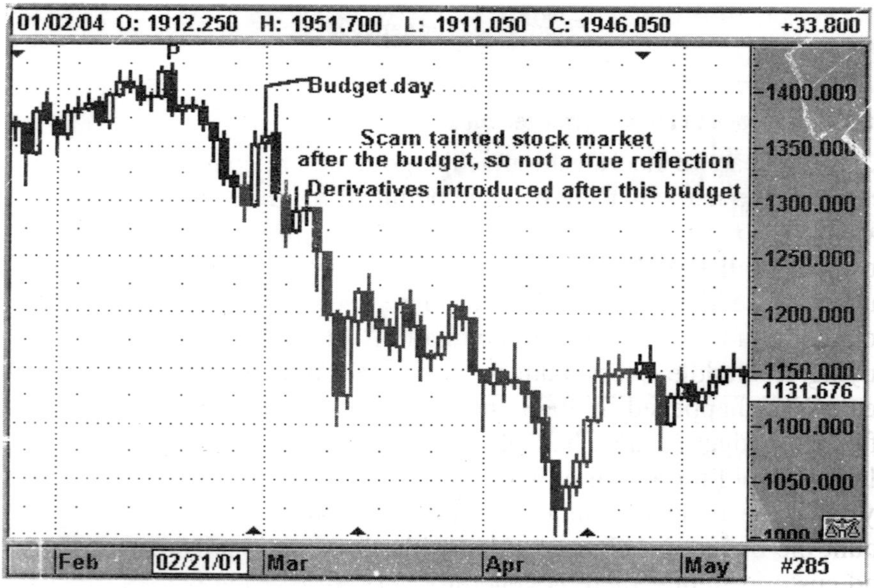

Figure 10.4: **Budget 2001**

Figure 10.5: **Budget 2000**

Market Response to the Budget After 2002

After ten years of liberalisation as the government control of business lessened, the markets have become delinked from the budget to some extent. Also, since economic announcements from the government now come all year long, the budget is further diminishing in importance. These days the market response seems to be turning range bound around the budget. But the retail investor still seems to bank on buying a straddle every budget, paying Rs.100 on the Nifty every year. What happened in 2003 and 2004 was that the option premium after the budget became half of pre-budget levels. So the Nifty straddle being sold for a total of Rs. 100 on the Nifty loses implied volatility once the budget is announced, because stock prices already discount the budget in advance. Also with all the rationalising of excise and customs duties, there is generally very little in the budget that affects stock prices. I do not know how the options premiums will be in the future but, as a benchmark, if I am getting 100 points on selling an at-the-money straddle or implied volatility substantially higher than usual, I would sell a straddle, which as traders would recall is selling both the call and the put of an at-the-money strike.

The key here is not to speculate on what announcements the budget might contain but to see if the implied volatility of the option premium is high enough to sell. Nifty's historical volatility in 2003-2004 was around 27%. An implied volatility of around 37-38% should be good enough to sell.

You must look to buy back both legs of the straddle as soon as the volatility comes down. In general, if I get 100 points in selling the straddle pre-budget and if after the announcement of the budget I can buy it back for anything less than 60, I would do so.

Company Results

Companies often declare results before the markets open or after they close. Accordingly, when the stock opens in the subsequent trading session it often does so with an up or down gap. Even if the expectations are good from the results, it's often not clear if the stock has run up enough before the result, or if the results would meet or beat expectations. I have found that most times the call premium discounts the uncertainty attached to the result. As with all covered call writing, the risk of downside needs to be thought through.

The parameters I would look at while deciding the stock on which to write a covered call are those which could minimise the downside risk. First, I would consider the growth of the industry and the sector; they should be in the early stages of growth and not in a matured phase. For example, in commodities I would like to write covered calls when people are discovering the uptrend in commodity prices and the results are likely to surprise on the upside.

In sunrise sectors like IT or pharma, I would write covered calls when the companies are in the early phase of their growth cycle. I would not do it at a time such as February 2000 when panic was ruling the roost and even good results were getting punished. I would like to see the results of one or two of the other bellwethers in the sector. The stock on which I would write the covered call should have great management quality and be a large-sized company. If the stock has corrected a bit before the results, I would buy the next available strike from the price of the stock. If the stock has run up significantly, I would write a lower call and take in as much premium as possible just to have protection against any post news sell-off. If the news turns out to be worse than expected, I would unwind the entire position without any further ado.

Ultimately, there are only two parameters in writing covered calls:

1. The implied volatility should be high, and
2. The stock should not be highly overbought.

If you pay sufficient attention to these two parameters, you should be fine. Even if you are wrong, remember you are better off than with a naked position.

Election Results

My view on the frequent elections and their results is that it does not matter in the long run whether the Congress or the BJP wins the elections. Both parties have similar views on economic policy and reforms are inevitable. Of course, the usual problems of a democratic polity are going to occur for both parties. These days with opinion polls and exit polls available, the market is able to take a view on the direction of the results. I have observed that the options of PSU shares, particularly the divestment candidates, tend to price in some volatility premium. But, broadly, like in the case of the budget, election results now have limited impact on the market so long as there is the prospect of a stable government.

Of course, the condition of the market should be taken into account when deciding about writing covered calls. In a bull market, there is no bad news. In a bear market, there is no good news. The usual due diligence of an overbought and oversold market for writing covered calls is a must. Generally speaking, writing a covered call should be based on the implied volatility of the options being written. If implieds are low, chances are the market believes the election results are inconsequential. In the long run they are inconsequential anyway.

Cabinet Committee Meetings

We all know about the famous cabinet on divestment meetings that the government holds from time to time. These meetings generally end with a bagful of announcement which are the names of the companies next on the block — and some weird solutions for HPCL and BPCL. There was a time when HPCL and BPCL used to rise and fall by up to 20% on favourable or adverse announcements. But the markets have now grown wiser to the fact that these behemoths are difficult to divest and now take these meetings in its stride. Still, before writing covered calls it's important to see if the stock has run up in the hope of any announcement, and by how much. If the stocks are not very overbought and have not run up, at-the-money call options can be written for well-run PSU oil companies. If they have run-up a lot, I would either write deep in-the-money options or let it pass. I would definitely ensure that the long term trend of all these companies is up. I do not believe that in today's market any one believes that any of these companies can be divested easily. So, the market never prices in extraordinary news.

Chapter 11

Trading Discipline

No book or seminar on trading is complete without a sermon on discipline — and with good reason. Most novice traders believe that once they understand the nuances of technical analysis, they will automatically be successful. This is far from the truth. Discipline forms 80% of a good trader's, make-up and only 20% of a trader's success is as a result of his trading knowledge. This is the reason why there are many successful analysts but very few successful traders. It is important to know whether the market is in a trending or trading phase. In a trending phase, you go and buy or sell breakouts, but in a trading phase you buy weakness and sell strength.

A lot of analysts have trouble implementing their own analysis. This is because the market is not there to favour anyone. It is there to punish the indisciplined.

The market takes away money from indisciplined traders and gives it to the disciplined ones. A trader can have cutting-edge software, the best trading system, he may be a master at reading charts and still be unsuccessful if he lacks the discipline to execute his analysis. Learning to read charts is perhaps the easier bit of technical analysis. Learning to overcome fear and greed and winning over one's emotions is a much bigger challenge. Looking at wins and losses with the same eye is never easy. Curbing human emotions of euphoria and panic is always difficult. Talking and writing about strategies is easier than putting money on the line and trading.

What is Discipline?

Discipline in any field means following a certain set of rules in order to achieve objectives one has set for oneself. Discipline is the foremost quality in all professionals. For example, in the defence forces discipline is inculcated in the recruits so that they can be trained to vanquish the enemy. Discipline is important for sales teams so that they can plan a strategy and achieve their targets. Discipline is important for doctors, lawyers and all other professionals who need to solve the problems of their clients. But nowhere is discipline more important than in trading. Lack of discipline can put a trader out of business faster than anything else.

Let's consider the differences between a disciplined and an indisciplined person in general. The objective of this exercise is to identify things that might peg us back in trading and to shun them out of our system:

- A disciplined person is likely to be disciplined in all his daily activities and much more likely to be a success.
- A disciplined person has a plan for everything he wants to achieve.
- He knows where to get the resources and the skills to implement that plan. Last but not the least, he has set himself goals to achieve.
- A disciplined person is an excellent time manager.
- A disciplined person builds frameworks for various situations and knows what to do within those frameworks.
- When a disciplined person fails, he looks at it as a stepping stone to success and learns from his mistakes instead of looking for scapegoats to blame.
- A disciplined person keeps his composure at all times.
- A disciplined person is positive about whatever he does in life and keeps negativity away.
- A disciplined person is confident of his success and is able to deal with the inevitable tough times and is thus able to keep himself mentally and emotionally stable.
- A disciplined person is patient in analysing all situations.

Now let's consider an indisciplined person. Some of the weaknesses of such an individual come naturally to most of us. These weaknesses are mercilessly exposed in trading as nowhere else:

- An indiscipined person is likely to fail at almost whatever he takes one.
- The indisciplined person is unlikely to have either goals or plans.
- An indisciplined person is negative in his approach.

- An indisciplined person loses his temper and sometimes his mental balance in tough times since he has no contingency plan.
- An indisciplined person is likely to blame everyone else but himself for his failures, thus failing to learn from his mistakes.
- An indisciplined person is not prepared for changing situations because he does not do his homework regularly.
- An indisciplined person looks to other people or equipment to make him succeed but fails to look at himself.
- The efforts of an indisciplined person do not pay off, leading him into a cycle of frustration and, hence, more mistakes.
- An indisciplined person is impatient, assesses situations incorrectly and takes incorrect actions.

The cost of not being disciplined is so high in trading that this topic deserves an entire chapter.

In trading, as in life, your success and failure depend on yourself. Every person is his own boss. When all is said and done, every person is responsible for his actions. Nowhere is it truer than in trading. In most businesses once you make certain systems and procedures, you may not need to worry a lot. But in trading, where decisions to buy and sell need to be taken every day, and taken constantly, it is impossible to succeed without discipline. All of us who trade for a living need to root out the weeds of indiscipline before it eats up all one's capital. The only way out is to be self-critical whenever you see indisciplined behaviour in yourself while trading and try to avoid it by setting rules for similar future situations.

Qualities of a Disciplined Trader

A Disciplined Trader has a Trading Plan and Does His Homework Diligently

Many traders take to trading because they think it is the simplest way of making money. Far from it, I believe it is the easiest way of losing money. There is an old Wall Street adage, that "the easiest way of making a small fortune in the markets is having a large fortune". This game is by no means for the faint hearted. This battle is not won or lost during trading hours but before the markets open.

Winning traders diligently maintain charts and keep aside some hours for market analysis. Every evening a winning trader updates his notebook and writes his strategy for the next day. Winning traders have a sense of the market's main trend. They identify the strongest sectors of the market and then the strongest stocks in those sectors. They know the level they are going to enter at and approximate targets for the anticipated move. Personally, I am not finicky about exact targets; I buy when the market is acting oversold on an intraday basis in a daily uptrend. This oversold level can come in even ten points before or after you thought it would. But it's important to have a general idea of where it might be located.

Similarly, I am willing to hold till the market is acting right. Once the market is unable to hold certain levels and breaks crucial supports, I book profits. Again, this depends on the type of market I am dealing with.

In a strong uptrend, I want the market to throw me out of a profitable trade.

In a mild uptrend, I am a little more cautious and try to book profits at the first sign of weakness.

In a choppy market, not only do I trade the lightest, I book profits while the market is still moving in my direction. The same goes for identifying the weakest sectors and the weakest stocks in those sectors for going short.

Good technical traders do not worry or debate about the news flow, they go by charting signals.

A Disciplined Trader Avoids Overtrading

Another reason to do your homework well and sincerely is to avoid overtrading. Only when a trader is clear about what he should be doing in the market can he take the right trades and back them up sufficiently. The market tries its best to mislead traders by swinging in both directions. The market wants to take away your trading capital from you. Unprepared traders who do not know if the market is trending or trading obviously can't decide whether to buy and sell breakouts, or to buy weakness and sell strength. They implement the wrong strategies in the wrong phase of the market and by the end of the day have a huge statement in their hands from their brokers, in which along with the losses that they have made, they have helped the broker rake in a lot of commissions.

Overtrading is the single biggest malaise of most traders. A disciplined trader is always ready to trade light when the market turns choppy and even not trade if there are no trades on the horizon. For example, my regular volume in the Nifty futures based on my money management policy is 3,000 shares of Nifty futures. But I trade full steam only when I see a trending market. I am open to trading 2,000 shares of Nifty futures when I am not confident of the expected move. I even go down to 1,000 Nifty futures if the market is stuck in a choppy mode with very small swings. A disciplined trader knows when to build positions and step on the gas and when to trade light and he can only make this assessment after he is clear about his analysis of the market and has a trading plan at the beginning of every trading day.

A Disciplined Trader Does Not Get Unnerved by Losses

A winning trader is always cautious; he knows each trade is just another trade, so he always uses money management techniques. He never over leverages and always has set-ups and rules which he follows religiously. He takes losses in his stride and tries to understand why the market moved against him. Often he gets important trading signals from his losses. I trade Nifty futures very actively and do most of my trades based on chart patterns. I often use a loss as an important indicator for taking a position in the reverse direction. Figure 11.1 is an actual trade I took based on a failed buy signal.

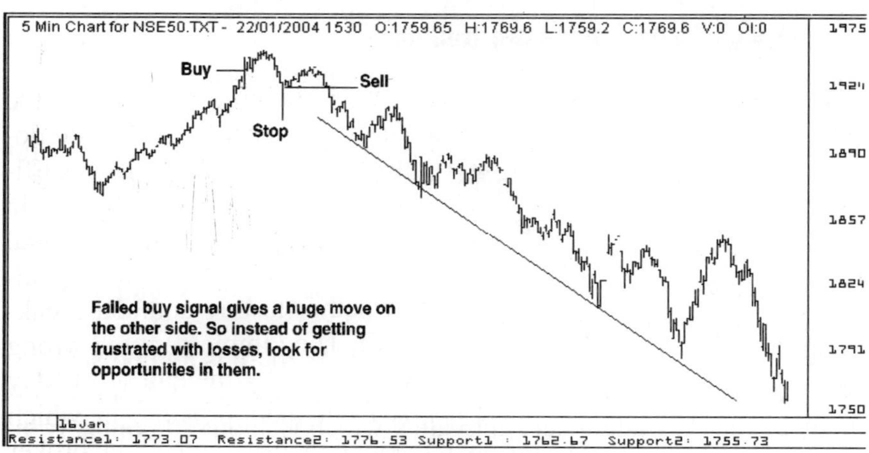

Figure 11.1

The conditions surrounding this trade were that the market had recently touched new highs (Nifty 2015), then corrected marginally, and was now about to again challenge the new high of 2015. The dilemma that every trader faces at such times is whether the market will just kiss the new high and fall back, or whether it would make newer highs. And the only reasonable way to find this out is to actually take a trade with a decent stop loss. Since I generally trade 15 contracts of Nifty futures, I decided that I would go long on 7 contracts before the Nifty touched new highs, and another 8 contracts once it convincingly crossed them. I must point out that though I was going long, I was also cautions because the market was extremely overbought. So I took the buy trade, as the market appeared to be holding some levels and had just started rallying after a minor corrections. (I believe in the adage that "in bull markets you do not but *some* pullbacks, but buy *all* pullbacks").

When I initiated the trade at 1,957, my stop loss was at 1,940. The market traded on the upside to about 1,963 and then turned hesitant for a couple of hours, trading in the 1,952 to 1,963 band. This was another warning; a market about to cross new highs should be much more active than that. Also, slowly the breadth was deteriorating. Then suddenly the market started selling off and hit my stop loss. That did not unnerve me but I thought that if even after a correction the market was not able to hold up, maybe that would be a signal to sell. After hitting my stop loss, it made a weak rallying attempt and then fell through the previous pivot. This signalled a short trade and I went short at 1,940 with all 15 contracts of the Nifty, keeping a stop at the highs and thus got a huge move on the downside. I covered at 1,794.

The key here was being alert and not worrying about the stops being hit. The clear message is that if a stop gets hit — provided it's not been placed too close — the market is not as strong in the direction of the trade as you thought.

The market kept going down for the next four days, an average of 50 Nifty points a day. So the stop loss cost me 17 points but put me on a trade that gave me 146 points.

Here I would like to mention that if I think there is a good set-up, I would always be willing to risk the normal amount that I generally do, about 1% of my trading account value, which is about 20 points. If the stop gets hit, I try to look for what the market is trying to tell me and reassess what the situation of the market is at that point — whether it is oversold or overbought. But I never try to get into an ego tussle with the market because the market is always right. If the market tells me I am wrong, I keep open my options of taking trades in the reverse direction as well. Sometimes the market gives confusing signals and whipsaws me; at that point, my effort is to avoid overtrading. I simply wait on the sidelines till the market gives a clearer indication of its direction. Treat the market as a lady and you will be happy. When a lady says no, gentlemen take it as no. It works well with the ladies, as it does with the market.

A Disciplined Trader Tries to Capture the Large Market Moves

Novice traders often book profits too quickly because they want to enjoy the winning feeling. Sometimes even on the media one hears things like, "You never lose your shirt booking profits." I believe novice traders actually lose their account equity quickly because they do not book their losses quickly enough.

Knowledgeable traders on the other hand, will also lose their trading equity — though slowly — if they are satisfied in booking small profits all the time. By doing that the only person who can grow rich is your broker. And this does happen because, inevitably, you will have periods of drawdowns when you are not in sync with the market. You can never cover a 15-20% drawdown if you keep booking small profits. The best you will do is be at breakeven at the end of the day, which is not, and should not, be the goal of trading full time, or even part time.

Those who trade for a living cannot sustain an equity account that is not growing. Thus when you believe you have entered into a large move, you need to ride it out till the market stops acting right. Traders with a lot of knowledge of technical analysis, but little experience, often get into the quagmire of following very small targets, believing the market to be overbought at every small rise — and uniformly so in all markets. Such traders are unable to make money because they are too smart for their own good. They forget to see the phase of the market. Not only do these traders book profits early, sometimes they even take short positions believing that a correction is "due". Markets do not generally correct when corrections are "due". The best policy is to use a trailing stop loss and let the market run when it wants to run. The disciplined trader understands this and keeps stop losses wide enough so that he is balanced between staying in the move as well as protecting his equity. Capturing a few large moves every year is what really makes worthwhile trading profits.

A Disciplined Trader Always Keeps Learning New Trading Techniques

You cannot learn trading in a day or even a few weeks, sometimes not even in months. Disciplined traders keep reading all the new research on technical analysis they can get their hands on. They also read a number of books every month about techniques, about trading psychology and about other successful traders and how they manage their accounts. A lot of very affordable seminars on trading are often held on weekends; experienced traders too should try to attend them, as even one great trading idea gained can be worth the seminar's fee. I often like to think about traders as *jehadis*; unless there is a fire in the belly, unless there is a strong will and commitment to win, it is impossible to win consistently in the market.

My educational background is in engineering, after which I completed an MBA in the US. But I can safely say that for trading I have read more than ten times the number of books that I read in both those courses combined. Whenever I see a bookstore where trading books might be available, I go in and buy whatever is new. I also visit a lot of Internet trading sites during the weekend, reading all the material that is written about trading. A lot of it is not of much use but you often find nuggets that help your trading. Learning how to consistently trade profitably is a lifelong struggle and winning it a most satisfying experience.

A Disciplined Trader Always Tries to Make Some Money with Less Risky Strategies As Well

In this book we have focused on three strategies of making money:

1. Position trading, swing trading and day trading in the futures market; I consider the last one to be the most risky.
2. Writing covered calls — less risky than the above and a more consistent winner.
3. Futures and cash arbitrage — no risk at all, but equally the returns are the lowest.

Futures trading is a very risky business. The best of chartists and the best of traders sometimes fail. Sure, it gives the highest returns but these may not be consistent — and the drawdowns can be large. Traders should always remember that no matter how good your analysis is, sometimes the market is not willing to oblige. In these times the 4-5% that can be earned in covered calls or futures and cash arbitrage comes in very handy. It improves the long term sustainability of a trading model and keeps your profit register ringing. Traders must learn to live with lower risk and lower return at certain times in the market, in order to protect and enlarge their capital. Futures trading should be thought of as an icing on the cake. I know it's not glamorous to tell anyone that one makes money on covered calls or cash and futures arbitrage, but then bread and butter activities are never glamorous.

Diversification is not a hollow term. Consistent profits not only add to a trader's equity over a period of time but also takes the pressure off a trader. I believe a trader should have some exposure in covered calls every month when the opportunity arises. When there is no covered call opportunity, i.e. when the market is stretched on the upside, you should keep a large arbitrate position. As the market goes into a correction and the cost of carry becomes negative, you can shift from the arbitrage position to the covered call position. If a trader can have some less risky returns to back up his futures trading, this adds to his confidence and improves the futures trading as well.

Disciplined traders have reasonable risk and return expectations and are open to using less risky and less exciting strategies of making money, which helps them tide over rough periods in the markets.

A Disciplined Trader Treats Trading as a Business and Keeps a Positive Attitude

Trading can be an expensive adventure sport. It should be treated as a business and should be very profit oriented. Disciplined traders review their performance at regular intervals and try to identify causes of both superior and inferior performance. The focus should be on consistent profits rather than erratic large profits and losses. Also, trading performance should not be made a judgement on an individual; rather, it should be considered a consequence of right or wrong actions. Disciplined traders are able to identify when they are out of sync with the market and need to reduce position size, or keep away altogether. Successful trading is like dancing in rhythm with the market. Unsuccessful traders often cut down on all other expenses but refuse to see what might be wrong with their trading methods. Denial is a costly attitude in trading. If you see that a particular trade is not working the way you had expected, reduce or eliminate your positions and see what is going on. Most disciplined and successful traders are very humble. Humility is a virtue that traders should learn on their own, else the market makes sure that they do. Ego and an "I can do no wrong" attitude in good times can lead to severe drawdowns in the long term.

Also, bad days in trading should be accepted as cheerfully as the good ones. There is a cost of trading that the family of every trader bears as well. They are the ones who need to live with the trader's frustrations and depression. So disciplined traders maintain composure whether they have made a profit or not on a particular day and avoid mood swings. A good way to do this is to also participate in activities other than trading and let the mind rest so that it is fresh for the next trading day.

A Disciplined Trader Does Not Blame the Market

Disciplined traders do not blame the market, the government, the companies or anyone else, conveniently excluding themselves, for their losses. The market gives ample opportunities to traders to make money. It is only the trader's fault if he fails to recognise them. Also, the market has various phases. It is overbought sometimes and oversold at other times. It is trending some of the time and choppy at others. It is for a trader to take maximum advantage of favourable market conditions and keep away from unfavourable onces. With the help of derivatives, it is now possible to make some money in all kinds of markets. So the trader needs to look for opportunities all the time.

To my mind, the important keys to making long term money in trading are:

- Keeping losses small. Remember all losses start small.
- Ride as many big moves as possible.
- Avoid overtrading.
- Never try to impose your will on the market.

It is impossible to practice all of the above perfectly. If you can, then you would not be reading this book. I certainly can't but I am improving on every aspect with every trade. I believe if a trader can practice all of the above with some degree of success, improvement in trading performance can be dramatic.

A Disciplined Trader Keeps a Cushion

If new traders are lucky to come into a market during a roaring bull phase, they sometimes think that the market is the best place to put all one's money. But disciplined and seasoned traders know that if the market starts acting differently in the future, which it surely will, profits will stop pouring in and there might even be periods of losses. So do not commit more than a certain amount to the market at any given point of time. Take profits from your broker whenever you have them in your trading account and stow them away in a separate account. I would go to the extent of saying that you might even consider investing in real estate as well if the profits are substantial. I say this because the market is like a deep and big well. No matter how much money you put in it, it can all vanish. So by having an account where you accumulate profits during good times, it helps you when markets turn unfavourable.

This also makes drawdowns less stressful as you have the cushion of previously earned profits. Trading is about walking a tightrope most times. Make sure you have enough cushion if you fall.

A Disciplined Trader Knows There is No Holy Grail in the Market

There is no magical key to this or any other stock market. If there were, the investment banks who spend billions of dollars on research would snap it up. There is no software or trading book which can give you enormous wealth. They can only give you tools and skills that you can learn to apply. And, finally, there is no free lunch; every trading penny has to be earned. I would recommend that each trader identify his own style, his own patterns, his own horizon and the set-ups that he is most comfortable with and practice them to perfection. You need only to be able to trade very few patterns to make consistent profits in the market.

In general, a good charting software is more than enough. I use 5-minute, 30-minute and end-of-day data for my trading and it's more than enough for me. No amount of gizmos can make a difference to your trading. There are no signals that are always 100% correct, so stop looking for them. Focus, instead, on percentage trades, trying to catch large moves and keeping your methodology simple. What needs constant improving are discipline and your trading psychology. At end of the day, money is not made by how complicated-looking your analysis is but whether it gets you in the right trade at the right time. On the Net, a lot of experts often suggest highly complicated strategies as well as indicators but remember nothing is perfect, least of all complicated strategies. Over-analysis can lead to paralysis and that is death for a trader. If you can't pull the trigger at the right time, then all your analysis and knowledge is a waste.

Remember analysts are paid a pittance of what successful traders can make. Also most analysts are not good traders, possibly because their focus is too wide, or because they get too involved with overvaluation and undervaluation. Analysis should be implementable in order to make trading profits. A lot of people believe that looking at the US market all night long gives an indication of the activity in Indian markets, or looking at Nasdaq futures would give a hint about how the Indian bourses would behave. I beg to differ with them. Unless there are extreme readings because of a specific reason, every market has its own rhythm and the chart patterns alone should be seriously looked at and taken as the final word. If you are wrong, the worst that can then happen is that your stop loss would get hit.

Traits of the Indisciplined Trader

I am qualified to speak on this subject because I was an indisciplined trader for a long time and the market hammered me into line and forced me to change my approach.

Indisciplined Traders Jump in During the First Half-hour of the Trading Session

The first half-hour of the trading day is driven by emotion, affected by overnight movements in the global markets, and hangover of the previous day's trading. Also, this is the period used by the market to entice novice traders into taking a position which might be contrary to the real trend which emerges only later in the day. Most experienced traders simply watch the markets for the first half of the day for intraday patterns and any subsequent trading breakouts.

Indisciplined Traders Fail to Hear the Market's Message

Personally, I try to hear the message of the markets and then try to confirm it with the charts. During the trading day, I like to watch if the market is able to hold certain levels or not. I like to go long around the end of the day if supported by patterns, and if the prices are consistently holding on to higher levels. I like to go short if the market is giving up higher levels, unable to sustain them and the patterns support a downmove of the market. This technique is called tape watching and all full-time traders practice it in some shape or form. If the markets are choppy and oscillate within a small range, then the market's message is to keep out.

Hearing the message of the market can be particularly important in times of significant news. The market generally reacts in a fashion contrary to most peoples' expectation. Let us consider two recent Indian events of significance.

One was the Gujarat earthquake that took place on 26 January 2001 and the other the 13 December 2001 terrorist attack on the Indian parliament. Both these events appeared catastrophic at first glance. TV channels suggested that the earthquake would devastate the country's economy because Gujarat has the largest number of investors and their confidence would be shattered, making the stock market plunge.

Tragic as both the events were, the market reacted in a different way to each by the end of the day. In both cases the markets plunged around 170 points when it opened, in both cases it tried to recover and while it managed a full recovery in the case of the Gujarat earthquake, it could not do so in the Parliament attack case. The market was proven correct on both counts. The Gujarat earthquake actually held the possibility of boosting the economy as reconstruction had to be taken up, and also because most of the big installations, including the Jamnagar Refinery, escaped damage. In the case of the attack on parliament, although traders assessed that terrorist attacks were nothing new in the country but the market did not recover because it could see some kind of military build-up ahead from both India and Pakistan. And markets hate war and uncertainty.

In both these cases what helped the cause of the traders were the charts. If the charts say that the market is acting in a certain way, go ahead and accept it. The market is right all the time. This is probably even more true than the more common wisdom about the customer being the king. If you can accept the market as king, you will end up as a very rich trader, indeed. Herein lies one reason why people who think they are very educated and smart often get trashed by the market because this market doesn't care who you are and it's certainly not there to help you. So expect no mercy from it; in fact, think of it as something that is there to take away your money, unless you take steps to protect yourself.

Indiscipline Traders Ignore the Phase the Market Is In

It is important to know what phase the market is in — whether it's in a trending or a trading phase. In a trending phase, you go and buy/sell breakouts, but in a trading phase you buy weakness and sell strength. Traders who do not understand the mood of the market often end up using the wrong indicators in the wrong market conditions. This is an area where humility comes in. Trading in the market is like blind man walking with the help of a stick. You need to be extremely flexible in changing positions and in trying to develop a feel for the market. This feel is then backed by the various indicators, such as the ADX, in confirming the phase of the market. Indisciplined traders, driven by their ego, often ignore the phase the market is in.

Indisciplined Traders Fail to Realise that Reducing Position Size Does Not Mean a Lack of Faith in One's Ability

Traders should be flexible in reducing their position size whenever the market is not giving clear signals. For example, if you take an average position of 3,000 shares in Nifty futures, you should be ready to reduce it to 1,000 shares. This can happen either when trading counter trend or when the market is not displaying a strong trend. Your exposure to the market should depend on the market's mood at any given point in the market. You should book partial profits as soon as the trade starts earning two to three times the average risk taken.

Indisciplined Traders Fail to Treat Every Trade As Just Another Trade

Indisciplined traders often think that a particular situation is sure to give profits and sometimes take risk several times their normal level. This can lead to a heavy drawdown as such situations often do not work out. Every trade is just another trade and only normal profits should be expected every time. Supernormal profits are a bonus when they — rarely! — occur but should not be expected. The risk should not be increased unless your account equity grows enough to service that risk.

Indisciplined Traders are Over-Eager to Book Profits

Profits in any trading account are often skewed to only a few trades. Traders should not be over-eager to book profits so long the market is acting right. Most traders tend to book profits too early in order to enjoy the winning feeling, thereby letting go substantial trends even when they have got a good entry into the market. If at all, profit booking should be done in stages, always keeping some position open to take advantage of the rest of the move. Remember trading should consist of small profits, small losses, and big profits. Big losses are what must be avoided. The purpose of trading should be to get a position substantially into money, and then maintain trailing stop losses to protect profits.

Most trading is breakeven trading. Accounts sizes and income from trading are enhanced only when you make eight to ten times your risk. If you can make this happens once a month or even once in two months, you would be fine. The important point here is to not get shaken by the daily noise of the market and to see the market through to its logical target. Remember, most money is made not by brilliant entries but by sitting on profitable positions long enough. It's boring to do nothing once a position is taken but the maturity of a trader is known not by the number of trades he makes but the amount of time he sits on profitable trades and hence the quantum of profits that he generates.

Indisciplined Traders Often Use Trading for Emotional Highs

Trading is an expensive place to get emotional excitement or to be treated as an adventure sport. Traders need to keep a high degree of emotional balance to trade successfully. If you are stressed because of some unrelated events, there is no need to add trading stress to it. Trading should be avoided in periods of high emotional stress.

Indisciplined Traders Don't Realise that Trading Decisions Are Not About Consensus Building

Our training since childhood often hampers the behaviour necessary for successful trading. We are always taught that whenever we take a decision, we should consult a number of people, and then do what the majority thinks is right. The truth of this market is that it never does what the majority thinks it will do.

Trading is a loner's job. Traders should not talk to a lot of people during trading hours. They can talk to experienced traders after market hours but more on methodology than on what the other trader thinks about the market. If a trader has to ask someone else about his trade then he should not be in it. Traders should constantly try to improve their trading skills and by trading skills I mean not only charting skills but also position sizing and money management skills. Successful traders recognise that money cannot be made equally easily all the time in the market. They back off for a while if the market is too volatile or choppy.

The above are general ideas on what should and should not be done. Obviously, there are no set ways on how to achieve these goals. As in most cases, the end is what matters and not necessarily the means.

My Trading Manual

Different traders develop their own methods to deal with the issues and psychology in trading. I am presenting below a manual of how I approach my trading and what I do before and after I initiate a trade. This is just one way of doing things; traders can improve upon this as they go along, or follow totally different methods to achieve similar goals.

Preparation for Trading

Here is how I do it:

- Every evening I get the end of day data around 4 p.m. That is when I began my analysis. My charts are religiously updated every evening. This is one ritual I do not miss if I have to trade the following day. Remember, a trader's day never ends.
- First of all I go through all the broad indices in the following order: Nifty, S & P CNX 500, Nifty Junior, Defty. This gives me a feel for the broad market and the breadth of any market move. The conclusion I draw from this is the underlying strength of a market move. If the indices are secular in their movement, I am more confident of the move. If the move is restricted only to index stocks while the other indices are moving in the opposite direction, I take it as a time to get cautious. If the index stocks are doing nothing and the midcaps are moving, these moves do not sustain because it's the retailers who are generally in the midcaps and unless the frontline stocks move, the midcap moves cannot be sustained. Also, I look at the ADX of all these indices to see the strength of the ongoing trend and identify the phase of the market in terms of whether it is trading or trending. The objective of this stage is therefore to identify the direction and the strength of the market.
- I then look at the various sectoral indices. In the Indian context, these are banking, pharma, technology, PSU, FMCG, auto, etc. and separate the strong sectors from the weak ones.
- Based on whether the main trend of the market is up or down, I select the strongest and the weakest sectors and then select their strongest and weakest stocks.
- I then look through the charts of all these stocks to see if any specific set-ups exist. At this point, I write all the set-ups that may breakout on the following day along with stop losses, entry and exit levels.
- Other situations I like to look for are volume breakouts. Most technical analysis software allows for checking the volume gainers. This can also be done at the Yahoo India finance site. I like to look at this list because the top volume movers can often be stocks which have broken out on heavy volume from set-ups and there could be likely follow-up. But here I try to ignore the cash group

stocks and concentrate mainly on ones which have derivatives. In India, it is wise to check the pedigree of the company before taking the volume leaders too seriously.

- At the end of this exercise I have a nice list of set-ups and trades written down to the last detail in my notebook. I try not to overanalyse, also, not to oversimplify things. If something is not clear, I move on to the next one. I like to trade only the surest patterns and set-ups.

Trade Execution

No matter how much net practice (paper trading) one does, the true test of a trader comes only on the real pitch and in playing with the big boys. Trade execution is very important to ensure that you do not end up buying tops and selling bottoms although that too will sometimes happen. The goal of good trade execution is to get into low risk situations which give you a wide stop loss and the trade gets enough room to gyrate before moving on and you need to actually be wrong for the stop loss to be hit. Buying oversold situations in an uptrend and overbought situations in a downtrend should be the goal of trade execution:

- The best entries are achieved in the latter half of the day. I avoid all trade execution in the market's first hour. The advantage of entering trades late, and particularly in the last hour is that by then the market has had all its intraday swings and is moving in the direction it finally wants to take.
- The one exception to the above rule is that if the market gaps down and the main trend is up; I like to buy when the market opens. This generally provides an excellent breakeven level and is usually a very high percentage trade. Once you get a trade that immediately moves about one average true range into the money, you just need to trail stops and let the profits roll in. The same applies to sell side trades.
- I have access to 5- and 30-minute data as well as I like to take trades when some kind of a breakout happens on a pattern on any of these charts; 30-minute charts for daily entries and 5-minute chart for intraday entries, provided the main trend is in place on the higher time frame.

- If a trade on, say, the Nifty is executed on the long side and the stop loss of one average true range is hit, I would like to see the breadth of the market and see if the market is making lower tops. If so, I reverse the trade. So I take a stop loss getting hit as a signal for a trade possibility on the opposite side. These trades are often big trades since, like me, other traders could also be trapped.
- I take profits on overnight positions at the opening if the market opens with a favourable gap, but new positions should not be initiated.
- Gap openings in the direction of the main trend should be dealt with very carefully. Personally, I like to wait a while till the market makes some kind of trading range beyond the gap, or the gap gets filled after the opening and takes support at some point before taking action. As risk free as the gaps in the opposite direction are, I have found gaps in the direction of the trend to be extremely risky. Keeping patience in the case of such gaps is the best strategy.

Trade Management

Contrary to what most people think, the part of trading that makes you the most money is trade management. Trade management is the part that happens once a trade has been taken on. Many traders do not get far enough to critically review their trade management skills, since most trading careers end while learning the mumbo jumbo of technical analysis.

Once the trade is on, three things can happen:

1. Trade moves deep in the money quickly

This is the situation all of us hope for. I start the trade with a one average true range stop and as the market moves into the money by one average true range, I move the stop to breakeven. This means I give the market room for at least one average true range to go through its intraday gyrations. Intraday pivots can be used as the stops for intraday charts.

I just let the trade reach its logical targets which have been identified in my trading plan. I will hold on to the trade as long as the market keeps acting right. This means unless there is overwhelming evidence of trend change, I would not get out of the trade. This might take away some profits from you if the markets turn exactly from the targets identified earlier but the tendency to stay longer with the trade will help in the long-term because the market operates on excesses. As the targets approach, however, stops can be tightened or partial profits booked but keeping some of your position will keep you in the trade till the end.

At this point, I would say at the risk of reducing the importance of charting that traders should not become a slave to indicators or charts — the market should have the final word. Indicators and charts provide the road map but these charts depend on actual market action, and not *vice versa*. Also, try to trade with the trend unless there is overwhelming evidence of a trend reversal. In counter-trend trades it's important to remember that technical targets may not be met and you should be prepared to book profits at the first sign of reversal.

2. The Trade Does Nothing for an Entire Session

This can happen in choppy markets where the index and stocks can stay in a narrow range for many days. The index or the stock may meander around the breakeven level, neither hitting the stop loss nor advancing any further. In such situations it's best to get out of the trade and make a fresh entry another day. Alternately, you could consider selling straddles or covered calls. But a trade that does not immediately move into profit seldom turns out to be a winner in the end.

3. The Trade Immediately Goes and Hits Your Stop

There are two reasons why the stop loss might be hit:

1. It was placed too close and got hit by the noise in the market. To check this out, observe the market for a while and try to enter the next breakout and also keep a wider breakout.
2. If a stop loss of one average true range gets hit, then you can be sure it probably was not noise. You should then consider the breadth of the market, look at intraday patterns on the index as well as key stocks, and consider selling on the next rally. The best moves occur when the market initially changes direction because a number of traders do not take timely action when the market is not acting in their direction.

Finally, remember the following thumb rules in all types of markets.

- Extraordinary market volatility indicates an impending decline and is a sign of distribution, particularly at the top of the market.
- If the volume drops in an upmove and the market goes extremely quiet, it means that the fuel needed to keep the market is running out and it would soon go into correction, or will reverse trends.
- If the volume drops in a downmove, and the market becomes quiet it means a slow accumulation might be taking place. Look to trade the first breakout from a consolidation pattern.
- If a market is dropping on heavy volume, it means there is more downside yet to come and people are getting out in a hurry.

Indians love speculation. They love taking risks with whatever they have. Often they are cheated by lottery owners and casino owners into thinking that huge riches await them. At other times they lose their shirts to frivolous ventures such as plantation companies. but derivative trading is different, it is a game of skill where the best man wins. It cannot be manipulated to give an unfair advantage to anyone.

Chapter 12

Money Management

The Size of Your Trading Positions should be Based on the Size of Your Trading Capital

To my mind, one of the most neglected aspects of trading is money management. So neglected and ignored is the topic that most traders never know it exists and go out of business without actually knowing what they missed out on. Most trading books and seminars focus on set-ups, entries and, sometimes, exits. The reason for this is that money management is not a particularly glamorous or marketable topic for any seminar or book. But traders of all time frames should take this chapter more seriously than any other because this is the topic that alerts traders about whether they can sustain their business.

People have different views on what money management actually is. Let's first be clear what money management is not:

- Money management is not the part of your trading system that indicates how much you can lose on a given trade. Most retail traders have the placement of stops drilled into them by technical analysts, erroneously, as the ultimate money management tool.
- Money management is not diversification. Many people believe that diversification is the best way to properly manage money. This would be taking too simplistic a view in terms of trading methodology.
- Money management is not risk control. It is certainly not buying call and put options.
- Money management is not risk avoidance. It is certainly not having all your assets in fixed income securities.
- Money management is not that part of the trading system that maximises performance.

- Money management is not part of the system that tells you what to invest in. It certainly has nothing to do with technical analysis or charting and all the other techniques we have discussed so far.

What is Money Management?

So, what exactly is money management?

Money management is that part of your trading system that answers the question "How much?" throughout the course of a trade.

Trading, like every other business, needs to start with a certain amount of equity or "seed capital". Traders remain in business so long as they have this seed capital with them.

Drawdowns

Drawdowns are, of course, a part of every trader's life.

Let's say a trader has trading equity of Rs 10 lakh and after a string of losses is left with Rs 7 lakh. He is thus said to have had a drawdown of 30%. After this, only when the trader is able to make back is original capital can he think about profits.

Let's consider a simple game to understand the effects of drawdowns on a trader's trading ability, something as simple as tossing a coin. Now the two possible outcomes of this game are either heads or tails. Our trader in the game wins if he gets heads and loses if he gets tails. He starts with Rs 1,000 and risks Rs 100 on every toss. Let's assume he tosses the coin three times and loses every time, a distinct possibility. Now he is down to Rs 700. If he were now to assume that he will win the next toss because he has had three losses in a row, that's a gambler's fallacy because his chances of winning the next toss are still only 50%, the probability of a favourable outcome. Let us assume that based on this fallacy he decides to bet Rs 300 because he is so sure he will win. However, he loses again and now has only Rs 400 left. From here on, he now needs to make 150% just to breakeven. It is, therefore, highly unlikely that he would:

- Breakeven in a short period of time, or
- Make any substantial profits.

Lesson: the trader failed in this simple game because he risked too much money on a single trade.

Recovery after Drawdowns

Table 12.1 clearly brings out that drawdowns upto 20% need only a 25% gain to recover; anything over 20% begins to get very difficult.

Most traders come to the equity markets with undercapitalised accounts but with pipe dreams of making millions and this is what ultimately causes their downfall. In India, particularly, the huge minimum derivative contract sizes suggest that only high net worth investors and institutions should participate in it. Still everyday millions of small traders try to profit from the derivatives market and fail. That is because these people are practicing poor money management — their account size is simply too small to begin with. And because of their inadequate account size, the mathematical odds of failure are very high.

In my opinion, if a person has Rs 50 lakh as total account equity, the total naked derivatives exposure (excluding covered calls) at any point of time should not exceed 10-15% of the portfolio, i.e. Rs 5 lakh to Rs 7 lakh, and the balance 85-90% of the portfolio should be in a covered calls with underlying stocks being held. This way the 85-90% of the account grows steadily, albeit at a slower pace, while the kicker is provided by the naked derivatives exposure. This parameter can equally be applied to accounts of all sizes. Positions can be added as one's trading account grows in size. This is my way of money management.

Notice in Table 12.1 how much your account has to recover from various drawdown sizes just to recover to breakeven.

Table 12.1

Drawdowns	Gain Needed to Recover
5%	5.3%
10%	11.1%
15%	17.6%
20%	25%
25%	33%
30%	42.9%
40%	66.7%
50%	100%
60%	150%
70%	300%
80%	900%

Position Sizing Strategies

Professional gamblers like to talk about two types of postion sizing strategies, namely martingale and anti-martingale strategies. Martingale strategies suggest increasing bet sizes when equity decreases during a losing streak. Anti-martingale strategies, on the other hand suggest increasing one's bet size only during winning streaks, i.e. when one's equity increases.

If you have played roulette or our very own "Lucky 7" at fairs or the local Diwali Mela, you might have considered the purest form of martingale strategies which simply amounts to doubling your bet size when you lose. For example, if you lose Re 1, you next bet Rs 2. If you lose Rs 2, then you next bet Rs 4, and so on. When you finally win, which you eventually do, you will be ahead by the original size of your bet.

Casinos love people who play such martingale strategies. First any game of chance will have losing streaks. And, second, when the probability of winning is less than 50%, the losing streaks can be quite significant.

Let's assume that you have a losing streak of ten consecutive losses. If you had started betting Re 1, and doubled every subsequent bet, then you would have lost Rs 2,047 over the streak. You will now be betting Rs 2,048 simply to get your original rupee back. Thus your win-loss ratio for less than a 50:50 bet is 1:4097. Looked at another way, you will need to be risking a loss of over Rs 4,000 to get Re 1 in profits. And most casinos might have betting limits. So the martingale strategies generally do not work — whether in the casino or in the market.

Most Indian traders will connect with this strategy as the loss averaging strategy which has never really worked for anyone. My take on loss averaging is that if you have made a good trade, it works from the word go. Usually taking the first loss results in the smallest loss. So it's important not to try and trade your way out of losses but to cut them straightaway.

On the other hand, anti-martingale strategies, which call for larger risk,.do work — both in the casino and in the market. Position sizing systems that work call for increasing one's position size when you make money. This holds for gambling, trading and investing. The purpose of position sizing is to tell you how many units — shares or contracts — you should take on, given the size of your account. A position sizing decision might even suggest that you don't have enough money to take any positions at all because the risk is too big. It allows you to determine your risk and reward characteristics by working out how many units you will risk on a given trade — and on each trade in a given portfolio. It also helps you equalise your trade exposure among the elements of your portfolio.

As a rule of thumb, I believe that the overall leverage used by a person should not be more than 33%. Thus, for a 200 share Nifty contract, which has a margin of Rs 32,000 at 1,600 Nifty (at a margin of 10%) and a total contract value of Rs 3,20,000, I would be comfortable having at least Rs 2 lakh in my trading account, which works out to approx. 66% of the contract value. Now some would wonder why I need Rs. 2 lakh in my account when the margin required in only Rs 32,000. This is to ensure that a drawdown of 15-20%, which is always possible, does not throw me out of business. Another contract can be added when the account increases by another Rs 2 lakh, but not before that. A more aggressive trader might believe Rs 1 lakh is enough to trade a similar contract. But in the long run my chances of sustaining in the market are much better than his. There is no need for the other 85-90% of the account equity to sit idle; it can be used to earn returns of about 4% a month with covered calls.

Some people think they are doing an adequate job of position sizing by having a "money management stop". Such stops can be placed through the trading terminal and are triggered if particular prices are hit. Most people decide on such stops by just considering the rupee loss they are willing to take. But this kind of stop does not tell you how many units you ought to buy in relation to the overall size of your trading capital, or what is appropriate for you for a given trade, and therefore such a stop has nothing to do with position sizing. Controlling risk by determining the amount of loss if you are stopped out is not the same as controlling risk through a position sizing model that determines "how many", and whether you can afford even one position.

We now turn to a discussion of the anti-martingale strategies for position sizing, in which your position size goes up with your account size.

We are going to use a trend following system for the purpose of explaining these strategies using the Nifty futures; volumes should in any case be kept lower in choppy markets.

Strategy 1: One Unit per Fixed Amount of Money

This method tells you the size of your position for every "X" rupees in your account. The system I use is to trade one Nifty futures contract for every Rs 2 lakh of my trading equity. This method has the advantage that a trade is never rejected simply because it's too risky.

Consider the following two money management strategies:

There is one trader who trades one Nifty contract for every Rs 2 lakh in his account. This trader has Rs 6 lakh in his account. There is another trader with a trading equity of Rs 10 lakh who does not take a trade if it has more than a 3% risk.

Now consider a Nifty futures set up which ends up being very profitable; the first trader took the trade and did very well for the month. The second trader, since he limits his risk to 3%, avoided the trade and thus had a below average month. The same trade could well have had the reverse consequences, making the second trader look very smart. As you can see, the benefit of the first strategy is that you take every signal.

On the other hand, there are certain disadvantages as well of the first trader's technique.

Not All Futures are Alike

1,200 shares of Nifty futures at a Nifty level of 1,500 will attract a margin of Rs 1.8 lakh (10%) which will allow you to hold contracts worth Rs 18 lakh. On the other hand, 1,200 stock futures of Reliance at an underlying price of Rs. 510 will attract a margin of Rs 122,400 at a rate of 20% margin (stock futures have higher margin) and allow you to hold contracts worth Rs 612,000.

At the time of writing this book, Nifty had an average daily range, also known as average true range of 30 point and Reliance had an average true range of 13 points. Let us assume that a stop loss of a day's average true range is put on both the futures contracts as is sometimes necessary in volatile markets.

The 6 Nifty contracts could lose you a maximum of Rs 36,000 whereas the 2 Reliance contracts could lose you maximum of Rs

15,600. So each trading opportunity in the futures market is different and the same criteria cannot be uniformly applied.

Very Low Leverage or a Very Small-Sized Account Can Hinder Raising the Position Size

This can occur in two ways. Consider a trader trading one Nifty contract for every Rs 5 lakh who has a Rs 10 lakh account. He will need a 50 per cent return for his account to go upto Rs 15 lakh which will enable him to increase his position size.

On the other hand, if a trader has a Rs 2 lakh account and trades only one unit, he would need to double his account to be able to add another unit to his position.

A third trader with a Rs 30 lakh account, trading one contract for each Rs 2 lakh, will need only to move up to Rs. 32 lakh to be able to add another unit; this is only a 6.6% increase. This is my preferred method of position sizing.

Strategy 2: Equal Value Units

The equal units strategy is typically used with stocks but can be used with futures as well.

Assume a trader has an account equity of Rs. 20 lakh. (I have assumed the figure of Rs 20 lakh for ease of calculation). The equal value units strategy says you determine the position size by dividing your capital into five, or any other number, of equal instalments. Thus, we can have five units of Rs 4 lakh each. In the futures market, you might decide that with Rs 20 lakh you want to control as much product as possible. One bottleneck with this strategy in the Indian derivatives market is the large contract sizes. This would be a major problem as at a Nifty level of 1,600, maybe not with a Rs 20 lakh account but with, say, a Rs 5 lakh account; for example a single contract of Telco, consisting of 3,300 shares, will control product worth over Rs. 10 lakh, and so on as shown in Table 12.2

Table 12.2

Futures	*No. of Shares*	*Margin* (Rs.)*	*You Control Product Worth (Rs.)*
Satyam@ 350	2,400 (2 contracts)	4,20,000 (50%)	8,40,000
Nifty@ 1600	1,400 (7 contracts)	3,84,000 (20%)	19,20,000
Reliance@ 492	3,000 (5 contracts)	442,800 (30%)	14,76,000
ACC@ 226	6,000 (4 contracts)	406,800 (30%)	13,56,000
Tisco@ 360	3,600 (2 contracts)	388,800 (30%)	12,96,000
Total		20,42,000	68,88,000

(*Margin percentages assumed are hypothetical and can vary depending on market conditions.)

Now some would call this a diversified futures portfolio, but personally I am not comfortable about putting all my money into a leveraged product such as futures. Shares for which derivatives are allowed all have very high beta and tend to rise or fall together. I would instead take an exposure on the Nifty for diversification and ease of tracking. But that is simply my personal preference. However, if the Nifty is not showing any trend, I would then look at individual stock futures, or at a basket of stock futures. But under no circumstances would I have a naked futures position totalling more than 15% of my total trading account.

Traders should always keep track of the total product value they are controlling and their leverage. This strategy has the drawback that you can increase the size of your position only very slowly, particularly considering the lot sizes in India.

Strategy 3: The Per Cent Risk Model

When entering a position, it is critical for a trader to have decided the point at which he would exit in order to preserve his capital. I think that no more than 2% of the trading capital should be risked on any single trade. Again, this could vary a bit according to the stock; for a technology stock it could be on the higher side than in the case of an old economy stock, but the maximum should stay at 2%. Thus the position can be sized in such a way that no more than 2% of your entire capital is at risk at any point. That's what I personally do.

Taking again an example of the Nifty contract for a Rs 10 lakh naked futures portfolio, and considering a 2% risk, the risk on the potion needs to be capped at Rs 20,000. Suppose the trade you are taking has a 20-point stop loss, then your futures position should be no more than 1,000 shares of Nifty.

If a trader has a system with very small stops, then he needs to adopt much smaller risk levels. Thus, for example, if the stops are less than the daily range of prices, then you need guidelines which are about half of 2%. Personally speaking, I focus a lot more on good entry set-ups and keep a little larger stop when I get into a trade, up to 5% of the naked futures portion of my account which again works out to about 2% of my total account. For a long time I traded futures with very small stops and my stop losses often got hit before the position finally moved in the desired direction. Accordingly, I decided to increase my stop loss and simultaneously filter my entries even more, and only enter once I had the market perfectly set up. In practice, no matter how good you are at charting, often positions initially move in the reverse direction, sometimes because of noise and sometimes because of a pullback after a breakout. So a wider initial stop can be used but then the position needs to be sized accordingly keeping the daily range in mind. My results have been dramatically different since I widened my stops, but this should be done considering the size of the account. Once a trade moves at least one daily range in the money, I use stops at breakeven. I keep close trailing stops only in trading markets. In trending markets, I would look for real evidence of reversal before keeping a close stop. I would keep at least half a daily range or a pivot as the stop, whichever is closer. Position resizing can be done as the account grows in size, so does the per cent risk.

Strategy 4: The Per Cent Volatility Model

Volatility refers to the amount of daily price movement of the underlying instrument over an arbitrary period of time. It's the direct measurement of the price change a trader is likely to be exposed to — whether favourable or unfavourable. If you equate the volatility of each position that you take by making it a fixed percentage of your capital, then you are basically equalising the possible market fluctuations of each portfolio element to which you are exposed in the immediate future.

Thus, if the various volatilities of stock futures are sized in terms of the percentage risk, the volatility of the entire portfolio would be standardised.

Let's try to understand this with the help of an example.

We shall assume an account size of Rs 40 lakh divided equally into four parts and a risk percentage of 2%

Now on a portfolio divided into four parts, the total risk on the entire portfolio allowed is Rs 80,000 and is divided into Rs 20,000 for each of the four parts. As you can see from Table 12.3, the problem that arises is that the appropriate sizes are sometimes not available. But this is again a very safe method, especially for beginner traders. Positions are sized according to the volatility as well as percentage of risk.

Table 123

Futures	*Daily Range (Rs.)*	*Risk Amount (Rs.)*	*No. of Shares*
Nifty	30	20,000	666
Satyam	11	20,000	1,818
ACC	7	20,000	2,857
Tisco	13	20,000	1,538

In my view, the two best strategies are the first and the fourth. The benefit with Strategy 1 is that you can measure the amount of leverage, vary it according to your comfort level, and increase positions a your account size goes up. The benefit of Strategy 4 is that position are sized according to volatility and risk percentage and hence defin the rules for traders.

Stops

In conjunction with the money management methods explained above, stops are a very important aspect of trading. A stop is that predecided point on a chart which defines the amount of risk a trader is going to take.

There are various methods of placing stops and then trading them. Stops are as much about initiating trades as they are about trade management once the position is in the money. It is very critical for a person to be clear about the methodology of placing stops, and adhering to it once the trade is initiated.

To my mind, keeping mental stops, or having very close stops, or changing stops mid-trade are all counter productive. Stops placed too close often get hit because of noise or random movements in th prices of futures, while stops placed too far may actually skew risk and return. However, a trader has to assume that no trade will be his last; all traders realise that sustainability in the business is key to making profits. When a trader goes out of business, the possibility of profits ends right there and then. We will discuss all of this in detail in this section.

Media analysts often talk of stops as a philosophy. I would say that putting rupee stops without any attention to one's position size is a colossal mistake. Often, stops suggested on television shows are 5-10% below the prevailing market prices. Following this, a trader will keep risking 5-10% of his capital on every trade, and a streak of losses will create such a bad drawdown that he will never recover from it. Stops on any trade or a basket of trades, at least initially, should not be more than 2% of the trader's account equity; the variable is the position size and not the size of the stop as is sometimes suggested.

The reason for putting stops is to pre-define your risk and also to avoid getting frozen into inaction when a position starts going against you. Any broker on NSE or BSE terminals will put the stop loss for you. The stop loss has both a trigger price and the limit price.

The Functions of a Stop

A stop has two useful functions.

First, it preserves capital when a trader is wrong. As sustainability in the business is the key to profits, it's important that the trader does not lose more than a predefined amount when he is proved wrong.

The second function of the stop loss is that it helps measure profit in terms of the risk taken. If a trader risks an X amount in every trade, he can thus measure his profit in terms of 2X, 3X ….. 10X, etc.

To illustrate this concept, let us assume a trader wins 50% of the trades he makes. Suppose he has a trading capital (account equity) of Rs 5,000 and, on average he makes Rs. 2X on every winning trade and loses X on every losing trade. Now take that X to be Rs 100 and assume the trader takes 100 trades. The two variables here are the number of times X and the winning ratio. Let's do a sensitivity analysis for both, for 100 trades, and varying the number of times X.

Table 12.3

Amount at Risk (Rs.)	*Winning Probability*	*Profit (Win) Multiple*	*Profit (Rs.)*
100	50%	2X	5,000
100	50%	5X	20,000
100	50%	10X	45,000
100	60%	2X	8,000
100	60%	5X	26,000
100	60%	10X	56,000

Table 12.4 clearly brings out how dramatically profitability improves if the win multiple improves even just marginally. This clearly proves you don't have to be right all the time to make big profits in the market. Many successful traders have wining probability only in the region of 30-40%, yet make most of their money on big trades.

Tackling Market Noise

Intra-day market movements usually have no material impact on the overall trend. In fact, most of these gyrations are caused by very temporary demand supply mismatches. Thus a trader needs to keep his stop losses far enough so that the noise does not throw him off the trade. This judgement is usually developed with years of practice. Although theoretically it appears a fine idea to buy breakouts out of ranges and patterns, or trade overbought and oversold levels, in reality a market often does nothing after these breakouts — and sometimes even reverses for a while before proceeding with the original trend. The key here is to keep a wider stop and size your positions as described earlier.

The key is to have a strong body of evidence before you enter a trade. Buy or sell signals should be matched across time frames, the breadth of the market has to be considered, and then the stops need to be placed in an area where the stop may not apparently logical. I say this because "logical" stops will usually be taken out by the market in case it reverses temporarily. Even after all care is taken, the stops may still be hit by strong countermoves called whipsaws but the number of such instances can be reduced. The average true range can be considered to be the measure of market noise. The charts in Figures 12.1 and 12.2 show examples where the market can have temporary reversals after a breakdown.

Figure 12.1

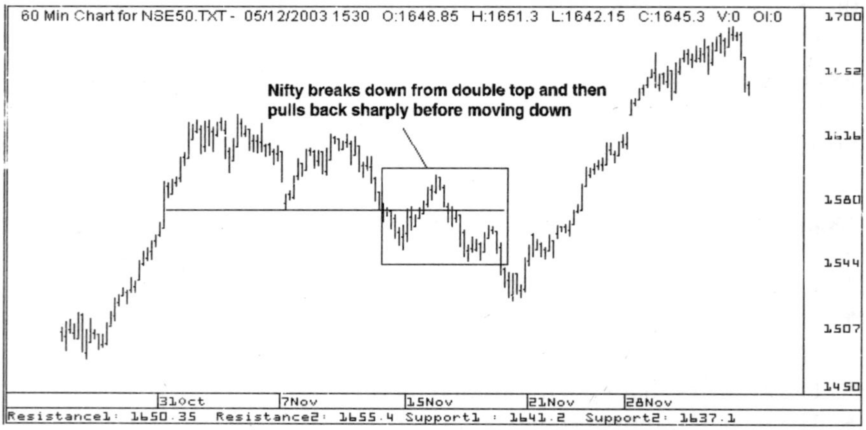

Figure 12.2

We now turn to some of the methods for placing stops.

Tight Stops

Being a swing trader, I generally hold my positions for four to five days. I use tight stops as trailing stops only once I am deep in the money in terms of profit. I do so as a method for protecting my profits rather than when entering a position. This is my opinion as a swing trader.

There are certain other advantages of tight stops. First, you lose much less money when a trade is aborted. Second, because of your small loss, you can make multiple attempts at re-entry. And, third, if you get such a move, your profit will be many times the amount of your initial risk.

Equally, tight stops have some serious shortcomings.

Tight stops result in many more trades in order to generate the same profits. In markets which are not trending very strongly, sometimes your stop can keep getting hit before the market moves in the desired direction. I used tight stops in the initial phase of any career and found that the number of times they got hit before a trade moved in the desired direction far exceeded the benefit of making high returns.

The other downside is that transaction costs add up since tight stops lead to overtrading. Cheap as trading is in India, a substantial part of the profit can be eaten away by tight stops.

My personal view on tight stops continues to be that they should be used when a trade is substantially in the money and the market is showing signs of reversing. You can then protect a large part of your profit by putting a tight stop.

Choosing a Stop

The factors which determine the nature of the stop are:

- A trader's objectives and the nature of his trading — i.e. day trading, position trading, or swing trading,
- The concept that is being traded, and
- The trader's temperament.
- Let's look at some of the stop strategies.

Rupee Stop

Rupee stops have certain benefits; for one, they define beforehand how much you can lose on a trade. These stops are also not predictable because they are not placed on the obvious supports and resistances on the chart. If these stops are placed some distance away from a support, they can be very effective. For example, a trader with a capital of Rs 10 lakh may decide to risk Rs 10,000 on a single trade.

But traders need to keep in mind the rules of money management and position sizing while using rupee stops. Personally, I believe in an upper limit on the amount being risked on every trade, but on the lower side each trade is different, each situation is different, and it would be a mistake to have a standard rupee stop loss for all situations.

Percentage Stop

Some people set stops by allowing the price to retrace a certain percentage of the entry price. For example, if the buying price in a trade is Rs 100, a stop is set 10% lower, at Rs 90. This practice is fine so long as the percentage is based on an objective criteria like a pivot. Arbitrary percentages on the other hand; will often lead to inefficient trade management, which usually means not achieving the entire profits possible.

Volatility Stops

Volatility stops are based on the assumption that, to at least some extent, the volatility represents noise. So if a volatility stop is placed at some multiple of the average true range, then the probability is that the stop is beyond the immediate noise of the market.

Time Stops

As I have said at other places in the book, a good trade works immediately. A trade which meanders around the breakeven level, or goes sideways; more often than not does not work out. Typically I wait for a couple days, including the day I initiated the trade, and use this time stop in conjunction with the pivot stop. I would also like to reiterate that technical analysis is not an exact science, and patterns and breakouts can and do fail, particularly in non-trending markets. So it's important for the trader to keep an open mind and if a trade is not working out within the time that he is comfortable with, he should re-evaluate the evidence and re-consider whether to continue in it. Getting out of a potentially unprofitable trade is also a strategy; the trader is not a loser if he gets out of a trade that is not working. You can always get back into the position if the stock or the index starts a move. Always remember, you cannot arm-twist the market to give you profits, so learn to observe its steps and dance with its rythm.

Pivot Stops

These are the stops that I use most extensively and have been very useful in my trading so far. I like to place these stops a couple of points above and below the previous pivots, since placing pivot stocks is a well known methodology. The larger the time frame on which the pivot is broken, the more is its relevance. Breaking of pivots often shows breach of support or resistance; also, it shows strength and weakness.

There are some rules I follow while using stops.

First I never change my stop; unless it's a trailing stop, my risk is the same on every trade since I do not differentiate trades on the basis of expectation.

Second, if my stops are hit and I take a loss, I stand back and review the market action for two possibilities:

1. My analysis was wrong. In that case, I try to see if I can reverse my position in the same trade because a failed breakout in one direction leads to a strong move in the other. (Figure 12.3)
2. I try to see if we are in a choppy phase of the market. If that is the case, I just fold my hands and sit back because my experience suggests that only market trends give traders money; and choppy markets take all of it, and more, back. The worst action in a choppy market would be to go on making trades in both directions in the hope of finding on profitable trades. Often I also reduce my volume to nominal if I do have to test waters. The market is like a girlfriend; if she says no, gentlemen must take that as a no.

I use pivots both to enter and exit trades. Breaking of an up pivot shows strength, breaking of a down pivot shows weakness.

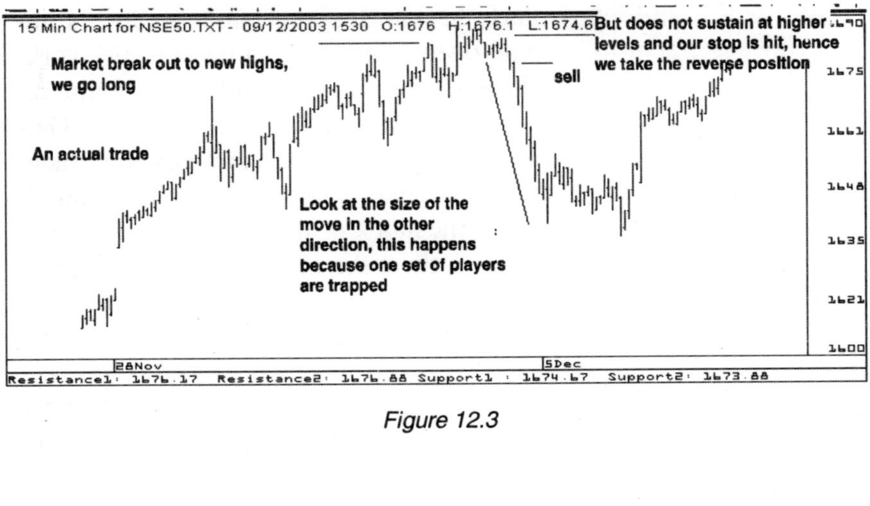

Figure 12.3

- I always buy a market which, along with other evidence of a market moving up, breaks the nearest upward pivot.
- I sell a market which, along with other evidence of market going down, breaks the nearest downward pivot.

So the pivot is trigger for all my actions. If a pivot is broken in either direction and the market whipsaws back in the opposite direction, it is prudent to wait till the market makes the next move and reduce volumes drastically on further trades.

But it is critical to be confident about the move that a trader anticipates is building up. In the market things are never clear till everybody is in the move. Taking a small position to test waters if you are not confident about the move is always advisable, the position can then be enlarged as the market moves in your favour. In other words, the position taken by a trader, within the parameters of money management, can vary with the amount of confidence a trader has in the move. (*see* Figures 12.4 and 12.5)

Figure 12.4

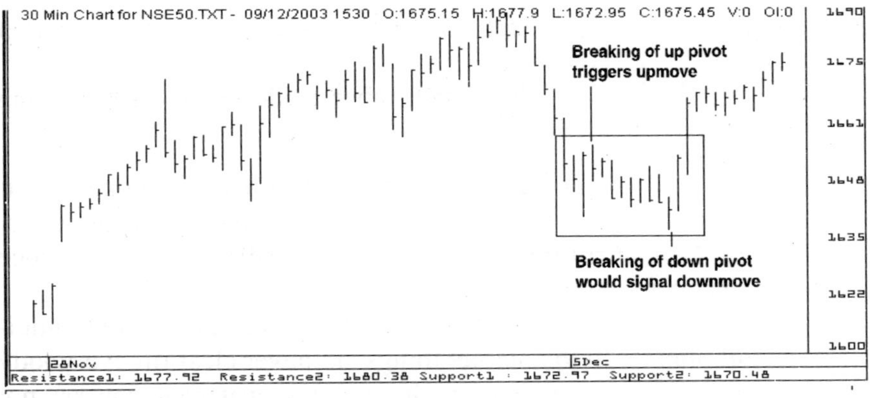

Figure 12.5

Exits

Most unsuccessful traders never really get to this part of the story. By the time they work through the entry methods, they have been beaten by the market. The exit aspect of trading is probably more important than even entries. On this point I am reminded of the mythological character in the *Mahabharata*, Abhimanyu, who knew how to enter a battle formation but did not know how to make a safe exit. He probably decided he would think about the exit once he was inside the formation, and we all know the tragic result of that misadventure. Most traders commit the same mistake in the markets. They begin to think about exits only once they are in a trade. And they meet with the same fate as did Abhimanyu.

I like to treat exits as a separate part of technical analysis, called trade management. I believe a good entry into a trade is only 25% of the job, albeit a very important one. The part that makes money is trade management. The skill of keeping a position through the gyrations of the market is as difficult to achieve, if not more, as are sound entries. As highlighted earlier in this chapter, most successful traders make most of their money from very few trades. So once you are in the right trade, it's critical to manage it well in order to get the maximum profit out of it. You can be assured that the market would try to shake you out more often than you think.

Rules for Good Exits

You Need to Decide the Exit Before Entering a Trade

Once you see an entry set-up, you must have two scenarios ready:

1. How do you exit if the trade moves against you; this is done with a stop loss.
2. How do you decide on an exit if the trade moves in your direction. This is done with the help of chart patterns and certain back-of-the-envelope calculations of various patterns. In my experience, I have found that these patterns are good approximations of the minimum objective. So that gives you the initial estimate of how far you are going to hold the trade. This includes locating targets on intraday as well as daily charts.

The methodology for targets on chart patterns has been described in the chapter on day trading (Chapter 5). Here we will look at a trading methodology which was not described there but which is very effective in trending markets.

All rallies pull back at some point, and then the rally resumes again. On average, a pullback is about 50% not only of the previous move but also the subsequent move. This rule works broadly even in a bear market. The important thing here is too use finesse. Targets do not mean that a trader needs to blindly exit his position at that point. Rather, he then needs to be a little cautious, lighten positions or tighten stops, etc. in order to protect his profits. (*see* Figure 12.6)

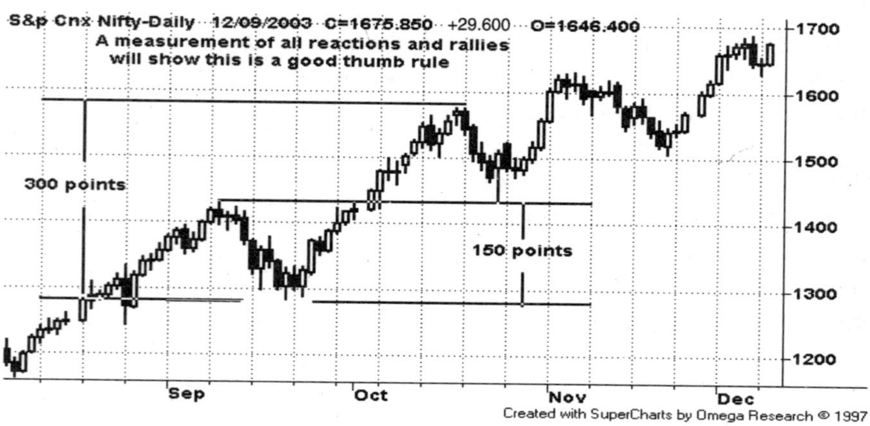

Figure 12.6

Let me describe a real trade that I took and how I managed it.

The Nifty was in an intermediate correction and had bounced back from 1,509. Looking at the intraday chart I decided to take the trade at 1,556, as the market broke out. I put my first stop right below the intraday pivot which was 1,540, which was also the day's low. Sure enough as soon as I took the trade the market went back to 1,546, and then started rallying from there. As it closed at 1,572, I moved my stop to breakeven. Now as the market kept moving up, I kept a trailing stop of one ATR for continuing in the position. As the market reached 1,670, very favourable election results were declared. The market initially rallied to 1,680 but then closed sort of indifferent at around 1,670. Now what was the message of the market here?

It was that the market was tiring out and even good news could not move it much higher. So I moved my stop to the previous intraday down pivot of 1,660. I decided that I should take my profits the next day, particularly as the market breadth had also deteriorated by the end of the day. On the intraday chart too there were bearish patterns. So the next day as the market rallied again to 1,680, I took my entire profits. After that, I waited. As the market began to break beyond 1,680, I went long again at 1,684, keeping my mind alert that a false breakout could have occurred. I kept the stop for this trade at the day's low at 1,676. The market tried to rally several times, even went up to 1,689 but could not sustain those levels and moved down sharply taking my stop with it. As soon as it took my stop, it also broke a downward pivot and I reversed the entire position and instead went short at 1,676 with a stop above the high of the day which in the case of Nifty futures was 1,685 and, lo and behold, the market went down sharply to close at 1,645 which gave me handsome profits on a day which had not begun so well. I would like to point out that I booked these profits on the downmove on the same day because the market was still in an uptrend and it could move back up at any point. If you are getting sharp profits on a countertrend day, you should take them because the main move can come into play at any time. This trade was described in parts in earlier chapters; Figure 12.7 shows the entire trade and the various stops I placed.

Figure 12.7

The point I'm trying to make is that it is critical for traders listen to the market, and if the market is not acting as they think it should, you need to book profits immediately and wait for the market's next move. If your stop loss is hit, it's not as if you have been proved wrong or have lost something. It can sometimes be the signal for bigger profits. If you can listen to the markets, you don't need most of the fancy indicators around. The market drops enough hints about what it's going to do next. Market re-entry at higher price should not be seen as an admission of failure, but as a prudent decision to wait for the market to show its hand more fully.

Trailing Stop

Once in profit, I like to keep a trailing stop at one ATR (average true range) so that the daily gyrations of the market do not throw me out of a position that is working. A trailing stop is one which trails the price. Putting it very close to the prevailing price can throw you out of a trade which has some way to go.

Scaling Out of Postions

Another good idea, though not my favourite, is to scale out of positions as they go into profits. Scaling in and scaling out are common strategies used by many traders. These traders take a small position first and then keep building if the trade moves in their direction. Some traders I know sell a part of the position and thus essentially make it a free position, or one that has a lower breakeven. Their profits are generally lower than for traders who take an entire position together. I prefer the latter because I look at entry set-ups very carefully and make an entry in a low risk situation. I do not enter into trades till the market is set up perfectly. Traders who scale positions can be a little more relaxed about their set-ups and entries, since scaling involves both gradual building of positions and gradual profit taking. This way, scaling reduces a trader's initial risk.

Other Methods

A lot of traders use a variety of other methods, such as some moving average or trend channel breakdown or multiple moving averages. All these methods can be found in most books on technical analysis. What is not found is the perspective on exits and the markets. As we all know by now, there are two kinds of markets, the trading market and the trending market. The trading market has shorter moves and has a tendency to reverse after brief periods of up and down movements. Thus the stops and targets need to be closer and traders should focus on booking profits keeping in mind the smaller moves. In trading markets, traders should try to trade overbought and oversold areas with the use of indicators such as the RSI and be comfortable with booking small profits. The trending markets, on the other hand, offer bigger profits as the main moves are much larger. So a trader needs to be in such a market till the market throws him out of a trade. A trader should also remember the time frame he is trading in and should look for hints in the lower time frame for topping out or bottoming out patterns which might suggest caution.

Also, a trader needs to have a plan and approximate targets in mind before he enters a trade so that he can manage his stop losses effectively. There are times when the markets want to give him huge profits; at other times only small profits can be made. Trade management to a large extent determines the trader's profitability. This game is not as much about the number of profitable trades as it is about the size of profits. Failure to remember this can lead either to traders not realising the full profit potential of their trades, or in giving back substantial amounts of profits.

Ordinary traders can win with the help of charts and good money management. As the country grows economically, a lot wealth will get created — and a lot of wealth will be lost as well. And most of it will happen on the stock market. The wealth creators and accumulators will be traders who align themselves with the market and make use of all the sophisticated trading tools available. People who lose wealth will be the buy and hold investors who get into expensive stocks and then don't get out even when the stocks goes down to half its value.

In a capitalist society, the opportunity of creating a large fortune is within the reach of all of us. The road is long and arduous and experience often a harsh teacher. But aligning risks to return expectations is possible like never before. Never before was so much flexibility available to individual investors and traders in terms of available instruments and liquidity. The derivatives market is changing the Indian investor's landscape forever. It is, finally, possible to make a fortune on the Indian stock markets.

Chapter 13

Selection of Stocks and Futures

Choosing What You Play

Early in 2006, TV-18 started a paid website, called Power Your Trade where a select team of technical analysts each give two trading ideas every day. This website became very popular and lots of people liked the recommendations I made. I often heard stories that people went to their brokers' offices simply to take the trades I'd suggested. As time passed, these recommendations almost acquired a cult status. In this chapter I will reveal the relatively simple methodology that I use every evening to come up with those daily recommendations.

You may well ask why I would share my secrets in a book priced at a mere Rs. 400?

Well, because actually there is no secret; it's just pure common sense which I figured out as a result of trading for many years.

Let's go back to the same cricketing analogy that we started with in this book's Introduction.

It is said that Indian batsmen are tigers at home. Why? Because on Indian pitches they just get on to the front foot and pulverize any bowling. But when they go abroad, they limply hang their bats outside the off stump and get out meekly to the moving ball. This difference in performance is because of the differences between Indian pitches and those found outside Asia. The same skill set which works great on one type of picthes fails when applied to different pitches. Another analogy is the difference between driving a great car on a smooth 6-lane highway, and on a small village road. The car is the same but the comfort and performance would be vastly different.

Similarly, if brilliant technical analysis is applied to the wrong stocks, you can't get right results.

Generally, there are two types of stock analyses that go on in the markets: top down and bottom up.

Bottom Up Analysis

Bottom up analysis consists of analysing each individual company based on its earnings, cash flow, growth prospects, a review of its balance sheets, profit and loss statement, etc., and is generally used by fundamental analysts and other market players who are hunting for value. Such analysis is of little value to technical traders as it does not sufficiently position the odds in their favour. Hence they typically look at top down analysis.

Top Down Analysis

The market's main trend plays an integral part in where any stock is headed. Just as a rising tide lifts all boats whether big or small, so too a rising market buoys up all stocks to a greater or lesser extent. So it is the main trend of the market that a technical trader first seeks to figure out. Such an analyst next looks at the trend of the particular sector or industry, and only then comes the trend of a particular stock. This is how technicians view the market.

By identifying situations where all three — namely, the market trend, the sector trend and the stock's trend — are moving in the same direction, the odds of making money in the shortest possible time are the highest. So traders need to first assess the market direction, and then the sector direction before taking trades in a leveraged market.

The methodology that I am about to explain below has a very simple premise:

All assets which attract money, continue to attract money till they become very expensive. Conversely, all assets which lose investor interest continue to slide till they bottom out.

We can identify such sectors and stocks by using the indicator called rate of change (ROC).

Thus as a trader with a month's view, if I could get a list of stocks sorted from highest to lowest in terms of ROC, it will give me the right list of stocks or futures to trade.

Rate of Change (ROC)

Rate of change is a very simple technical indicator and is available in most proprietary trading software. ROC provides information regarding the change in the price of a stock in a given time period. For a swing trader, the rate of change can be calculated over 20 days. Stocks which have the highest rate of change are obviously the ones attracting the most amount of money. The stocks with the lowest rate of change are the ones which are either not attracting money, or money may even actually be deserting them.

One can add some additional parameters, such as looking at stocks which are priced over Rs. 200 — this reduces the chance of a stock being cornered and manipulated, though it's still possible — and those that have an average daily trading volume of at least 1 lakh shares.

The ROC parameter for the number of days can be 20, as a month has about 20 trading days. A medium term trader can look at 60 as his ROC parameter, as he is trading a larger time frame. Such medium term traders, on the other hand, may actually be interested in buying stocks which seem to have completed their corrective phases, in which case may want to use this list upside down.

Let's now see how this strategy works.

A trader who needs about a month's point of view uses a 20-period ROC, 100,000+ volume, and a stock price of over Rs. 200.

The Indian market had a large correction when Nifty fell from 3,770 (May 2006) to 2,600 (June 2006), followed by a pullback rally in which Nifty bounced back to 3,200 before resuming its decline. At that point we were anticipating a retest of 2,600. So we needed to look for stocks which were showing weakness. In case 2,900 held, we would've reassessed the situation again.

Figure 13.1 depicts the market situation around 23 July 2006, and it's clearly visible that the market formed distributive patterns between 3,770-3,380 on the Nifty, and then again at 3,200-2,900. Also we can see that the 50 DMA (daily moving average) was then about to cross and slip below the 200 DMA, clear signs that the market would soon be heading down.

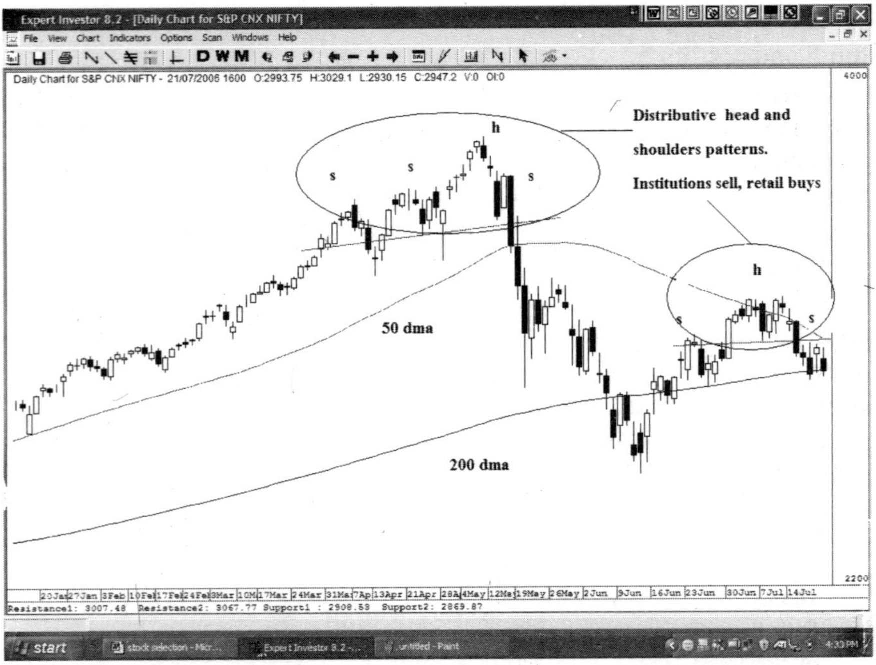

Figure 13.1: **Nifty**

The first quarter results were also then coming in. Technology, cement, metals, etc. turned in great results, actually better than what the market had expected. As each brilliant result was announced, the market, however, beat the stock down. Since the market continued to sulk, it was sending out a message that it was looking at a possible earnings decline in future quarters as a result of rising interest rates and inflation. It's important not to react to results like a news channel does but like the market which, in its wisdom, tries to look ahead and drive while keeping an eye on the rear view mirror.

As noted earlier, at this point we needed candidates to sell. Accordingly, we generated a list of stocks, based on their ROC in descending order, from the futures and options segment using the above listed parameters. This methodology is similar to the relative strength methodology. Generally we look for the weakest stocks in a weak market, but when the markets are ready to break down we should also look at strong stocks which are beginning to weaken. However, since many stocks had already lost a lot of ground it was important to identify stocks which still had room to decline further. I often start with the top

10 and bottom 10 stocks in such a list, but here let's review only the top 5 and bottom 5.

Another important piece of information that such a list gives us is about the sectors which are becoming stronger and those which are weakening. This key information helps me back strong or weak sectors. All things being equal, I would rather buy a strong stock in a strong sector — rather than a strong stock in a weak sector — and short a weak stock in a weak sector.

So as shown by the list in Table 13.1, the sectors growing strong were technology, FMCG, and cement, while the weakening sectors were auto, metals, oil. Such information, along with the rate of change of individual stocks, will keep you positioned in the right stocks even in a sideways market. This is because even when the market is in a sideways mode, there is a bull or bear phase playing itself out in some sector or the other.

Table 13.1

Name	*ROC Value*	*Name*	*ROC Value*
PUNJLLOYD	-28.3	BHEL	-4.73
JETAIRWAYSEQ	-25.77	ICICI BANK	-4.43
REL.CAPITAL	-20.7	HDFC BANK	-4.26
PATNI EQ	-17.58	RELIANCE	-3.94
TATAMOTORSEQ	-13.32	MATRIXLABSEQ	-3.91
STER EQ	-13.26	INDIAN HOTEL	-3.54
MAH & MAH	-11.29	CESC LTD	-3.52
IPCL	-10.98	NSE NIFTY	-3.45
RANBAXY LAB.	-9.56	CIPLA	-3.04
TATASTEEL	-9.26	HOUS DEV FIN	-2.87
BHARAT FORGE	-9.02	SATYAM COMP	-2.68
NATION ALUMI	-8.57	BHARTIARTL	-2.27
BHARAT PETRO	-8.53	PNB	-1.94
MARUTI	-8.44	SUN PHARMA.	0.22
CENTURY TEXT	-8.33	GRASIM IND.	0.73
TITAN IND.	-8.28	A.C.C.	0.92
SIEMENS	-8.06	HIND.LEVER	1.11
HERO HONDA	-7.14	COLGATE	1.38
VIDESH SANCH	-6.08	SUZLON	2.51
ONGC CORP.	-5.59	TATA POWER	3.2
WIPRO	-5.54	TCS EQ	3.95
G.E.SHIPPING	-5.18	INFOSYS TECH	7.18
STATE BANK	-5.08	I-FLEX	8.03
GAIL	-5.04	HCL TECHNOLO	8.7
REL EQ	-4.81		

Let's consider the chart of the stock at the very top, Punj Lloyd (Figure 13.2):

Figure 13.2: **Punj Lloyd**

My assessment was that though the chart was weak, the share had already declined a lot and did not have room for significant further decline, so I wouldn't pick this stock for my short list.

Let's now look at the chart of the second stock from the top, that of Jet Airways (Figure 13.3):

Figure 13.3: **Jet Airways**

Again a weak stock, but one which in the short run had possibly already declined too much. Let's move on.

Let's now look at the weekly chart of Reliance Capital (Figure 13.4), to get a better assessment of its weakness at that point. This stock initially held firm when the entire market was collapsing, and had only recently started its decline. Now look at the last black candle, the best short is one that initially rises in price and then later on starts its decline. This gives it a closer stop. The high and low of the previous black bar is 482 and 407, respectively. The weekly low before that was 450. So we design the trade as follows:

> Sell above 407 (so that we sell into a rally), keep a stop of the previous week's low of 450, so that the stop is close.

The target of this move is 328 so you are broadly getting a 1:1.5 risk-reward on the trade, which is fine in a sideways market.

Figure 13.4: **Reliance Capital**

Figure 13.5: **Patni Computers**

Let's now move along to the daily chart of the next stock in our ROC list, Patni Computers (Figure 13.5), which had then been a consistent underperformer in the technology sector. The stock had just undergone a 3-4 day pullback and looked ripe for another shorting opportunity above 276. The top of the pullback was 292, which could be used as a stop. A target of this short can be calculated by measuring the length from the lowest pivot (250) to the top of the pullback (292-250=40), and then subtracting it back from that lowest pivot (250-42=208), which now becomes a target.

So the trade for Patni Computers took the shape:

Sell above 276, stop 292, target 208.

Now we look at the daily chart of Sterlite Industries (Figure 13.6). As money then seemed to be leaving the metals sector, Sterlite appeared to be in a huge range, 270-450. As its chart shows, Sterlite was then in a short term downtrend and saw a weak pullback rally to 387. This seemed another good candidate for shorting. Following the same rules, we design the following trade:

Figure 13.6: **Sterlite Industries**

Sell above the close 377, use a stop of 412 instead of 387 which is the top of the pullback because you want the trade to have some room. A good target for this swing could be 270-280.

Let's now consider some of the top positive ROC stocks. The breakdown of the strongest stocks would happen only when the whole market goes into a decline. It's worth keeping an eye open for such an eventuality because when the market does break down, the stocks with the strongest gains sometimes see the maximum declines. Since the market at that time appeared a little sideways, so there weren't a lot of shorting opportunities among the strong stocks.

Nevertheless, let's take a look.

Tata Power had gone through a pullback rally after a sharp decline (Figure 13.7). The stock would weaken below 445-450, so we continued to watch it. Another way is to look for a break of the upward sloping trendline.

Figure 13.7: **Tata Power**

IFlex (Figure 13.8) also showed strong gains but then seemed to have entered a strong resistance area between 1350-1380 — but it was too early to enter shorts here.

Figure 13.8: **IFlex**

The results season was just over and, the techs had produced great results. Yet, they were unable to take out resistances on the upside as can be seen from the charts of TCS (Figure 13.9) and Infosys (Figure 13.10). So though they were outperforming, they were unable to move to new highs. Were the markets break down, there could be some downside post the results.

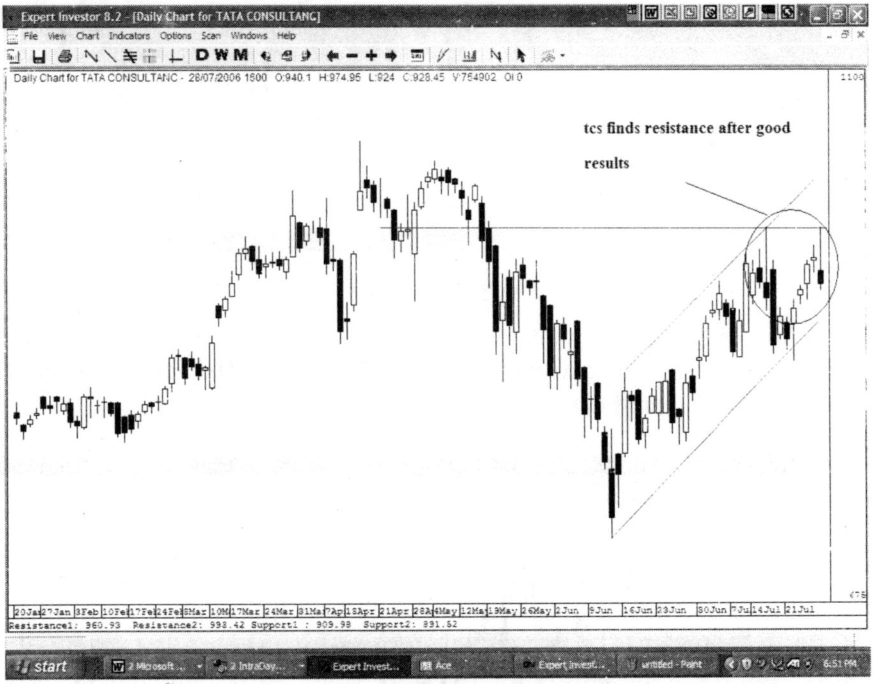

Figure 13.9: **TCS**

Here, then, is the drill that I follow on a daily basis for selecting the right stocks and futures to trade:

- Take a view on the market, i.e. determine the market's main trend;
- Generate an ROC-based list of stocks sorted from the highest to the lowest;
- Identify the strong and weak sectors;

Figure 13.10: **Infosys**

- Based on the market and sectoral trends, choose the strongest and weakest stocks;
- Look for patterns on individual stocks which show a breakout;
- Design the trade with a logical stop which allows enough room for market noise.

Why is it necessary to choose the right stocks? This is because technical analysis is the science of graphically assessing strength and weakness of stocks. It's impossible to apply all the rules to the thousands of listed stocks. Hence we need a short list of the strongest or the weakest stocks among the group that we are interested in trading. Technical analysis too has a failure rate, hence a successful trader tries to put as many odds in his favour as possible. Knowing the market's direction, and the strength of different sectors, is an important key to success as stocks move in groups and trends.

It is important to emphasise here that the above methodology works very well in a trending market because stocks generally move in a directional trend in trending markets.

Also this relative strength methodology works best over the short term.

This brings us back to the important distinction between the concepts of trading and trending markets.

In a range-bound sort of market, it's important to look at the list both from the top — and from the bottom. This is because when the entire market is ranging, most stocks are also range-bound. So the ones which have made their move either rest for a while, or correct. And the underperformers then start moving. You should, therefore, not be looking for breakouts in such a market because attempted breakouts tend to fail. You need to try to buy support, and sell resistance.

As you can see, it is important to be understand whether the market is trending or range-bound before you can decide how you will look at the list.

Figures 13.11 to 13.20 demonstrate a few other charts outlining some typical patterns I want from an ROC list in a trending market. These are the kinds of stocks that will get into my daily trading list.

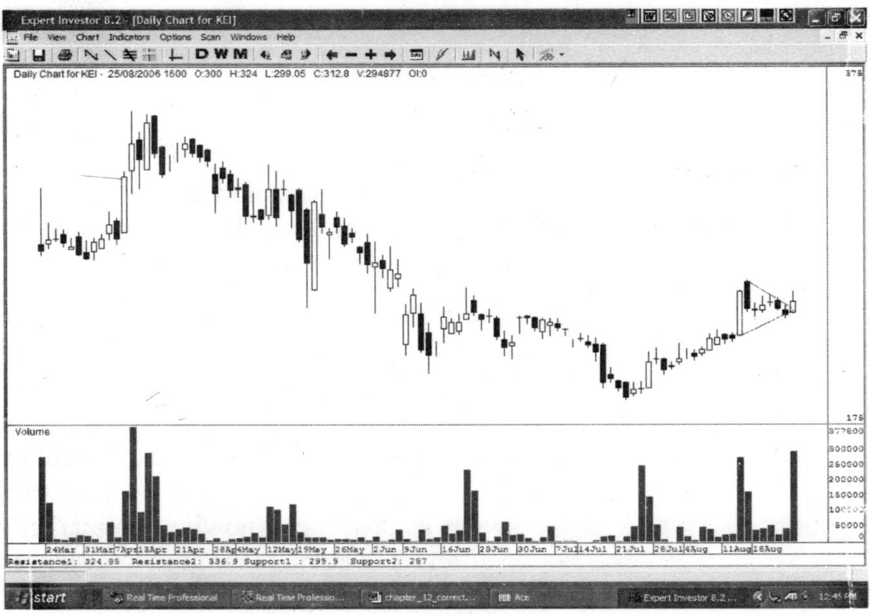

Figure 13.11

Figure 13.12

Figure 13.13

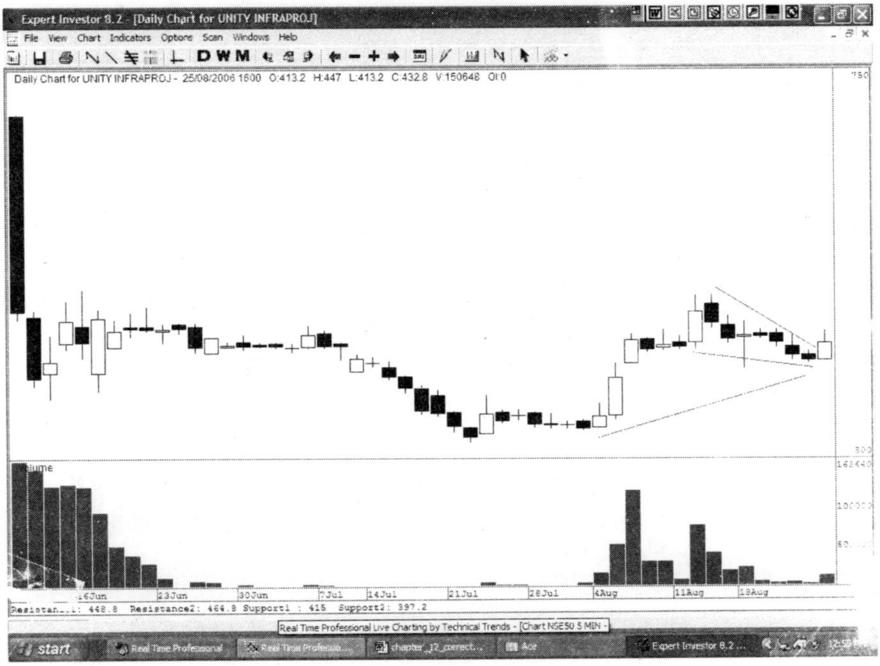

Figure 13.14

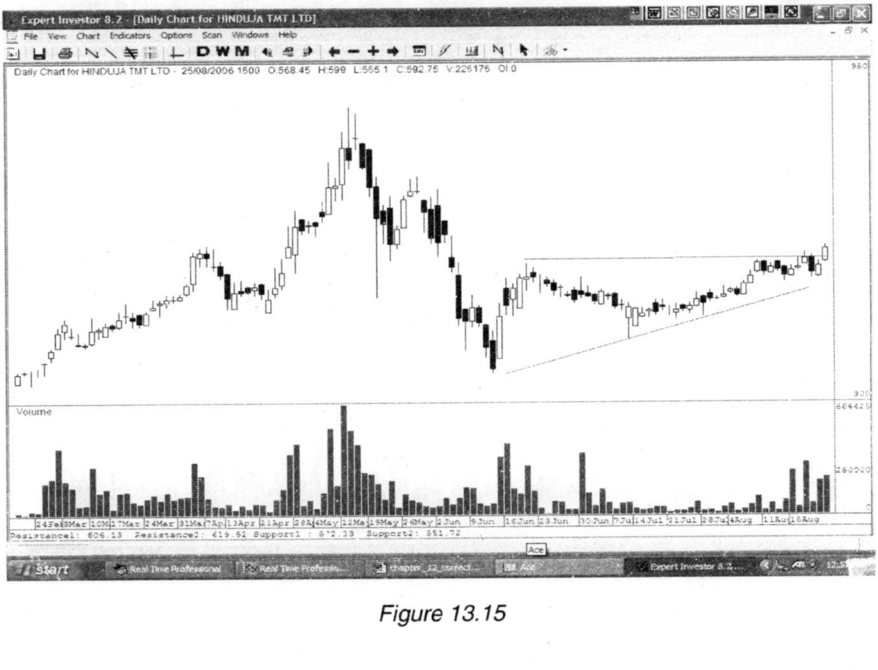

Figure 13.15

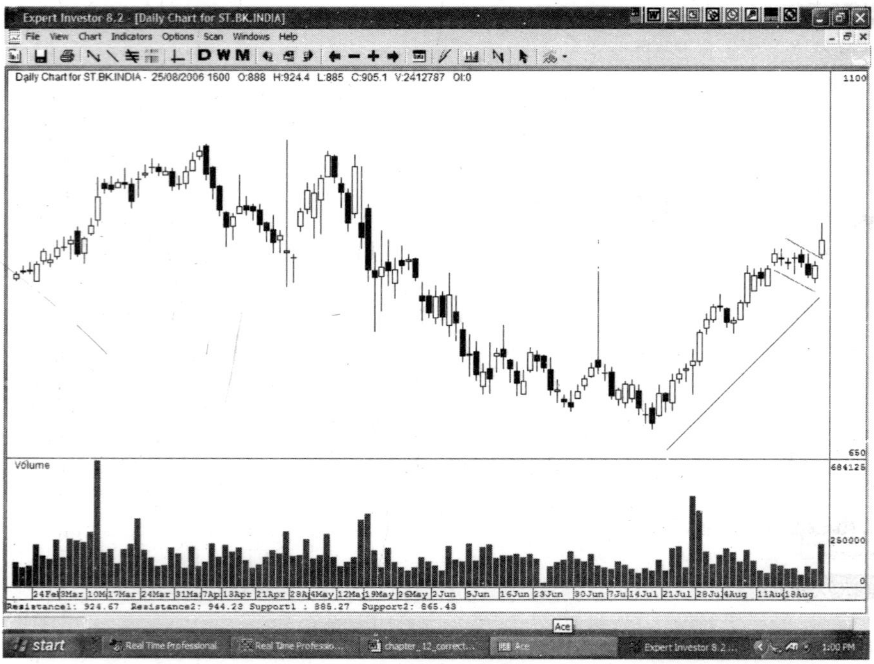

Figure 13.16

Figure 13.17

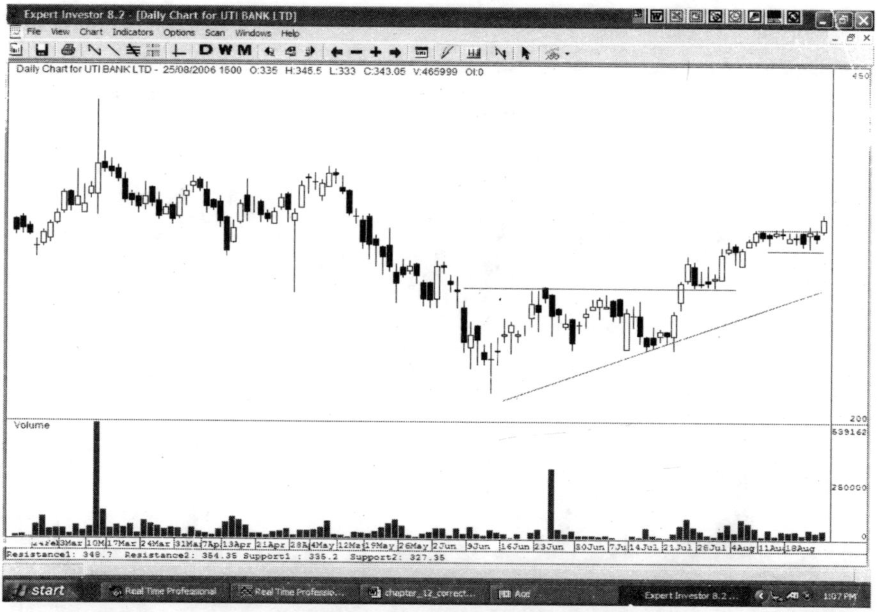

Figure 13.18

Figure 13.19

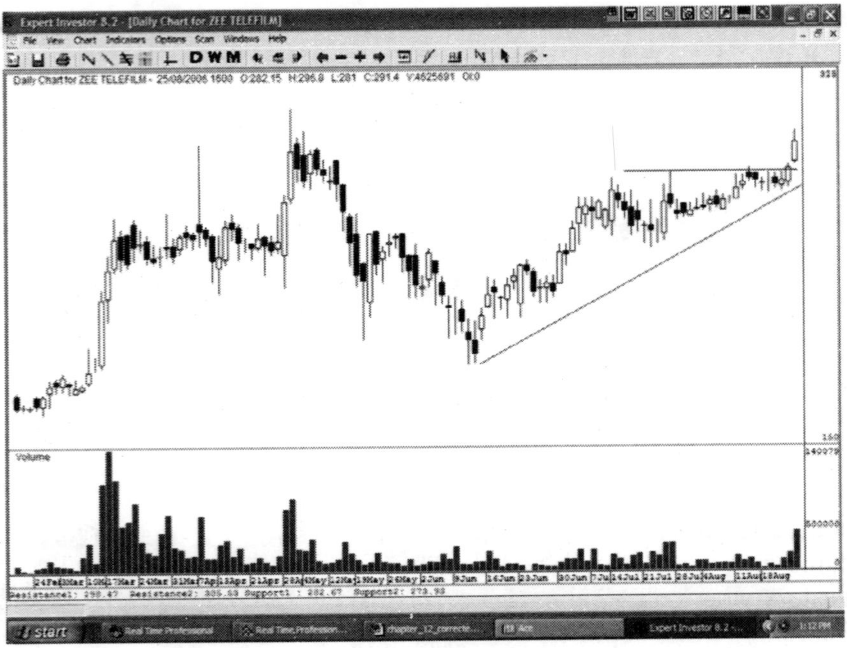

Figure 13.20

Adding a Fundamental Valuation Parameter

I have recently added a fundamental valuation parameter, such as price to sales for most companies, and price to book value for banking and commodity companies. Thus, when using at the ROC methodology, I would also look at the historical price to sales and price to book value of the particular stocks both over a period of time and across the industry. I would avoid any company which is selling several times its past ratios. An example would be the choice between Ansal Infrastructure and Unitech in the latter part of 2006. While Unitech sold for 23 times sales, Ansal sold for 4 times sales. It's clear that given strong technical picture in both the stocks, I would choose the one which was not overly frothy.

Chapter 14

My Trading Diary

The Bubble and the Crash: February-June 2006

Nifty was at 2,100 when this book was first published in early 2005. From there it had risen almost 80% to 3,770 by May 2006, after which there was a correction of 40% to 2,600 by June 2006.

As the Nifty's weekly chart (Figure 14.1) shows, the bubble had started to form between February and May 2006. Many people who came into the market after February 2006 were wiped out totally. Investors who kept a rational head had started booking profits beyond February, while sophisticated traders kept looking over their shoulder from then on for a correction.

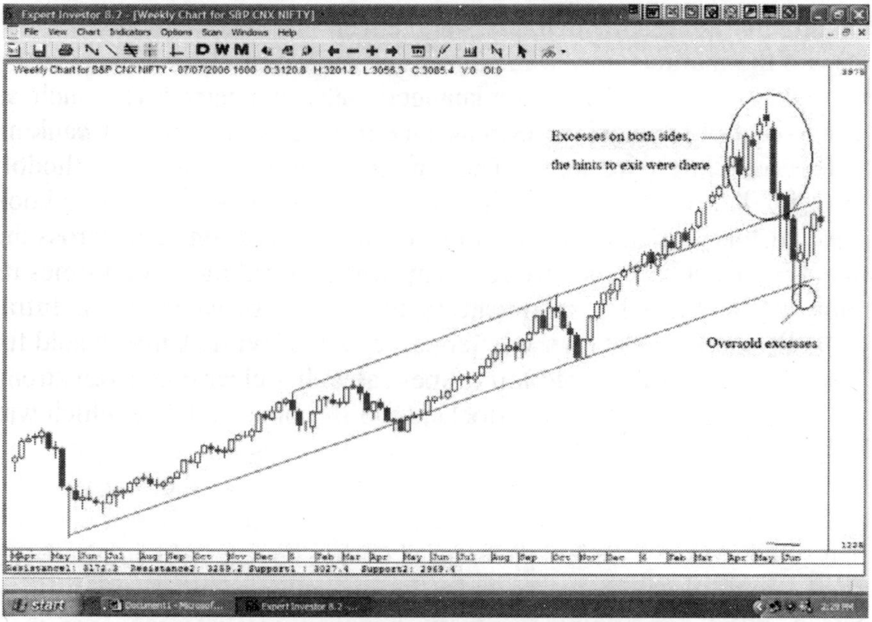

Figure 14.1: **Weekly Chart of the Nifty (April 2004-June 2006)**

So the creation of a bubble was clearly visible and one could also observe a situation of euphoria. The market offered several opportunities to get out and some analysts kept warning of an impending correction. But to the unwary, the market seemed to offer extremely easy opportunities of making money. As prices began to scale even the most optimistic predictions, and vaulted over all the real triggers which could push the markets higher, analysts started justifying their predictions of a further uninterrupted rise on the basis of the real estate which companies owned. It was clear that an end could be near, but people just did not want to listen.

The same excesses can be observed on the downside: as the Nifty went below the downward sloping trendline, a bounce was expected and it retraced about 50% of the fall as of the writing of this chapter (July 2006).

The apprehension of a bubble hit home to me when a former domestic help phoned me for suggestions about investing in the market. I started getting inquiries from army officers posted in Kashmir and, equally, from housewives wanting my services to impress their husbands, with greed in their voice as if they had found a magical key. My phone would not stop ringing; every five minutes there was a new person interested in the markets. People who had absolutely nothing to do with the markets now wanted to jump in. When my wife's friends, with whom till then I'd only exchanged pleasantries, and who had no background of the stock market, wanted to take up futures trading as a profession, I knew we were approaching a moment of truth. This was in April 2006.

As all this was unfolding, I went to buy a car in March 2006 and was only just able to squeeze my loan application through ICICI Bank at the old interest rates, as it had already hiked its interest rate on car loans. By the time the loan was passed, it was already April 2006. All these events together suggested to me that while on the one hand there was extreme euphoria in the markets, on the other hand liquidity on the ground was starting to tighten. Observing these dichotomies I put my ear extremely close to the ground, ready to exit at the first sign of trouble. Other alert investors and traders too would have taken note of such signals. In my media appearances during this period I continually urged people not to increase their trading volume and book profits instead, but I don't think too many people were listening over the euphoric roar of the market. It happens every time when a bull market is about to take a break.

Were the charts at all indicating how one could have gotten off without damaging oneself too much? Maybe they were.

After the market made a new high at 3,770 on 11 May 2006, and then closed lower, we had a very normal down day. There always are several one-day corrections even in a strong bull market. So the next day (12 May 2006), we looked for a support and went long. The market did not quite close strong on the second day but since it closed as a doji (see the section on candlestick charting in Chapter 3), we carried forward our longs. On 13 May, after a lukewarm opening the market started tanking and broke through the first strong support of 3,590 and closed almost near its intra-day low at 3,480. Now I was seriously worried, but we still carried our longs since 100-point corrections were normal at that time. Also, my final stop of 3,430 had not yet been breached though the market had shown enough weakness for me to be on my guard. As it happened, the market turned from 3,430 and started moving higher.

But I had seen enough. I used Fibonacci retracements on the fall from 3,770 to 3,430, and found 50% retracement at 3,630. So the instructions were clear: as soon as we saw levels higher than 3,600, it was Control+Alt+Delete from the market. On 17 May 2006 the market touched 3,643 and I closed all my positions. When the ship is on fire, you just jump off and save whatever you can. The deck of a burning ship is not the place for a lot of analysis. Leave analysis to the analysts, traders should think only about making and losing money. The same day I left for a fortnight's European vacation advising investors on CNBC that they, too, should sell and go on holiday. In hindsight, that was great advice. So this was the story of my exit from the bull market. At this point I knew I was saving money by not putting it at risk. In such situations, traders should stand aside and wait; not losing money is, in effect, making money. Often at market turns, things are not clear enough to act, so it's wise to wait for some clarity.

So I actually got out of the market as I was already on the alert. Some of you may say that everything seems clear in hindsight. Yes, I accept I could have been wrong here, and I did actually exit the market a couple of times earlier too, looking at several signs of a top. The important thing here is not whether I rode the entire move exactly till

3,770; the important thing is that I protected most of my profits and my capital to live to fight another day. If you survive in the market, you finally make money, that is my mantra.

Let's now consider Figure 14.2.

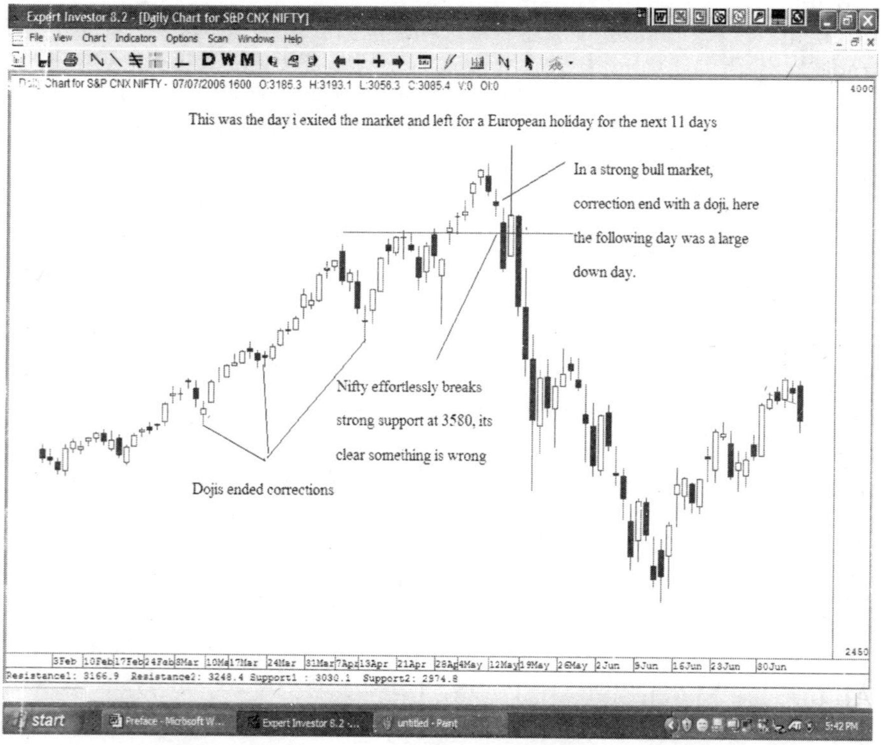

Figure 14.2: **Market Mayhem in May 2006 on the Daily Chart**

By the last week of July 2006, people wanted to know whether we were then in a bull or a bear market. Basically what they wanted to know was whether the Nifty was going to quickly top 4,000, or slide back to 2,100. My answer to them was that in the short term probably it was going to be neither, and probably in the medium term as well — and that anyway it's not all that important to know where the market is going so long as you can ride the short term swings which can often be as large as 600 points on the Nifty.

I believe that a bear market is a more than 20% fall from the top and its beginning is accompanied by all kinds of excesses, such as leveraged money and extreme euphoria, which were all present in May 2006. So in July 2006 it was possible that the market could break through 2,600 and go lower, and as people grew increasingly disenchanted, bottom out only around 2,100. The other option was that the market could hold on to 2,600 and keep moving sideways for the next few months before moving to new highs. Equally, neither of the above might have happened. What is important for a trader is to be able to trade as many of the market swings as possible. A near approximation of such a scenario is the way S&P 500 had moved since March 2001; for more than five years till July 2006 it kept moving in a range without making fresh new highs.

A lot of traders and investors told me stories of how much they lost in the savage fall of May 2006. In each case, I found that money management principles were put on the back burner as greed took over and people abandoned all common sense. Where I had reduced my volumes from 150 Nifty futures per Rs. 1 lakh of capital to almost 50 Nifty futures per lakh during this period, there were people who held on to their leveraged positions without any stop losses, and without any regard to sound money management principles even while the markets came crashing down. It was like giving a person an aeroplane to fly, when all he had experience of was driving a car. I think the difference between smart traders and amateurs is that smart traders know when to take their foot off the gas pedal, while amateurs press it even harder during such times and that is the reason they lose.

There are some hard lessons that the crash of May 2006 taught us. All through March and April 2006, I repeatedly suggested that traders should reduce their trading volume. My TV anchors would ignore and laugh at such advice for the need of caution. Finally, I believe what had to happen would have happened anyway, but being rational and reducing one's trading volume at the right time — i.e., when things appeared overheated — would have done much less damage. In the overwhelming number of cases it was not the fall in price which destroyed people, it was the heavy volume they traded.

The other advice I have for people is to not come into market undercapitalised, or merely for the short term, or for the lack of another occupation. All of these reasons misfire and rip people off capital all the time. Futures trading, in particular, is not a part-time occupation. Some people mistakably believe that it does not need too much attention, and that they can become expert futures traders while staying focused on another career. If it were so easy, I would not be writing this book, and neither would I have spent a good part of my life learning how to trade better. Unless you are willing to do the hard work, and have the time and commitment to make a success of it, trading may not be right for you.

Chapter 15

The AG Last Hour Trading Technique

It is said that 95 per cent of day traders lose money. Well, not any more if you operate in the right time zone of the day and in the right stocks. In fact, you can day trade the markets with 80 per cent accuracy.

The overall market volatility seems to be increasing every year. So, more the time you spend in the markets, the greater the risk you are taking. On the other hand, it has now become possible to slice the trading day into the most active and most profitable time periods and the least profitable and least active time periods.

The AG Last Hour Trading Technique is a "buy today, sell tomorrow" — or, conversely, "sell today, buy tomorrow" — day trading strategy. It can be used for entry in the last hour of a trading day and exiting in the first hour of the next trading day.

This strategy has been crystallized by the "mother" of all inventions, namely necessity.

I have been appearing daily on the Indian business television news channel, ET-Now. The last hour every day has a programme which is like the Indian version of the famous US "Fast Money" programme. This has led to real time back testing of this strategy on a daily basis for one year. The strategy has a documented back testing accuracy, within given parameters, of about 80 per cent odds of getting 2 per cent, or better, return on a daily basis. Another beauty of this strategy is that you always have a play for the day, and you do not break your back watching a quote screen all day. I know of people holding regular jobs who take extended lunch breaks from 2:00-3:30 p.m. in order just to trade this strategy. They often take home more money in a day than the entire month's salary from their regular jobs.

What's So Special about the First and Last Hours of a Trading Day?

It's a well documented fact that the first and the last hour are the most active periods of any trading day in terms of price and volume. This is so because most large institutions tend to operate in the post-lunch session. Also, usually there are several up and down swings during the day, with the market revealing its final hand only in the last hour.

The first hour of a trading day is also interesting and active but for a different reason. The underlying reason here is that stocks which have closed strong, or weak, in the previous session, tend to open next morning in the same direction as their close. This is also true for the overall market because all the television technical analysts, newsletter sellers, and retail traders are looking at daily charts for breakouts. So a strategy can be created where you buy / sell in tandem with the big institutions in the last hour of the day and book profits when the rest of the market tries to get on to the bandwagon in the first hour of the next trading day.

Presently, Indian markets trade from 9:15 a.m. to 3:30 p.m. So the technique described here is keeping these market hours in view. Thus the first hour is 9:15-10:15 a.m., and the last hour is 2:30-3:30 p.m. These principles are valid and can be applied in all markets and time zones.

The Context of the Market

By sitting it out till the last hour, the trend for the day becomes absolutely clear. Hence, by the last hour you know which side you need to act on; whether you need to look for shorting candidates or you want to go long on something:

- If the market has moved higher throughout the day, or generally kept a positive bias, you look for stocks to buy.
- In case the market is heading lower for the day, or keeping a generally negative bias, you look for stocks to sell.
- If it's a narrow range day, cut your trading volume to half.

How to Select the Right Stocks to Trade

So, as we have seen, on a daily basis by the last hour it's clear which is the strongest or the weakest group, what stocks are breaking down / out on the daily charts, and on what kind of volumes. A larger than usual volume results in a volume bar which, around the last hour, is bigger than the closing volumes for most days. The bigger the volume, the better the move.

In my experience, it's possible to identify at least one idea which works because there is always some action or the other somewhere in the market. And you need only one good idea to work in the market every day.

Personally, I tend to use one of the following two set-ups to select the stock to trade.

Set-up 1: Breakdown / breakout from a narrow range on a larger than usual volume (*see* Figure 15.1)

Narrow range breakouts and breakdowns generally give large moves in a particular direction. The move is particularly significant in the other direction if a narrow range occurs after a significant move in one direction.

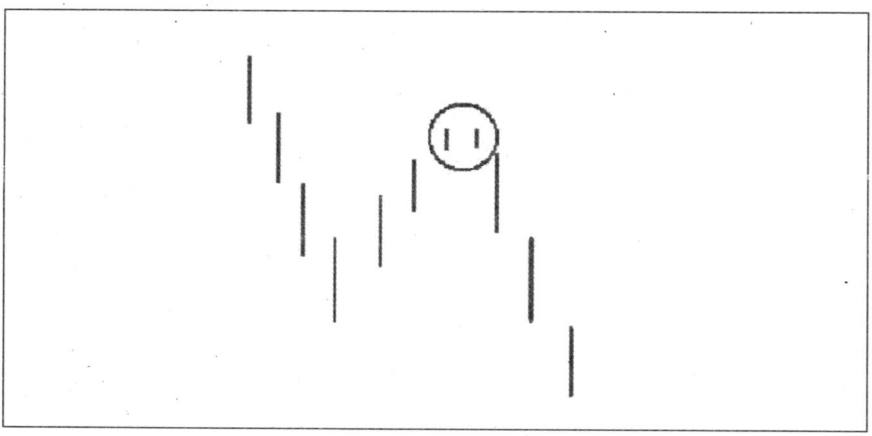

Figure 15.1: **Narrow range breakdown**

Set-up 2: Breakout / breakdown of a previous up or down pivot on larger than usual volume (*see* Figure 15.2)

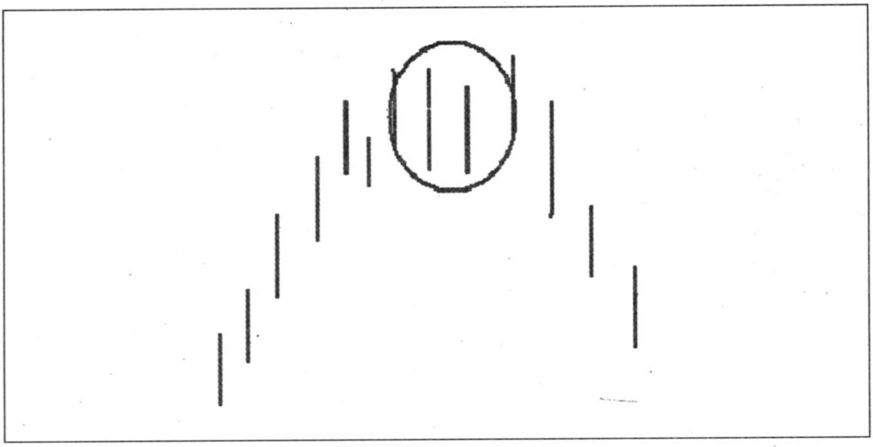

Figure 15.2: **Pivot breakdown on larger than normal volume**

This set-up is achieved by maintaining a market watch which lists gains or losses in percentage in various stocks according to a minimum traded volume criterion. It takes only about half-an-hour to scan through the 20 top losers or gainers amongst that list. I would much rather choose a high beta stock than a dead defensive one. We have only a couple of hours and we need to make the most of it.

You can add your own high probability set-ups to the two above.

For Best Results

- All of the above analysis should be done having a view on what kind of market we are dealing with — bull, bear, or sideways market.
- Which groups or sectors are leading and lagging.
- Which stocks have been the best and worst performing ones.
- The breakout / breakdown bar should be at least 3 per cent.
- On the chart, I generally have 20 and 30 simple DMA to give me an idea of the location of price on the chart.

- A Donchian channel makes it easier to see whether a pivot or a narrow range is getting broken on any time-frame. I use an ordinary 20-period channel.
- Try to get 7-8 per cent on 3 to 4 days in a month, although average profits will be 2 per cent plus.
- Choose at least two stocks so that if even one of them works, it makes your day.
- The technique fails 20 per cent of the time. When it does so, just get out fast, as "something is wrong".
- All exits must happen in the first hour of the following trading day.
- All of the above are used as additional information which may or may not be used with a trigger.

Having this sort of a context helps in choosing the best stocks to go short or long on. This will become clearer by looking at the examples that follow (*see* Figures 15.3 to 15.8).

Examples

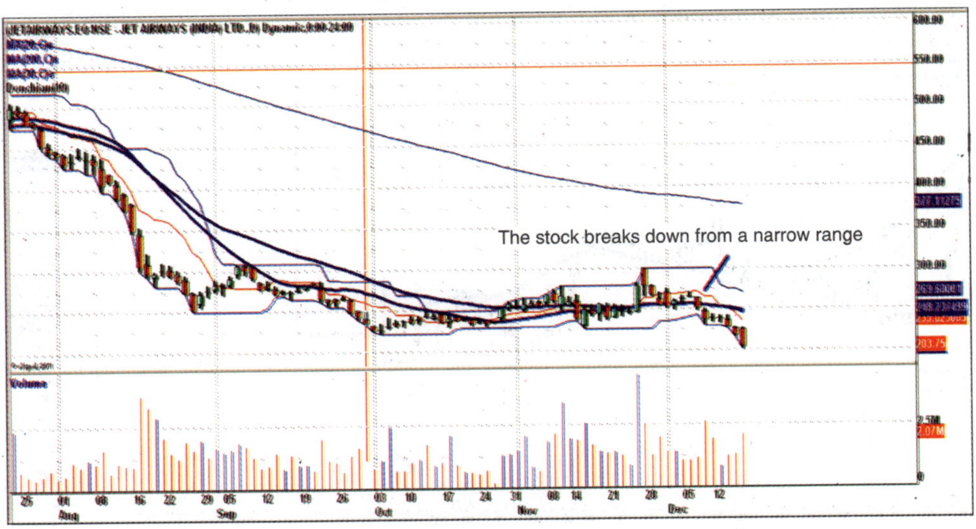

Figure 15.3: **The daily chart of Jet Airways shows how the stock broke down from a narrow range on 8 December 2011.**

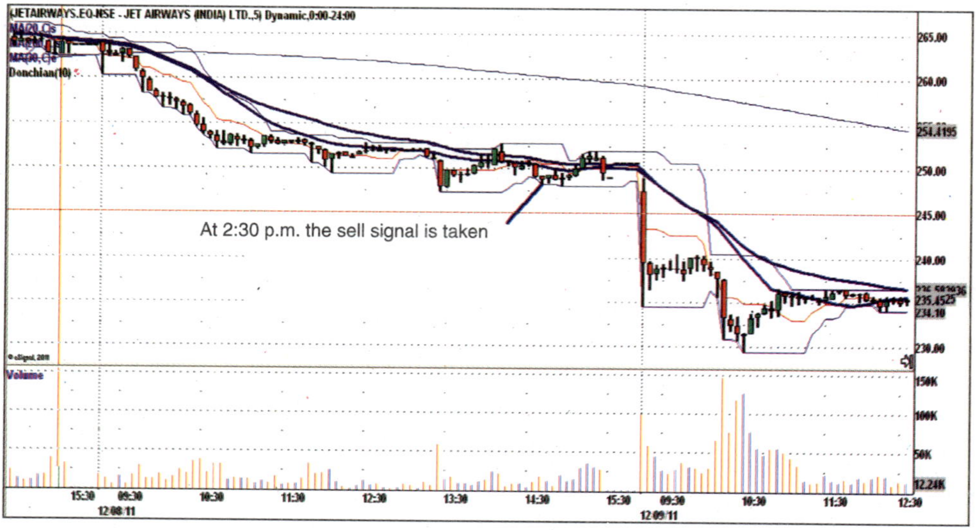

Figure 15.4: **This is the 5-minute chart of Jet Airways for the same day as depicted in Figure 15.3, i.e. 8 December 2011: At 2:30 p.m. the sell signal is taken because there is a narrow range breakdown on the daily chart (*see* Figure 15.3). The market context was weak and so was the airline group. In the first hour the next day, Jet fell on large volume.**

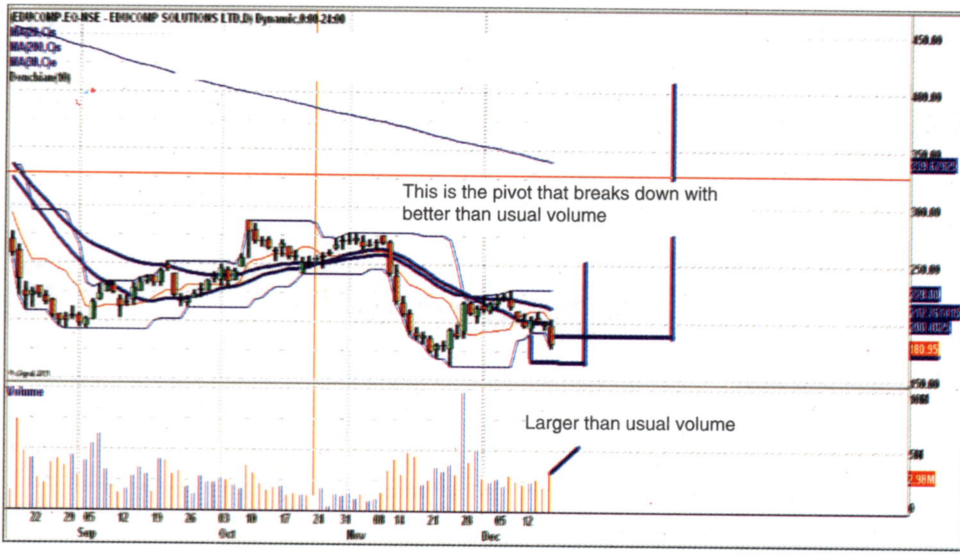

Figure 15.5: **The daily chart of Educomp, signal date 16 December 2011: The last traded day is the breakdown bar, plus you can add confirmation such as breakdown of a 20-day Donchian channel. Larger than usual volume is always a plus.**

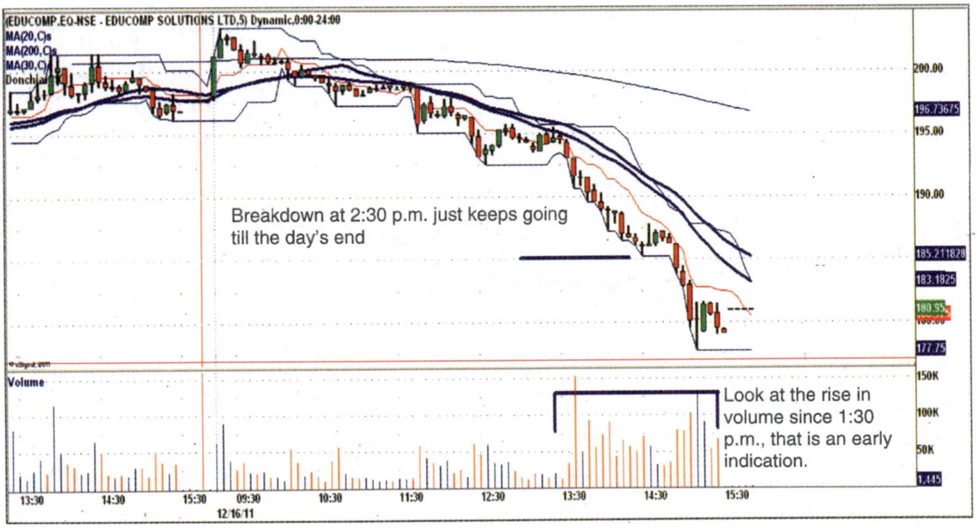

Figure 15.6: **The 5-minute chart of Educomp for 16 December 2011: The break-down at 2:30 p.m. just kept going till the day's end. Also, note the rise in volume since 1:30 p.m. — that was an early indication of the impending fall.**

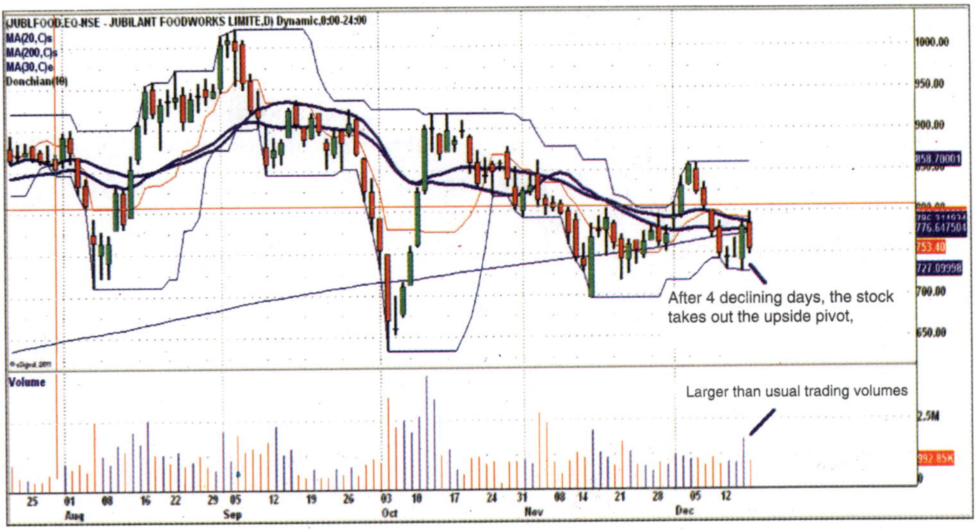

Figure 15.7: **Daily chart of Jubilant Foodworks, signal date 15 December, 2011: After four days of decline, the stock took out the upside pivot with good volume and hence came on our list. Notice, too, the larger than usual trading volumes.**

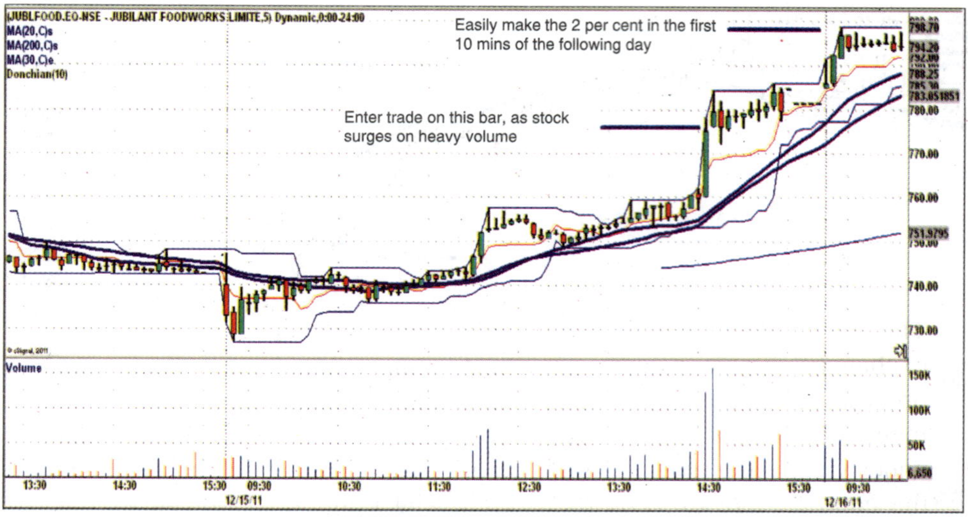

Figure 15.8: **5-minute chart of Jubilant Foodworks for 15 December 2011: Enter trade on the lower bar as stock surges on heavy volume and easily make 2 per cent in the first 10 minutes of the following day.**

Conclusion

Most day traders lose money because they crave too much action. A lot of losing trades happen during the dull period of the trading day. If nothing else, The AG Lost Hour Trading Technique sharpens your day trading by keeping you away from the choppy period in the market and makes you a net profitable trader. The key idea is that it's most profitable to participate in the market only during these two hours — it is similar to participating in a trending market in any other time-frame.

Appendix-I

Permitted Contract Sizes

The contract sizes in the Indian derivatives markets are decided by the exchanges. These can be important in a trader's decision making process, since the larger the contract sizes, the more likely the movements can be and greater the risk for every unit of movement in the underlying. As a rule of thumb, traders should avoid contracts where the contract size exceeds Rs. 5 lakh. The minimum allowed by the exchange is Rs. 2 lakh.

Please note: Contract lot sizes can be changed by NSE from time to time. You can always check the current position at NSE's website — www.nseindia.com

No.	*Underlying*	*Symbol*	*Market Lot*
1	S&P CNX Nifty	NIFTY	200
2	CNX IT	CNXIT	100
	Derivatives on Individual Securities		
1	Associated Cement Co. Ltd.	ACC	1,500
2	Andhra Bank	ANDHRABANK	4,600
3	Arvind Mills Ltd.	ARVINDMILL	4,300
4	Bajaj Auto Ltd.	BAJAJAUTO	400
5	Bank of Baroda	BANKBARODA	1,400
6	Bank of India	BANKINDIA	3,800
7	Bharat Electronics Ltd.	BEL	550
8	Bharat Heavy Electricals Ltd.	BHEL	600
9	Bharat Petroleum Corporation Ltd.	BPCL	550
10	Canara Bank	CANBK	1,600
11	Cipla Ltd.	CIPLA	1,000
12	Dr. Reddy's Laboratories Ltd.	DRREDDY	200
13	GAIL (India) Ltd.	GAIL	1,500
14	Grasim Industries Ltd.	GRASIM	350

No.	Underlying	Symbol	Market Lot
15	Gujarat Ambuja Cement Ltd.	GUJAMBCEM	1,100
16	HCL Technologies Ltd.	HCLTECH	1,300
17	Housing Development Finance Corporation Ltd.	HDFC	600
18	HDFC Bank Ltd.	HDFCBANK	800
19	Hero Honda Motors Ltd.	HEROHONDA	400
20	Hindalco Industries Ltd.	HINDALC0	300
21	Hindustan Lever Ltd.	HINDLEVER	2,000
22	Hindustan Petroleum Corporation Ltd.	HINDPETRO	650
23	ICICI Bank Ltd.	ICICIBANK	1,400
24	I-FLEX Solutions Ltd.	I-FLEX	300
25	Infosys Technologies Ltd.	INFOSYSTCH	200
26	Indian Petrochemicals Corpn. Ltd.	IPCL	1,100
27	Indian Oil Corporation Ltd.	IOC	600
28	ITC Ltd.	ITC	300
29	Mahindra & Mahindra Ltd.	M&M	625
30	Maruti Udyog Ltd.	MARUTI	400
31	Mastek Ltd.	MASTEK	1,600
32	Mahanagar Telephone Nigam Ltd.	MTNL	1,600
33	National Aluminium Co. Ltd.	NATIONALUM	1,150
34	National Thermal Power Corporation Ltd.	NTPC	3,250
35	Oil & Natural Gas Corp. Ltd.	ONGC	300
36	Oriental Bank of Commerce	ORIENTBANK	1,200
37	Punjab National Bank	PNB	1,200
38	Polaris Software Lab Ltd.	POLARIS	1,400
39	Ranbaxy Laboratories Ltd.	RANBAXY	400
40	Reliance Energy Ltd.	REL	550
41	Reliance Industries Ltd.	RELIANCE	600
42	Satyam Computer Services Ltd.	SATYAMCOMP	1,200
43	State Bank of India	SBIN	500
44	Shipping Corporation of India Ltd.	SCI	1,600
45	Syndicate Bank	SYNDIBANK	7,600
46	Tata Consultancy Services Ltd.	TCS	250
47	Tata Power Co. Ltd.	TATAPOWER	800
48	Tata Tea Ltd.	TATATEA	550
49	Tata Motors Ltd.	TATAMOTORS	825
50	Tata Iron and Steel Co. Ltd.	TISCO	1,350
51	Union Bank of India	UNIONBANK	4,200
52	Wipro Ltd.	WIPRO	600

Appendix-II

Calculating Implied Volatility

Implied volatility is possibly the most important concept in options trading. All traders should learn to calculate the implied volatility or know of websites which offer implied volatilities of the indices and individual stocks. One of the methods of calculating implied volatilities is described below. This calculator is a part of the options strategy evaluation Excel spreadsheet available at www.hoadley.com/options.

For example, if we need to calculate the implied volatility of the Satyam 320 call option, the inputs required are:

- **Risk Free Rate:** This can be the prevailing interest rates on bank deposits, annually 6%.
- **Dividends:** These need to be included if it's a dividend month. Generally options of stock which go ex-dividend in the current month should be avoided.
- **Option Type:** Call
- **Option Market Price:** This is available from the broker.
- **Strike Price:** 320
- **Value Date:** It's the date on which the valuation is being done.
- **Expiration Date:** This is the date where the contracts in question expire.

(The number of days to expiry is calculated automatically.)

All dates need to be entered in the American date format which is mm/dd/yy.

Once all the inputs are entered, you get the following output on your computer screen.

Implied Volatility Calculator

Risk Free Interest Rate:	6.00%
Underlying Asset:	
Market price:	318.00
Dividends:	
Ex date	
Amount	
Or	
Continuous rate	
Option:	
Option type:	
Option market price:	20
Strike price:	320.00
Value date:	5/7/04
Expiration date:	5/27/04
Days to expiration:	20
Pricing:	
Pricing model:	
Number of steps for binomial model:	100
Implied Volatility:	68.91%

Now this implied volatility needs to be compared with the historical volatility in order determine if higher volatility is priced into the option than what is historically appropriate.

Appendix-III

Using the Peter Hoadley Options Strategy Software

This software can be used to test various strategies and construct profit diagrams. Below we will go through an example of a selling a straddle and how the software is used with this strategy. More help is available at www.hoadley.com/options. The software is available free of cost from the above site. There are a number of inputs which you need to change in the default screen. This should be done very carefully as a mistake here can spoil the calculation.

Step 1

When you open the options strategy software, you see the first screen as shown below. We'll consider the example of Nifty options for the purpose of this illustration.

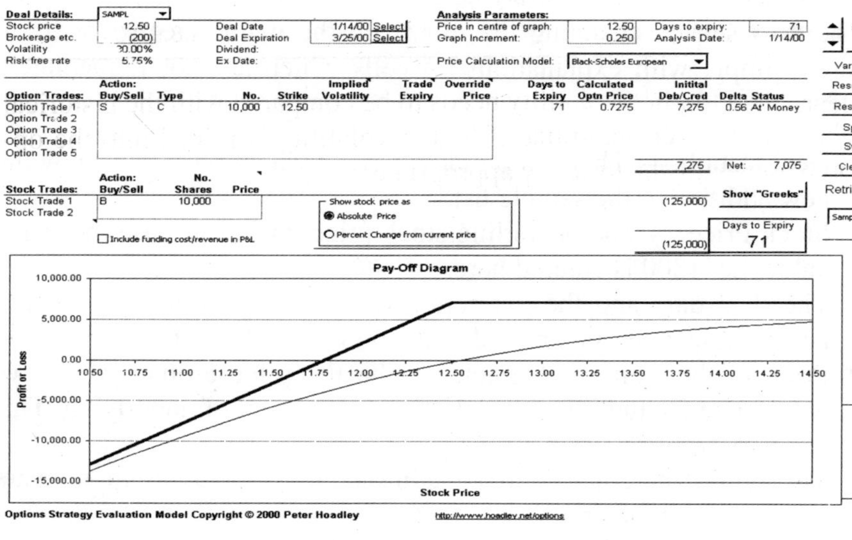

Step 2

Now the inputs to this main screen need to be set up. This can be done by clicking on the underlying assets settings module. As you can see that the Nifty option is added at the end.

The historical volatility of 17% is available at various websites with information on Indian derivatives and with some big brokers as well. Another change that is to be made here is the risk-free interest rate which we will change to 6%.

Peter Hoadley's

Options Strategy Analysis Tools

Risk-free interest rate:	6.00%
Binomial tree steps:	100

PC graphics card resolution: 1024 x 768

		Dividends -	Dividends - Discrete							
Stock		Continuous	Payment 1		Payment 2		Payment 3		Payment 4	
Code	Volatility	Annual Yield	Ex Date	$.cc	Ex Date	$.cc	Ex Date	$.cc	Ex Date	$.cc
$IND	20.00%	1.75%								
GE	30.00%		1/21/00	4.65	2/25/00	4.80				
MSFT	35.00%									
SAMPL	30.00%									
TRW	23.00%									
Nifty	17.00%									

Step 3

The next step is changing the inputs on the main screen which are fairly simple with explanations on cells which are not immediately clear.

- Deal Details — This is a pulldown menu which will now show the new addition to the sample list.
- Stock Price — The prevailing stock price, or in this case the index value, i.e. 1800 is entered here.
- The deal date and the expiration date of the options are entered here. These dates are entered in the mm/dd/yy format.
- Price in the centrer of graph can be the price around which we would like to study the impact of the movement of underlying. This can vary from case to case.
- The graph increment can be adjusted to get maximum relevant movement on the graph.
- The option details are fed into action, buy/sell, number and strike cells.

- Now the next 3 entries are not used all the time but only when there is a particular situation:
  - (i) Implied volatility needs be entered if it's different from the volatility set up of the stock under the "underlying assets settings" sheet.
  - (ii) Trade expiry date needs to be entered if it's different from the deal expiry date, for example, in a calendar spread.
  - (iii) Override price — Enter an option price here if it's different from the option price calculated by the option model. In the case of Nifty they are and so those different prices are entered.

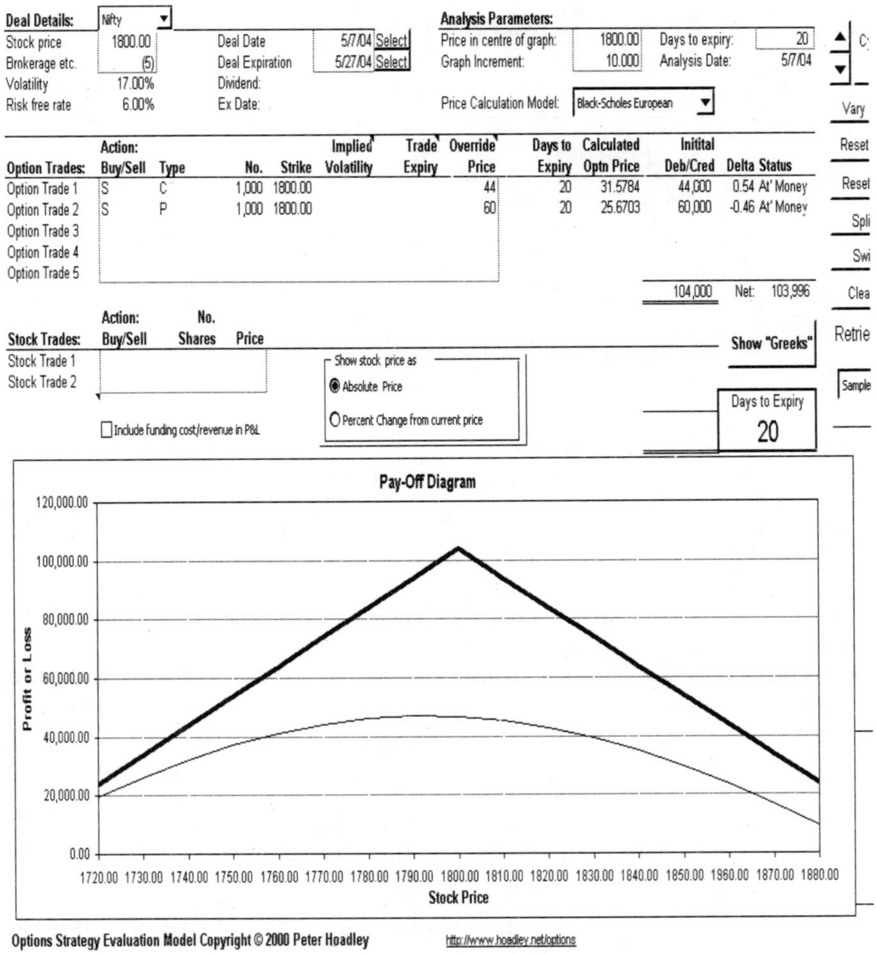

- Right next to the foregoing screen is the profit diagram which shows profit/loss position on the deal date as well as at the expiry date.

Profit/LossTables:

Show Greeks at Analysis Date | Return to Payoff Diagram | Switch to comparison area table | Vary option parameters

P/L at Expiry: 5/27/04

Stock Price:	1720.00	1730.00	1740.00	1750.00	1760.00	1770.00	1780.00	1790.00	1800.00	1810.00	1820.00	1830.00	1840.00	1850.00	1860.00	1870.00	1880.00
Brokerage etc.	(5)	(5)	(5)	(5)	(5)	(5)	(5)	(5)	(5)	(5)	(5)	(5)	(5)	(5)	(5)	(5)	(5)
Options:																	
Option Trade 1	44,000	44,000	44,000	44,000	44,000	44,000	44,000	44,000	44,000	34,000	24,000	14,000	4,000	-6,000	-16,000	-26,000	-36,000
Option Trade 2	-20,000	-10,000		10,000	20,000	30,000	40,000	50,000	60,000	60,000	60,000	60,000	60,000	60,000	60,000	60,000	60,000
Option Trade 3																	
Option Trade 4																	
Option Trade 5																	
Stock:																	
Dividends																	
Stock Trade 1																	
Stock Trade 2																	
Net Funding:																	
Total P/L:	23,996	33,996	43,996	53,996	63,996	73,996	83,996	93,996	103,996	93,996	83,996	73,996	63,996	53,996	43,996	33,996	23,996
	-4.4%	-3.9%	-3.3%	-2.8%	-2.2%	-1.7%	-1.1%	-0.6%	0	+0.6%	+1.1%	+1.7%	+2.2%	+2.8%	+3.3%	+3.9%	+4.4%

P/L at Analysis Date: 5/7/04

Stock Price:	1720.00	1730.00	1740.00	1750.00	1760.00	1770.00	1780.00	1790.00	1800.00	1810.00	1820.00	1830.00	1840.00	1850.00	1860.00	1870.00	1880.00
Brokerage etc.	(5)	(5)	(5)	(5)	(5)	(5)	(5)	(5)	(5)	(5)	(5)	(5)	(5)	(5)	(5)	(5)	(5)
Options:																	
Option Trade 1	38,810	37,141	35,082	32,590	29,620	26,140	22,123	17,551	12,422	6,739	518	-6,214	-13,424	-21,074	-29,120	-37,517	-46,219
Option Trade 2	-19,281	-10,951	-3,009	4,498	11,529	18,048	24,031	29,459	34,330	38,647	42,426	45,694	48,484	50,834	52,788	54,391	55,689
Option Trade 3																	
Option Trade 4																	
Option Trade 5																	
Stock:																	
Dividends																	
Stock Trade 1																	
Stock Trade 2																	
Net Funding:																	
Total P/L:	19,524	26,185	32,069	37,083	41,145	44,184	46,149	47,006	46,747	45,381	42,940	39,476	35,055	29,756	23,664	16,870	9,465

Position "Greeks:"

Delta (ESP)																	
Gamma (ESP)																	
Theta																	
Vega																	
Rho																	

(Press button at top of screen to calculate) For help: www.hoadley.net/options